Praise for The Art of Coaching Teams

"There are many books on coaching, but this one you must have. Covering everything from working with teams to conflict resolution, from decision making to school culture, this book details ways to become a more effective and self-reflective leader. Take time to integrate these ideas into your own practice and share the approaches with others. It is well worth the effort."—Kent D. Peterson, emeritus professor, University of Wisconsin-Madison, author of *Shaping School Culture*

"Elena's latest book provides leaders with a framework to create, coach, and manage effective teams—with both compassion and clarity. The powerful personal anecdotes humanize a daunting process, and the detailed scripts allow for ample opportunities to practice."—Maia Heyck-Merlin, author, *The Together Teacher* and *The Together Leader*

"This book is the logical next step to support our collaborative structures and empower teacher leadership. I implore all school leaders to engage in Elena's work, and utilize this resource to support their collaborative teams and enhance their school culture."—Brian Duwe, principal, Aurora West College Preparatory Academy, Denver, Colorado

"Elena Aguilar uses her coaching experiences with both struggling and successful teams to teach clear lessons on how to build emotional intelligence in ourselves, in our teams, and ultimately in our students. With a solid foundation of extensive research, *The Art of Coaching Teams* provides the tools and inspiration educational leaders need for fundamental, long-lasting change."—Katie Ciancetta, instructional coach, Salem Keizer Public Schools, Oregon

"This book is a 'how-to' manual for building, leading, and facilitating teams. It's packed with practical tools, tips, and protocols! Elena writes straight from her heart, coaching her readers every step of the way to develop the skills they need to lead transformational teams."—Meredith Melvin Adelfio, instructional coach, Sidwell Friends School, Washington D.C.

"Administrators seeking to develop effective teams that transform schools must read this book. Offering tools that translate aspirations into practice, Elena Aguilar possesses a deep compassion for the work of educators and an unwavering commitment to making schools more equitable for all children." —Charlotte Worsley, assistant head for student life, The Urban School of San Francisco, California

"In *The Art of Coaching Teams*, Aguilar succeeds in translating her transformational coaching framework into a practical and heartening resource for all who coach and manage teams. She infuses 30+ years of research on emotional intelligence, team development, and leadership with her unique blend of empathy, clarity, and hope."—Laurelin Andrade, manager of coaches

"This book comes at the right time for teachers and leaders committed to creating more equitable outcomes for diverse students. Aguilar gives us the tools to work together effectively for real change."—Zaretta Hammond, author, *Culturally Responsive Teaching and the Brain*

"Drawing deeply on her lived experiences, Aguilar offers readers a path to leadership characterized by reflection, intention, and humility. In balancing the practical and profound, *The Art of Coaching Teams* lives up to its promise as a guide for leaders who seek to transform themselves and their teams."—Brianna Crowley, high school teacher and instructional coach, Hershey, Pennsylvania

"A guide for leaders to move collaborative learning teams beyond superficial engagements about surface level dilemmas and toward authentic relationships to produce meaningful dialogue and to change essential practices."—Dr. Jacqueline Kennedy, executive director of teaching and learning, Arlington Independent School District, Texas

"Anyone who believes that a school's student culture is only as strong as a school's adult culture would greatly benefit from reading this book. Aguilar's guidelines elevate the technical 'how-to' and offer adaptive moves for building a transformative community in any environment."—Yanira Canizalez, founding head of school, Lodestar—A Lighthouse Community Charter Public School, Oakland, California

"Many leaders working in marginalized communities feel an urgency to tackle problems immediately, even when we are not as equipped as we need to be. This book is a perfect antidote to this pressure: by taking a step back to reflect and consider approaches that Elena shares, we may in fact lead our teams towards lasting solutions and achieve our collective goal of transforming lives. Elena not only presents an array of tools, but she also calls out what is best in all of us as we aspire to leave a lasting impact on communities we love deeply."—Tiffany Cheng Nyaggah, executive director and cofounder of Dignitas, Nairobi, Kenya

The *Art* of Coaching Teams

Building Resilient Communities That Transform Schools

BY ELENA AGUILAR

JJ JOSSEY-BASS™
A Wiley Brand

WILEY

Published by Jossey-Bass
A Wiley Brand
One Montgomery Street, Suite 1000, San Francisco, CA 94104–4594 — www.josseybass.com

Figure 2.1 Copyright Joshya/Shutterstock

Exhibit 4.4 Modified and used by permission from the National Equity Project

Jossey-Bass books and products are available through most bookstores. To contact Jossey-Bass directly call our Customer Care Department within the U.S. at 800–956–7739, outside the U.S. at 317–572–3986, or fax 317–572–4002.

Wiley publishes in a variety of print and electronic formats and by print-on-demand. Some material included with standard print versions of this book may not be included in e-books or in print-on-demand. If this book refers to media such as a CD or DVD that is not included in the version you purchased, you may download this material at http://booksupport.wiley.com. For more information about Wiley products, visit www.wiley.com.

Library of Congress Cataloging-in-Publication Data

Names: Aguilar, Elena, 1969– author.
Title: The art of coaching teams : building resilient communities that transform schools / by Elena Aguilar.
Description: San Francisco, CA : Jossey-Bass, 2016. | Includes bibliographical references and index.
Identifiers: LCCN 2015046841 (print) | LCCN 2015049516 (ebook) | ISBN 9781118984154 (pbk.) |
    ISBN 9781118984178 (pdf) | ISBN 9781118984161 (epub)
Subjects: LCSH: Teaching teams — United States. | Team learning approach in education — United States. |
    Teachers–In service-training — United States. | Mentoring in education — United States.
Classification: LCC LB1029.T4 A38 2016 (print) | LCC LB1029.T4 (ebook) | DDC 371.14/8 — dc23

Cover image: Wiley
Cover design: Pgiam/iStockphoto

Printed in the United States of America

FIRST EDITION
HB Printing   10 9 8 7 6 5 4 3 2 1
PB Printing   10 9 8 7 6 5 4 3 2 1

FOR STACEY AND ORION,
MY HOME AND HEART TEAM WHO MAKE IT ALL POSSIBLE

Our goal is to create a beloved community and this will require a qualitative change in our souls as well as a quantitative change in our lives.
—Dr. Martin Luther King Jr.

CONTENTS

EXHIBITS

INTRODUCTION

Artists are notoriously messy. Their physical work spaces can be disorganized (at least this is true for the artist to whom I am married), and their processes can be haphazard, full of false starts, revisions, and crumpled pieces that never make it to completion. The drafts and sketches left in studios suggest that the messy creative process itself may be essential to produce to great work.

If coaching teams is an art, and the skills necessary to lead great teams take years of messy practice to develop, we are in a tough place. While artists often refine their practice in private, much of our growth and development as facilitators is public, evident when we lead team meetings or present professional development. Furthermore, there isn't a formula that can be used to build an effective team. All teams inevitably look and feel different—they are made up of people, after all, and it is these people who make teams potentially transformational and also challenging to lead.

Our big dreams for transforming schools depend on highly functioning groups of educators working together. This is a daunting challenge—and one I'll admit that I avoided for years. I hoped that our individual efforts would amount to transformation; I preferred working alone, and I hadn't experienced teams that could accomplish great things. When I was first in a role where I was asked to facilitate a team of adult learners, I didn't have the skill set I needed. I'm now ready to proclaim not only that yes, we have to build teams, but also that yes, we can.

It's been over a decade since I began coaching. My early efforts at facilitating teams included false starts and little grace or beauty. Over the years, I've worked on my craft with great commitment—I acquired knowledge and theory, I practiced skills over and over, and I figured out who I want to be as a leader.

The Art of Coaching Teams is deeply informed by my lived experiences and chronicles key moments of my journey toward powerful leadership. As much as it makes me cringe to reveal my rough drafts as a team leader, I hope that you will see that the art of coaching teams can be developed. Most important, I hope the tools, tips, protocols, and theory contained in these pages will help you find your own conviction and confidence that you can develop the skills to lead transformational teams.

A TALE OF TWO TEAMS

I would like tell you a story, a tale of two teams. The first team is a humanities team that I facilitated some years ago when I was a novice instructional coach working in a middle school that I'll call Wilson Middle School. (All names of people in this school are fictitious; see the note on anonymity following this introduction.) From my perspective, this team was disastrous. There was little trust, we didn't get much done, and I struggled as a leader. The second team was a team of coaches that I led after I'd had several years of experience as a facilitator. This team thrived, and I thrived as a leader. Based on many indicators, this team was a success.

Think of this tale of two teams as a serial: with each chapter of this book, I offer another episode from the stories to illustrate the art of coaching teams. So let me start the story—by starting at the end, with the successful team, so that I can offer you a vision for perhaps what might be. I'd like to transport you back to a typical Friday afternoon and offer a glimpse of what you might have seen in our small office.

Transformational Coaching Team, 2014

In one corner of the room, four coaches sit on the floor engaging in a role-play. Two take copious notes—as *observers* they're responsible for capturing what the *coach* and *client* say and do. Han is playing the coach in this scenario, trying to help Manny—who is playing a teacher—reflect on why his math lesson didn't go well.

Han listens, nods, validates Manny's challenges in the classroom. She asks probing questions, asks him to clarify his ideas, and paraphrases what he says. Her face is open, smiling, compassionate. But Manny is being difficult, authentically portraying the teacher he was depicting.

Han breaks protocol. "You guys, I'm stuck!" she says as she dramatically throws her hands in the air. "I don't know what else to say!"

Angela laughs. "I'm so glad I didn't have to be the coach first in this one—I don't know what I'd say either."

I'd been sitting close by, listening to the role-play, but as I hear the observers start to offer their feedback I move away. I know they can offer each other excellent feedback, and I want to check in with the other group of coaches.

"Wait, Elena," Han says. "I want to hear your thoughts, too! I know you were listening to all that, so what do you think?"

"I'll come back. I want to let you guys debrief first."

As I roll my chair to the other side of the room where the other four coaches are debriefing their first role-play round, I hear Dave make a comment that sends his group into a fit of laughter. He puts his arm around Michele, comforting her. She'd just played the coach, and I pick up that Dave, who had been the client, hadn't gone easy on her.

Anna looks at me. "Michele was trying some new approaches today—you should have seen it."

"What did you do?" I ask Michele, who looks flustered.

"I don't know." She smiled and shook her head. "I was trying to use the confrontational stance—that's one of my professional goals this year. I guess I don't know how to do that."

"She was brilliant," Dave says. "She even asked us to record it so she can watch it later. Maybe she'll let you see it."

"Wow, that's great, Michele," I say. She groans. "I don't want to see that, and I don't want you to see it, either." I smile. "That's your decision, of course," I say.

Anna, who was an observer, shifts the group back onto the protocol. "I can start the debrief," she says. "I noticed some moments that were really powerful, Michele, and some where you might have been able to get more traction if you'd just rephrased your question."

I slide my chair a couple feet away from the group so that I can listen but let them have space to debrief. They know enough, they trust each other, and they don't need me there. Michele takes notes on Anna's sharp insights. Noelle grabs a document from her desk, a tool she created for herself that she offers to Michele. Dave commends Michele's bold moves.

At the end of the meeting, we regroup at our oval table that fits the eight of us perfectly. As we debrief the role-play, coaches reflect on their professional growth and identify additional areas of learning. They make suggestions for readings and activities and commit to plan a coaching session in the upcoming week. In pairs they reflect on the intention they'd set for the day, and Michele shares that she knows she demonstrated her intention to take risks. They fill out the feedback form for me, some of them writing much more than others. And then I open a few minutes for appreciations and begin by offering my own. Everyone is appreciated. Everyone offers at least one appreciation. The words are important, but more important is the feeling that envelopes the room, one of indescribable respect and admiration—the feeling of a group of people who care deeply for each other, who enjoy each other's company, and who learn with and from each other.

For two years I was the manager of this team of coaches, and I felt that my primary role was to develop their skill, knowledge, and capacity to coach. When I created the model for our coaching program, I included an entire day of professional development every week. Monday through Thursday, the coaches were at sites—working with individual teachers and administrators, leading professional development sessions, facilitating department and grade-level meetings, participating in instructional leadership teams, gathering and analyzing data, and much more. On Fridays, without exception, we came together to reflect, learn, plan, and reenergize.

By the time I first met with this team in August 2012, I had a lot of ideas about how to create a highly functioning team. I knew that I'd be in a unique position with these eight coaches: although I was their boss, I viewed myself primarily as their coach, as the person responsible for helping them become the coaches and leaders that they wanted to be and that, ultimately, our students needed them to be.

We saw impressive results in the schools we supported, including growth in student learning, growth in teacher professional practice, increases in teacher retention, and improvements in collaboration among teams—all indicators of the work of an effective team of coaches. Perhaps most significant was what we learned about teams—about the utmost importance of teams and what it's like to be on a high-functioning team. Although many of us knew that teams were essential in transformation efforts, we hadn't experienced one that was collaborative and deeply caring and that got stuff done. The health of our team allowed us to go deep into individual and shared learning and into the scariest nooks and crannies—the ones where conversations about race and class, fear and despair, ego and emotions all reside. We challenged each other, pushed each other's thinking, celebrated learnings and growth, and encouraged each other to go deeper, go further, and then stop and rest. We all mourned when after two years forces beyond our control dissolved our team.

Now let me transport you briefly back to a meeting of the humanities team that I facilitated at Wilson Middle School some years prior.

Humanities Team, 2008

"Ok, are we ready to get started?" I looked around at the group of teachers. "I'll need to adjust the agenda since we're starting 20 minutes late," I said, my voice conveying my irritation at the behavior of a few teachers who trickled in late every week. "If we're going to reach our meeting objectives," I continued, "we all need to be here when we start." Bess made a snide comment under her breath that contained the phrase, "be sent to the principal's office." Margaret laughed, got up, and said, "I'll be right back; I left my drink in my classroom."

Per my request, the group looked over the agenda. "Any clarifying questions?" I asked. Bess raised her hand. "Yes. When are we going to talk about the abysmal student behavior here? When are we going to talk about how young men and women should be treating their elders? You would not believe what that little fool Keymonte said to me today when I asked him to take his hood off. Where does he think he is anyway? Is that how his mama lets him talk? I would have never spoken to a grown-up like he does. And when I sent him to the principal's office, he came back 15 minutes later with a big grin on his face. They get away with everything here."

"Bess," I interjected. "This is our department team time. That's not what we're supposed to talk about here."

"Oh, I'm so sorry," she said, her voice laden with sarcasm. "Ok, let's get to it. Let's get on with our learning target for today. 'I can identify two formative assessment strategies that I'll use next week,'" she said, reading from the agenda.

Sam put her head down on the desk. She often fell asleep during our meetings. Megan looked back and forth from me to Bess. Cassandra doodled in the margins of her notebook.

"Great. Thanks for reading the learning target, Bess," I said disingenuously. "Let's start by reviewing the article I brought for us to read on formative assessment. I'm going to ask you to count off and then work with your partner."

Before we could pair up, Margaret came back in. "There are three children running through the halls. I tried to catch them, but they took off laughing. This school is out of control."

"I was just saying that," Bess said. "But we have to stick with the plan today."

"This school is in Program Improvement Year 5!" I said, aware that my frustration levels were soaring, "Aren't you concerned about that at all?" Bess glared at me, and Margaret shrugged. "Our kids go to high school reading at a fifth-grade level—their reading skills actually drop while they're here. They won't pass the high school exit exam. Don't you think we need to do something about that?"

Margaret's phone rang. "Gotta take this," she said and walked out.

Bess moved her papers to the side and leaned forward. "We can't do anything about their reading levels until they learn to sit down, shut up, and act like human beings," she said. "Until then all of this professional development is a waste of time."

I stared at her. I could feel my hands trembling under the table.

Megan cleared her throat. "Well, I wouldn't mind if we got to the reading," she said. "How about you, Sam?" She said. Sam opened her eyes, sat up, and nodded.

"Sounds good to me," Cassandra said. "Megan, we're partners; want to sit by the window?"

"I prefer to work alone," Bess said. "I'll be in my room and come back for the discussion." She walked out.

I moved to sit with Sam and followed the protocol I'd created, but I couldn't stop ruminating over what Bess had said. Her words looped over and over in my mind.

I thought about the times I'd seen her shaming children in public, making fun of their names, and delivering lessons that seemed entirely disconnected from their learning needs. I'd never let my child be in her class. Those were other people's babies I felt responsible for protecting, but I didn't know how. I hadn't known how to respond in those moments or to her behavior in meetings. "What am I doing here?" I thought over and over. I missed teaching—the reward, satisfaction, and connection with people who appreciate me. "I'm doing nothing of value here," I thought. "I just want to quit."

I worked in the Oakland Unified School District (OUSD) in Oakland, California, for almost 20 years. During that time, I was a member of many teams and a leader of a few teams. The humanities team was the most difficult team I led and also one from which I learned a great deal. It was a couple years after I led this team that I wrote *The Art of Coaching* (Jossey-Bass, 2013), in which I originally intended to include a chapter about coaching teams. As I drafted that chapter, however, it became apparent that the content deserved a book of its own. But there was another reason that I couldn't yet write a chapter on coaching teams. Although I had a plethora of ideas about how to build effective teams, I had never been a member of a truly transformational team of educators. I had never led a team to a high level of performance. I acknowledged that I couldn't write about something I had never experienced—not as a participant or as a leader.

Even though it's true that we can learn a great deal from our struggles, our moments of success also yield deep learning. It wasn't until my experience leading the transformation team that I truly believed great teams could exist—a conviction that was essential for writing this book. It wasn't until that experience that I became confident in my ability to acquire the skills of leadership—and if I was able to do this, you can too. And it wasn't until that experience that I could say yes, try this approach to team building, conflict management, decision making, adult learning—*because I know it can work*. I've seen it work. I believe that many of these strategies could have worked with the Humanities Team, had I known how to use them. I can now precisely name the conditions necessary for transformational teams to develop and attest to what's possible when they are in place. Finally, I can tell you that it's worth it—all the time and effort you'll put into honing your leadership skills, to designing agendas, to one-on-one conversations with teammates: there's little that can compare to the reward of bringing together a group of people in healthy relationships who do good work in service of children.

I am forever grateful to the members of OUSD's transformational coaches, a team that over two years included Noelle, David, Rafael, John, Anna, Manny, Angela, Han, and Michele. I think of these people as my professional soul mates. For our team to become what it did, it took their willingness to be vulnerable and courageous, to be fully present in mind and body, and to put forth their questions and contributions. They were my teachers in many moments.

WHAT'S IN THIS BOOK?

This book is a how-to manual for building teams—how to design agendas, make decisions, establish communication protocols. Included are dozens of tools that you can use or adapt to meet your needs. All of the tools are available for download on my website (http://www.elenaaguilar.com). There you'll also find video clips demonstrating some of the strategies described in this book.

This is also a book about leadership. I hope to offer new perspectives on the kinds of leaders who can bring a group of people together to do hard work in service of others, work that in the process nourishes the minds, hearts, and spirits of all involved. I hope to offer you strategies to cultivate these adaptive qualities of leadership, including strategies to explore and boost your emotional resilience—the ability to understand your emotions, manage them, and use them to help you meet your goals and enjoy life.

Building teams requires us to hold both a macro and micro perspective. In this book, I'll take you back and forth between looking close up at elements including our emotions as leaders, meeting agendas, and language for difficult conversations and then back out to the macro structures including the alignment between teams in a school, leadership models, and organizational culture. For example, to offer suggestions for how to respond to someone who dominates a discussion, we need to look at the big picture and consider how systemic oppression impacts the development of trust among teachers and how communication and conflict are influenced by a school and district's adult culture. We'll explore how a leader can cultivate a team's emotional intelligence and how to deal with resistance. And we'll reflect on what leaders can say and do in the moment that someone is dominating a discussion.

If you lead groups that primarily engage in learning together—perhaps a professional learning community of coaches, a department, or a grade-level team—then the content of this book will help you establish the conditions so that adults can learn together. Over and over, we'll return to the conditions in which effective groups of educators work and learn together. There's a tremendous amount that you can do to create optimal conditions.

I encourage you to read this book in the order that it's presented because each chapter builds on previous ones. However, Exhibit I.1, located after the introduction, will help you identify where in this book you'll find answers to your most pressing questions about building teams. A tool you might want to look at and use right away is the facilitator core competencies (Appendix A). This tool identifies the set of skills that a facilitator needs and offers an opportunity to reflect on your abilities. Although my intention in this book is to boost the massive skill set laid out in the facilitator core competencies, you'll also find many resources to strengthen these competencies in my book, *The Art of Coaching*.

When I began writing this book, I asked one question of everyone with whom I came into contact in workshops I offered as well as through social media. I asked, "What's the hardest thing about coaching a team?" I received more than 1,000 responses and grouped them into the categories in Exhibit I.1. One of the most common responses was, "Dealing with one person who dominates conversations." I remember when that was also my most pressing question about managing group dynamics, and even though I wish I could offer five easy steps toward managing the verbal dominator it has in fact taken an entire book to answer that question in a way that leads to lasting change. As I hope you'll see, my intent is to offer a transformational approach that will allow us to create the kinds of healthy adult communities that will be able to serve the social, academic, and emotional needs of all children.

After reading this book, I hope that you'll be able to write a plan for developing a team you lead. Whether you're embarking on a leadership path and preparing to lead a team of colleagues or planning for a team you've led for some time, my intention is that you can cull through the strategies in this book and use them to formulate a plan. Appendix F offers a template for a team-building plan. On my website you can see examples of such a plan.

WHO IS THIS BOOK FOR?

This book is for anyone building, leading, or facilitating teams—and for those who hope to build the capacity of others to do so. This is for instructional coaches, professional learning community facilitators, grade-level leads, data team coaches, department heads, committee leads, and anyone else in a formal or informal leadership position. This book could be considered the companion to *The Art of Coaching* since it expands on many of the approaches described for working one-on-one with another educator.

The Art of Coaching Teams will help principals who seek to be a lead learner, as described by Michael Fullan in his book *The Principal* (2014). Fullan makes a compelling case for principals to focus their energies primarily on creating cultures of learning in their schools and to work with *teams* rather than individual teachers. His argument is backed by research conducted by the highly respected educators Richard DuFour and Robert Marzano, who argue, "Time devoted to building the capacity of teachers to work in teams is far better spent than time devoted to observing individual teachers" (2009, p. 67). Principals, imagine if you could reduce the number of observations and one-on-one conversations you have each week and see even greater impact on student learning. I hope this book might help you strategically develop teams of learners.

Administrators in all corners of our education system build teams: instructional leadership teams, culture and climate teams, student behavior teams, curriculum teams, and many more. This book is intended for those site leaders, directors, managers, coordinators, and superintendents who seek to strengthen their teams. The material offered in this book is relevant across roles wherever someone holds an intention to bring a group of people into healthy relationship with each other to accomplish something in the service of children.

TOWARD A BELOVED COMMUNITY

I am often daunted by the amount of change we need to see in our schools. The progress we've made feels slow. So many children are not receiving the education they need, they aren't treated with the love and kindness that all children deserve, and they aren't in communities where they can thrive. I've been working in education for 20 years, and sometimes it feels like little has changed.

However, when I think back on the places where change was made and children got more of what they need and deserve, those were uniformly places where the adults at the site worked in high-functioning teams together and where there was respect and trust between teachers and between teachers and administrators. In those places, when storms hit (and they did), the communities of adults and children weathered them well and emerged stronger than before. At the schools where I experienced this, teacher and administrator retention was high, institutional memory was preserved, and a culture of learning was maintained. Above all, people liked coming to work—there was laughter and meaningful conversations and sharing of resources, experiences, ideas, and accomplishments. In these contexts, creativity was abundant and evident—teams collaborated on projects and initiatives in innovative ways and with admirable results. At those moments, from within those healthy communities, I observed firsthand the positive impact of good teams on our children.

My purpose in my work is to interrupt the inequities I see in our education system and schools. Every morning I awaken hoping to contribute to building equitable schools where every child gets what he or she needs in school every day. My vision for a transformed society extends beyond what children experience in school—I hope to contribute to creating a just society where acceptance and kindness exist between all people of all ages, to creating a beloved community. While providing children with a different kind of experience in school, I also strive to create the world that they'll one day be a part of as adults.

I know that we can't create what we want to see for children without also attending to the adults who work with them—we just can't separate these two things. At the same time, I recognize how building healthy communities of adults is also working toward a more expansive vision of society. For some, I've found that this notion poses a challenge that we can and need to work toward both ends at the same time: what our children need and the larger picture of transformation. We can't do one without the other. Building high-functioning, healthy teams is a means to an end—to being able to improve student learning—but it is also the end itself, because at the core of a high-functioning healthy team is a beloved community.

AN ELEPHANT IN THE DARK

Some Hindus have an elephant to show.
No one here has ever seen an elephant.
They bring it at night to a dark room.
One by one, we go in the dark and come out
saying how we experience the animal.
One of us happens to touch the trunk.
A water-pipe kind of creature.
Another, the ear. A very strong, always moving
back and forth, fan-animal. Another, the leg.
I find it still, like a column on a temple.
Another touches the curved back.
A leathery throne. Another the cleverest,
feels the tusk. A rounded sword made of porcelain.
He is proud of his description.
Each of us touches one place
and understands the whole that way.
The palm and the fingers feeling in the dark
are how the senses explore the reality of the elephant.
If each of us held a candle there,
and if we went in together, we could see it.

By Rumi

This poem, "An Elephant in the Dark," by Rumi, the thirteenth-century Persian poet and mystic, offers a metaphor for the potential of a team working well. It was brought to my attention by Anna, one of the coaches in the team I led, when she offered it on one of our Friday learning sessions. That day, I remember the wave of gratitude I experienced as I took in this poem's meaning: alone we can only see one part of the big something we can't understand, and if we each hold a candle, we might be able to see what we cannot even yet imagine. In that moment, I also recognized that had it not been for this team and Anna's presence on it, I may not have come across this poem. Anna offered us each a candle.

Reflect: "An Elephant in the Dark"

Share this poem with a team you lead and offer these prompts for discussion:

- Within our context, what is analogous to the elephant in this poem? What are we trying to figure out?

- What are the different ways that members of our team contribute to this understanding? What does each one—because of his or her background, experiences, or knowledge—understand?

- Within our context, what is analogous to a candle? What do we need to be able to see the whole thing?

- What gets in the way of us going in together? What are you willing to do to go in together? What do you need from your teammates to do so?

A NOTE ON ANONYMITY AND PSEUDONYMS

The names of the coaches in the transformational coaching team are indeed their real names. To the very best of my abilities, I've depicted them and shared their words with as much accuracy as possible. In a few instances, for the sake of the narrative, I modified the sequence of events to make this more readable.

The names of every other teacher, coach, or leader mentioned in this book are pseudonyms. To protect privacy, I've also changed identity markers and some aspects of the narrative with the hopes that the people about whom I write will be unidentifiable.

EXHIBIT I.1: WHAT'S IN THIS BOOK?

This exhibit shows where to find answers to your most pressing questions about building teams.

Chapter	Guiding questions	Common challenges addressed (*"What's the hardest thing about coaching or leading a team?"*)	Truths about building teams
Chapter 1: Refining a Vision	What is an effective team? Why do we need teams? What kind of teams can have a positive impact on children?	• I'm leading a team, we're really struggling, and I can't figure out why. • Cultivating a sense of urgency in a team. • Getting everyone to work together effectively to a common goal. • I don't know if I believe in teams. I feel like I work better alone.	Teams that work in or with schools exist to serve the social, emotional, and academic needs of children.
Chapter 2: Knowing Ourselves as Leaders	How will my awareness of myself as a leader enable me to build a strong team? What kind of leader do I want to be?	• I don't feel I'm qualified to lead this team. • I'm leading a team, we're really struggling, and I can't figure out why. • My relationship to members in a team has changed, and now they seem to me differently. • I can't remain neutral as a leader—I'm not neutral. But how do I not impose my beliefs on others? • When teams look to me for confirmation or affirmation instead of talking with each other about what they believe and what they want to do. • I get really frustrated by some team members. • I can't stand working with stubborn people. • There are so many problems in our team I don't know where to start.	Who you are as a leader has the greatest influence on a team.
Chapter 3: Creating a Culture of Trust	What can I do to build trust in a team?	• Getting veteran teachers to change and do something different. • Dealing with adults who have fixed mind-sets and who are not willing to take challenges or learn by mistakes. • There are so many problems in our team I don't know where to start. • Getting people to trust each other. • Dealing with high team member turnover.	Teams thrive with trust.

Chapter	Guiding questions	Common challenges addressed ("What's the hardest thing about coaching or leading a team?")	Truths about building teams
Chapter 4: Defining Purpose, Process, and Product	How do we figure out what to do in our team? How do we make sure we're doing work as a team that will positively impact students?	• Figuring out which direction to go with my team—I don't know what will help us the most. • There are so many problems in our team I don't know where to start. • Dealing with conflicting needs from different group members. • We have such different styles, personalities, beliefs, and values. • Lack of implementation and follow-through. • Cultivating a sense of urgency in a team. • Ensuring everyone is on the same page about norms, expectations, beliefs, and goals. • Staying focused. • Getting everyone to work together effectively to a common goal. • Supporting others in moving past personal agendas.	Teams that work in or with schools exist to serve the social, emotional, and academic needs of children. Building teams takes time.
Chapter 5: Laying a Foundation for Trust	What can I do to build trust in a team? How can norms or community agreements help us become an effective team?	• Getting people to trust each other. • The negative voice that affects the whole group. • The dominant voice that contradicts and challenges all others. • Getting veteran teachers to change and do something different.	Teams thrive with trust. Building teams takes time.
Chapter 6: Developing the Emotional Intelligence of a Team	How can I help everyone get along? How can we deal with the stress of working in schools?	• Getting veteran teachers to change and do something different. • Getting team members to make changes or do something different when they're stuck. • The negative voice that affects the whole group. • The dominant voice that contradicts and challenges all others. • Many different personalities and styles—someone always seems to be offended. • The feeling of the coach being against the loud, dominant voice. • Some people just do not work well with others. • When one or two teachers consistently bring negativity and resistance to the group.	A team's collective emotional intelligence is the key factor in its level of performance.

(continued)

Exhibit I.1   **xxxi**

Chapter	Guiding questions	Common challenges addressed ("What's the hardest thing about coaching or leading a team?")	Truths about building teams
Chapter 7: Cultivating Healthy Communication	How can I facilitate effective communication in a team?	• Getting veteran teachers to change and do something different. • What to do about that one person who takes on a leadership role without being asked. • The negative voice that affects the whole group. • The dominant voice that contradicts and challenges all others. • Dealing with people's cynicism that their voice and time are not valued. • When one team member is not onboard with the other members. • When people don't push back on the dominant voices. • Drawing out the quiet participants. • Dealing with those who want to be heard but don't want to listen.	Communication between team members is the thread that connects everything.
Chapter 8: Making Good Decisions	How can decisions be made in a way that builds trust? What are different ways to make decisions?	• My team disagrees with all the decisions I make. • My team says I'm a top-down leader and that I don't give them input on decisions. • When one member of the team speaks for the team and sways things in a direction that others may not want to go. • When one team member is not onboard with the others. • Being unable to reach consensus because everyone has such strong opinions. • When we need to make decisions, our conversations go around and around, and we never seem to make them.	Teams thrive with trust. Communication between team members is the thread that connects everything.
Chapter 9: Supporting Adult Learners	How can knowledge of adult learning help me facilitate a team? How do I apply principles of adult learning to coaching teams?	• When teachers are in different places in their learning. • Meeting the needs of all. • Getting teachers to take responsibility for their own learning. • Lack of implementation and follow-through. • Getting veteran teachers to change and do something different. • Dealing with adults who have fixed mind-sets and who are not willing to take challenges or learn by mistakes.	Learning is the primary work of all teams.
Chapter 10: Orchestrating Meaningful Meetings	What should we do when we meet?	• Deciding what activities to do in meetings. • Finding ways to facilitate or use protocols that help teams collaborate rather than feeling led by me. • I need to talk less and listen more. • Teams look to me for affirmation instead of talking with each other about what they believe and want to do. • We are stuck doing the same kinds of things every time we meet, but I don't know what else to do.	The health of a meeting reflects the health of the team.

Chapter	Guiding questions	Common challenges addressed ("*What's the hardest thing about coaching or leading a team?*")	Truths about building teams
Chapter 11: Setting the Stage for Artful Meetings	How can I design meetings that develop an effective team?	• How to understand feedback when it contains extremes. • Feeling calm and confident when I lead meetings. • What to do about that one person who takes on a leadership role without being asked. • Getting everyone to work together effectively to a common goal. • Keeping people awake during my meetings. • Dealing with people who use technology inappropriately.	The health of a meeting reflects the health of the team.
Chapter 12: Navigating Conflict	How can healthy conflict make us a more effective team? How do I manage unhealthy conflict in my team?	• Getting team members to make changes or do something different when they're stuck. • When a team is not getting along because of the mix of personalities, different teaching styles, and so on. • The negative voice that affects the whole group. • The dominant voice that contradicts and challenges all others. • The mentality of, my kids are different from yours. • Teachers who are unwilling to examine their biases. • When one or two teachers consistently bring negativity and resistance to the group.	Conflict can be healthy, but unhealthy conflict needs to be managed.
Chapter 13: Assessing Organizational Conditions	How can I assess the conditions in which I'm leading my team so that I can figure out where to best focus my energy?	• We have no time to meet. • There are so many teams in our school, but no one has any idea what we're all doing. Everyone is doing something different. • How to make sure that what we're doing in our team actually has an impact on our school. • When we are in conflict with administration. • Dealing with high team member turnover. • Getting everyone to work together effectively to a common goal. • Our team is in conflict with the larger organization. I'm stuck in the middle. • I didn't choose my team, and we don't get along.	All teams exist within systems and power structures.

Exhibit I.1   **xxxiii**

CHAPTER 1

Refining a Vision

Humanities Team, 2008

We meet because all departments meet on Wednesday afternoons. We meet because our school has bad test scores and we're supposed to do something about that. We meet because—I have no idea, actually, why this team is supposed to meet. The department chair communicates information from the district—testing schedules, textbook changes, new initiatives. Then there's me, the coach, and I'm supposed to do what? When I came onboard, I asked the principal, "What do you hope I'll do with this department?" He said, "Get them to work better together." So we meet on Wednesdays.

To build something, we need to know what it is we want to build. I suspect that sometimes we struggle to build teams because we haven't even decided what we're trying to build or what describes this end goal. We need to start with articulating these elements of a vision before we start construction. The rest of this book offers you tools and strategies for team building, but in this first chapter we're consider the what, why, and when of teams. First: a quick clarification of terminology.

A NOTE ON TERMS

For the sake of simplicity and flow, there are sets of terms I use interchangeably in this book. First, I use *team* and *group* to mean the same thing—a unit of people who convene to work together interdependently for a shared, meaningful purpose.

To describe the kind of team I aspire to create, the kind I believe has potential to serve our schools and children, I also use a set of adjectives interchangeably: *great*, *effective*, *high-performing*, *high-functioning*, and *successful*. I don't want to confuse you, nor do I want to bore you with repetitive terminology. So if you wonder, "Well, what does she mean now when she says a team is high functioning?" I mean the same thing as when I say a team is effective.

I also use the terms *leader* and *facilitator* interchangeably. There are some differences between how we are identified by others—whether we are appointed to lead or facilitate a team, whether those in our team see us as a leader or a facilitator. Leaders often have more positional or situational authority, which often grants them more decision-making rights. Facilitators are more likely to guide a process and to have either decision-making power equal to the rest of the team members or no decision-making powers at all. Even though it's important to distinguish your role (and I'll return to this in Chapter 2), I hope that this book will have a wide range of readers—from site administrators to department heads to centrally based coaches to superintendents. Therefore, I'll alternate between the terms *leader* and *facilitator* so you know that regardless of your role I'm thinking of you.

WHAT IS A GREAT TEAM?

When I reflect on the transformational coach team that I led, I often think, "That was a great team, an incredible team, an awesome team that rocked." For the sake of simplicity and transferability to other contexts ("rocked" might not translate in some places), I've settled on using *great* as the broadest and widest descriptor of the kinds of teams I aspire to create.

J. Richard Hackman's (2011) work assisted me in defining the following three dimensions of great teams. Exhibit 1.1 can help you to consider these as they relate to a team you are a part of now, or once were a part of. Here are the three dimensions of a great team.

Exhibit 1.1. Dimensions of a Great Team: A Tool for Reflection

Dimension	Indicators	Yes/No
Product Something of quality gets done that is valuable, useful, and appreciated.	Was our product well received?	
	Did our clients (students, teachers, parents, staff) think that our product was high quality?	
	Did what we do make a difference to our clients?	
	Do I feel proud of the work we did together?	
Process The group's collaboration skills increase as a result of working together.	Did our ways of working together improve over time?	
	Did our ability to communicate with each other, manage unproductive conflict, and have healthy conflict increase?	
	If I was to continue working with this team, do I feel confident that our work products would continue to improve because we've figured out how to best work together?	
	If the team has disbanded: If this team were to reconvene, would I want to rejoin it?	
Learning The team experience is a learning experience that increases the skills and knowledge of individual team members.	Did I learn in this team?	
	Did being a part of this team help me improve my skills in my primary area of practice (e.g., teaching, coaching, leading)?	
	Did I feel I could take risks in my learning in this team?	
	Did I trust the other people in this team most of the time?	
	Did I feel like I belonged to a community?	

1. Product: A great team gets something done that is valuable, useful, and appreciated.

For many teams in our context, our products might be hard to identify. However, this is a primary indicator of a great team: that we get something done. Furthermore, the opinions of the recipients of this product count, so we need to know what they think of the work we do and we need to meet their expectations.

An instructional leadership team (ILT), for example, may be responsible for building the instructional capacity of staff. The ILT's primary role is to design and deliver professional development and to lead department teams. In this case, the ILT's products would be PD sessions and department meetings. We can evaluate the value and usefulness of these products on feedback forms and surveys.

In some teams, it's harder to identify products, but it's still worth an attempt. A grade-level team might convene to address a range of business items, including logistical issues that arise in their band, specific students who are struggling, and curriculum. The product of their work together might be schedules, new agreements, or insights into instructional practices. Although these activities may be valuable, if a team needs to think about product it can push members to reflect on what they're doing together. We'll come back to this question of what we're doing together in Chapter 4.

The product for a team of coaches is the impact they have on the clients they serve. In the case of the transformational coach team, our primary clients were teachers and administrators, and we measured impact in many ways, including on anonymous surveys, through growth in teacher performance, and on feedback forms after professional development sessions. Given that during the two years we offered coaching support more than 95% of the feedback we received was positive and clients reported high levels of satisfaction, I conclude that our team did something valuable, useful, and appreciated.

2. Process: A great team's collaboration skills increase as a result of working together.

The end product is only one part of what makes a great team, and you can't be great if that's all you do because process counts. A great team strengthens its way of working together as a unit, which sets it up for future success. The way the group works together and the group dynamics (e.g., how members communicate, how they manage conflict) fosters its ability to work together interdependently in the future. A great team periodically reflects on how its members are working together and uses this reflection to improve its work. Great teams perform more capably when they have finished a chunk of work than when they began.

Let's consider the example of a high school art department that collaborates during the spring semester to put on its annual festival of the arts (the team's big product).

As the team navigates conflict—Whose art gets to go up in the main building? How do we divide our budget equitably when the visual arts teachers need more money for materials than the dance teacher?—it finds ways to bridge the challenges that arise. At the end of the semester, as group members reflect on the success of the festival and the record high attendance of students and parents, they compile a list of guidelines that they'll use in preparation for the event the following year. There is laughter as they reflect on the experience with comments like, "We'll never do that again" and "I had no idea you had those skills; I hope you'll do that again next year." Each member feels confident that next year's festival will be easier to prepare for and even better. This team's process results in a stronger ability to work together.

3. Learning: Members of a great team learn.

A team is great when its members learn things that they wouldn't have learned had they been alone. Their skills and knowledge about their primary area of practice increase as a result of being a member of this team. This means that teachers in an English department increase their skills and knowledge of teaching, curriculum, and pedagogy because of their participation in their department team. Coaches working together as a team improve coaching conversation skills as knowledge of working with adult learners increases. In an ILT, members learn about leadership. In a response to intervention team, members learn about individualized and systemic ways to support struggling learners. In a culture and climate team, members learn ways to lead for transformational change.

For learning to occur, members must feel safe with each other. It's important to extract this assumption to think about whether a team was truly great. Underneath a successful learning experience is that members trusted each other, built community with each other, and had overall positive feelings toward each other. This is the only way that members can explore perspectives that differ from their own.

Although feeling good is not an end goal in itself for a great team—and it's not one of the three dimensions of a great team—it is an essential condition for a team to truly engage in transformative learning. Learning, not emotional safety, is the goal, but we can't learn unless we feel safe.

"The stars we are given. The constellations we create." Rebecca Solnit, Storming the Gates of Paradise

WHAT MAKES AN EFFECTIVE TEAM?

Members of a great team know that they must work together in certain ways to produce results—to be effective. How a team functions is inseparable from its potential for success. Members of an effective team know, in the moment, whether a meeting will lead them down a path to results or whether their efforts will be detailed or stalled.

Harvard education professor Richard F. Elmore notes that virtually every school he's visited has had some kind of team structure in place and a regular schedule of meetings. However, Elmore explains that " … only about one in ten teacher teams that I observe functions at a level that would result in any improvement of instructional practice and student learning in the classroom" (quoted in Troen and Boles, 2012, p. xv). This is a startling observation, and it demands that we direct our attention to *how* we function in teams.

For a team to be effective, high performing, and successful (descriptors I use interchangeably), we need a concrete definition of what makes a team effective. Exhibit 1.2 could be used as a definition or as a springboard for a team to articulate its vision for the indicators of an effective team. Having such an articulated vision is essential. Appendix B contains the Team Effectiveness Self-Assessment, which can be used for team reflection. As with all self-assessment tools, the purpose is to have a guide for a discussion about how a team is working together so that reflection can be promoted, thus leading to improved performance.

Exhibit 1.2. Indicators of an Effective Team

1. **Purpose:** Team members understand and agree on the team's purpose and goals.
2. **Results:** The team accomplishes what it sets out to achieve.
3. **Meeting Process:** Meetings are well facilitated and focused and result in clear outcomes.
4. **Decisions:** There are clear and articulated agreements about how decisions will be made.
5. **Commitment:** Team members buy in to decisions without hidden reservations or hesitation; actions reflect their commitment.
6. **Contributions:** Member contributions (ideas or information) are recognized and utilized. Different styles are embraced.
7. **Creativity:** Team members experiment with different ways of doing things and are creative in their approach.

8. **Collaboration:** Team members share their experience and expertise in ways that enhance team productivity and development.
9. **Respect:** Team members feel valued as an individual member. All members are treated with respect.
10. **Interpersonal Communication:** Communication between members is open and balanced at meetings.
11. **Productive Conflict:** Members engage in unfiltered debate around ideas and issues related to the work.
12. **Unproductive Conflict:** Members work constructively on issues until they are resolved.
13. **Procedures:** There are effective procedures to guide team functioning both during meetings and outside of meetings.
14. **Accountability:** Team members hold each other accountable.
15. **Evaluation:** The team regularly evaluates its process and productivity.

WHY DO WE NEED TEAMS?

At Learning Forward's 2013 annual conference, Professor Pedro Noguera delivered a keynote address on how to create equitable schools. He offered 10 equity practices that support the academic growth of all children and interrupt systemic inequities. After he concluded his prepared speech, the moderator asked, "What can people here do *now*? Tomorrow?" Dr. Noguera responded by urging us to find communities and to "build teams of people" who can take up this work. "We can't do it alone," he said.

This reminder is so simple yet so challenging: We can't do it alone. No individual alone can transform our schools into places where all children get what they need every day. Many of us are acutely aware of how much work needs to be done and of how far we are from an ideal of education. We might also be aware of our own individual limitations, including our capacity to do the amount of work that needs to be done and our individual scope of knowledge and skill set.

Teams have great potential for solving hard problems in challenging contexts. They bring together more skill, knowledge, and experience to work than any single individual can. They can integrate individual members' diverse contributions into a creative problem that is what is needed. Of course, as many of us know, teams can also go badly—not getting anything done or falling into groupthink. The challenge is to identify what it takes for teams to maximize their potential.

Some of us might suspect that we're stronger and more effective in teams, but we haven't had such an experience. Until we do, it can be hard to fully invest in building a team. We might be apprehensive about taking risks or trusting a leader. A leader needs to surface past experiences and beliefs about building teams to get buy-in to the process.

REFLECT: On the Need for Teams

1. Why do you think we need teams? What can we do in teams that we can't do alone?
2. What are the advantages of working in teams? What are the challenges?
3. Describe the most effective team you've ever been a part of or observed. What did this team do that wouldn't have been possible by a single individual?
4. What did you learn by working in a team that you might not have learned from working alone? What did you learn about yourself?
5. What's the hardest thing for you about facilitating a team?

WHEN DO WE REALLY NEED A TEAM?

In some organizations, there's a glorification of teams. A team is convened every other day, individuals belong to 17 different teams, and every task of every size is done collaboratively. However, sometimes what an organization needs is not a team but a working group or committee, and sometimes tasks might be better accomplished alone by one individual. The major distinctions between a team and a committee are listed in Exhibit 1.3.

Ideally, the classification of *team* is reserved for a limited number of groups. This number fluctuates based on the size of the school, the ability of the site leader to monitor teams, and the capacity of leaders and the organization as a whole. It is hard for an individual to lead more than three or four teams at the most—given that each team requires a work plan, regular monitoring, thoughtful agendas for each meeting, and so on. Leading teams takes a lot of time and energy. In addition, participants struggle if they belong to more than three or four teams at the most. To form strong teams, members need to develop trust between each other, effectively communicate with each other, and efficiently get things done. The solution to all the work that needs to be done in schools isn't to create dozens of teams—it is to have a handful of really effective, high-functioning teams.

Exhibit 1.3. Do We Need a Team?

Convene a Team When ...	Convene a Committee or Working Group When ...
• The work to be done is adaptive. It requires learning and changing people's hearts and minds.	• The work to be done is technical. It addresses a problem we know how to solve.
• The reason for existence will be ongoing, long term, and instrumental to the ability of the organization to fulfill its mission.	• The work is episodic and organized around a specific task or project.
• The tasks the team will engage in require more resources than one person alone can provide.	• One person or a couple people can do what needs to be done.
• The team's goals are directly in support of the larger organization's goals.	• There are tasks to complete, events to hold, and so on. The work done in this group may feed into or support the work of a team.
• Membership will be consistent for at least a year and it's important that this team develop trust in each other.	• High levels of trust aren't essential to meet the group's goals and membership can fluctuate.
• Diverse skills and perspectives are required to accomplish the work.	• Divergent perspectives aren't essential. A limited skill set is needed.
• There is someone with the skills to lead or facilitate the team.	• The success of the group doesn't weigh heavily on a leader or facilitator with skills.

Working Alone

Don't be afraid of individuals working alone—either within or apart from a team. Many people (especially introverts) need quiet, independent work time to effectively contribute to the greater whole. Teams can work *interdependently* and *independently* at the same time. For example, if a team of coaches is charged with designing and leading a 3-day summer training, some of the planning might be collaboratively decided, and much of the planning might be done in pairs or by individuals. The entire team may want to review plans after individuals have worked on them alone, but the actual planning of the work is sometimes best done individually. Every part of a team's work doesn't need to be done collaboratively, with everyone sitting around the table. A good indicator of team members trusting each other is that work can be divided up and people can go off and do parts of it alone or in pairs.

HOW DO WE BUILD TEAMS?

Although my intention in this book is to offer you strategies for building great teams, I can't dictate a sequence of steps that will ensure success. Furthermore, although I'll pay close attention to your role as a leader and what you can do, I also know that leaders cannot *make* a team great. You can put conditions in place to increase the likelihood that a team will be effective, but even your ability to put these conditions in place does not guarantee a successful team. Unfortunately, there is so much outside of our immediate control and influence that impacts a team's ability to thrive. That said, there's a whole lot you can do to build a great team. Let's get on with it.

Recommended Reading: *Seedfolks*

Sid Fleischman's *Seedfolks* is a novella about community building unlike any other I have read. It tells the story of how neighborhood residents transform a vacant, rat-infested, garbage-filled lot in Cleveland, Ohio, into a community garden. A different character narrates each chapter: a young Vietnamese girl who mourns her father, a Haitian immigrant, an elderly longtime resident, and many others whose poignant stories describe the pain and struggle of life. Together, these people transform the vacant lot; in turn, the garden transforms the community.

This is a story of grassroots organizing, of the power of sharing stories, and of our yearning to open our hearts to strangers. It depicts how abstract systems intersect and heap challenges on the individuals who exist within them. It is a story about transformational change.

When I taught middle school, I opened the year with this text as a suggestion of the community we could build together. It is a powerful read for young adults, and it also offers a blueprint for leaders who seek to build teams. If there's only one additional book you read related to team building or leadership, read *Seedfolks*—perhaps with your team. It may inspire you and offer you ideas for building a resilient community.

Transformational Coaching Team, 2014

"How has Michele influenced you?" I ask the eighth-grade English teacher about her coach, Michele. "She's helping me be the teacher I always wanted to be," she says. The teacher tells me that she's developed a peer coaching structure in her class where students coach each other—not give each other answers but build each other's capacity through supportive questioning. They're preparing for Socratic seminars, using peer coaching to ensure that their rich conversations end up expressed in their written work. The teacher says, "I think about how Michele has coached me, the way she's asked me questions and believed in me, and I'm teaching my kids to do that because it works."

This teacher's interactions with her students have changed dramatically over the period that she's worked with Michele. She is much more patient, kinder, and gentler with her kids than when I observed her teaching years ago. She tells me how much she trusts Michele, and when I observe her class I see how her students trust her and trust each other. I see vertical communities emerging, radiating out from points throughout our system.

My vision for my coach team was that it would be a community of resistance—resisting obsession with test scores, hierarchical leadership, oppressive urgency, transactional schooling. My vision was that it would be a resilient community, a beloved community, a microcosm of the humanity that our schools need. I wonder if I'm seeing echoes, reflections of this vision in the teacher's classroom, or whether her emerging vision aligns to mine, visions meeting in space and time.

CHAPTER 2

Knowing Ourselves as Leaders

Humanities Team, August 2007

It's the first morning of several days of staff professional development. I was briefly introduced ("our new literacy coach") during a short meeting yesterday, but I don't know everyone's name and have barely talked with those on the team I'll lead. Only 2 days ago, I was asked to design and facilitate this PD, and wanting to be useful and unsure of how to say no I agreed. After a quick community builder, I pull out the standardized test results from last spring: it shows that the great majority of students at this school are far below grade level in math, reading, and writing.

As I sit at the table with the principal and assistant principal during various activities, I realize I might be perceived as being on the "other side"—the side of administration. Technically I'm a teacher on special assignment, I still belong to the teacher's union, and I'll play no role in evaluation; however, I sense that teachers may see me as having abandoned their ranks.

I hope that looking at test scores might be an activity to guide teachers to consider changing the reading program—I hope their analysis will lead to a realization that a different approach needs to be used. But I also admit to myself, as I move to sit with the humanities team, that I want to use the data to shame them. I want them

---

to explain how it is that the great majority of their students are so far below grade level, how it is that eighth graders read at a lower level than when they entered sixth grade.

Their data analysis, however, is disconnected from their own teaching practices—they blame the kids, their parents, their community, their elementary school; they blame the current principal and previous ones. Regardless of the reflective prompt I offer, their reflections avoid looking inward. As the activity progresses and the conversation devolves, my anger rises, my arms fold across my chest, my heart hardens. I'm afraid that I've made a horrible mistake in taking this job. I want to walk out of the room.

We can't talk about building teams without exploring who we are as leaders—and who we want to be as leaders. Who we are as leaders is a composite of factors. Our emotions and the ways we express them are core elements of our leadership presence. Our emotions are influenced by our awareness of our personality as well as the skill set we possess. These components of who we are become nuanced and complicated when we situate ourselves within social constructions of leadership and power, constructions that include our race, ethnicity, class, gender, age, and sexual orientation. These constructions—both externally imposed and internally interpreted—then impact our emotions.

Before we create agendas and facilitate meetings, we need to explore our identities as leaders, which is what we'll begin in this chapter. There's really no point of origin in the complex interplay of these factors, so we'll start with our brains and emotions since it's possible that these reside deepest within our sphere of control. Then we'll circle out into personality and ability and explore how those affect who we are as leaders. Our cultural competence plays a role in who we are as leaders, so we'll briefly consider that impact. From there we'll leap into the big picture—into how leadership and power are socially constructed. Finally, we'll bring those reflections back and return to our brains, our emotions and to the implications of all of this when we show up to lead a meeting and analyze data with a team.

THE AMYGDALA IN A STRANGE LAND

If you aspire to transform schools, you'll need to know about and make friends with your amygdala. You can blame the emotional responses that you don't like in yourself and in others on this ancient little structure in our brains. When a teacher scoffs at a suggestion you make or you want to scream at an eighth grader who rolls her eyes at you, it's the amygdala's fault. The secret to our success as leaders might lie within our relationship to this hidden master.

Here's why: the way the human brain is organized means that you can't avoid having feelings. Everything you hear, see, touch, taste, and smell travels through your body in the form of electrical signals, passing from cell to cell until they reach your brain. Stimuli enter your brain near the base of the spinal cord and travel to your frontal lobe (behind your forehead), which is where rational, logical thinking takes place. But here's the challenge: along the route to your thinking place, these electrical signal pass through your limbic system where emotions are produced.

The amygdala is an almond-sized bunch of neurons in the limbic system. It is activated when, for example, we are strolling through the forest and we hear a rustling in the trees. The information about that noise is sent (within a few tenths of a second) into our limbic system for processing: our mammalian ancestors needed to know quickly whether the noise could be a predator; we had no time to wait for our rational mind to think through the options for a response. Another part of our limbic system, the hippocampus, compares the sound with what it already has on its danger list. It decides that, yes, a rustling sound could be a saber-toothed tiger and therefore could be fatally dangerous, so it sends an alert to our amygdala.

And then the trouble really begins because our amygdala pulls all the alarm bells in our brain, which activate our neural and hormonal systems. Within perhaps a second of hearing the rustling, adrenaline pumps through our body, our muscles constrict in preparation for running, and our heart beats faster. Some of us with particularly jumpy amygdalae might have even sprinted down the trail away from the perceived danger. We leave the forest feeling afraid of the woods, upset by our tendency to startle, and perhaps even a little embarrassed that we reacted in a way that we later recognized as inappropriate—after all, once we were 20 yards away and glanced back we saw a bunny hop across the path.

That's the trouble with our limbic system: it can cause us to respond unnecessarily. Even though we can learn strategies for intervening in this process and for using our mind to change our brain, the fact is that because of the physical organization of our brain, the way we experience stimuli means that we have emotions before reason is activated. The rational area of our brains can't stop the emotion felt by our limbic system, and we constantly experience feelings whether we're aware of them or not. To temper our amygdala we have to learn about feelings—they are often the cues that our amygdalae are active. This is where emotional intelligence (EI) comes into the conversation.

Understand Emotional Intelligence

EI is most simply the knowledge and awareness we have about our feelings. The definition I favor has four components (Goleman, Boyatzis, & McKee, 2002): self-awareness, self-management, social awareness, and social management. Self-awareness is the ability to recognize your own feelings—to know when you're experiencing emotions and to name them. Self-awareness allows you to recognize the impact of your emotions, to know your strengths and limits, and to have self-confidence and an awareness of your capabilities. For example, let's say that in a staff meeting you ask your principal a question and he responds brusquely. You might notice your flushing face and say to yourself, "I feel hurt and embarrassed." This would reflect self-awareness. Without this kind of emotional intelligence, you might unconsciously file this experience away as "yet another time when I was ignored."

The second component of EI is self-management, the ability to make conscious decisions about how to respond to emotions. Self-management includes emotional self-control, transparency, adaptability, and initiative—the readiness to act and seize opportunities. It allows you to anticipate the consequences of the choices you make and respond to the emotion in a way that feels aligned to your values and to the social context in which you find yourself. This doesn't mean that you suppress feelings; it means that you make a conscious choice about how to respond that in the core of your being (not in your panicky limbic system) feels appropriate.

Returning to the example of your principal, after acknowledging that you feel hurt and embarrassed, you might take a deep breath and plan to bring this up with him later. You might wonder whether he is rushing through the meeting, or you might recall that he is usually respectful or even that he often responds like this to questions, which means it's not personal. You might recognize that embarrassment surfaces in you because of a seeming recurring pattern in your life where people in positions of authority don't listen to you. When emotional management is undeveloped, we can get consumed by feeling embarrassed, we might mutter something to a colleague about our rude principal, or we might even walk out or decide we'll never ask another question again. The way we respond could have negative consequences and probably won't help us feel better.

Social awareness is the third element of EI and involves the ability to recognize and understand the feelings that other people experience. Social awareness includes empathy (sensing others' emotions, understanding their perspective, and taking active interest in their concerns), organizational awareness (reading the currents and politics at the organizational level), and service (recognizing the needs of others and meeting them). Therefore, back to the brusque principal, with social awareness you might say to yourself, "I've noticed him checking his watch multiple times during this meeting, and I also see that he looks especially tired. He seems preoccupied. I wonder if he's okay."

Relationship management is the final component of EI and involves the ability to manage conflicts with others, to form healthy relationships, to collaborate, to offer feedback and guidance, and to motivate and inspire others. This skill set enables you to approach your principal the next day and say, "You're usually so receptive to questions in meetings, so I was hurt by your response to my question yesterday. I want you to know the impact that had on me because I value the way we work together. I'm also wondering if everything is okay with you because you seemed distracted yesterday." Your skills in relationship management could also be behind your ability to say, "Yesterday I asked a question at the end of our meeting, and your response felt brusque. I felt embarrassed. You've responded like this on a number of occasions to my questions. For us to collaborate and meet the needs of our students, I want to feel comfortable asking questions, and I need to trust you. Can you help me understand your response yesterday?"

These competencies build on each other. You can't manage your emotions effectively if you're not aware of when you're experiencing them, and it's challenging to navigate other relationships when you aren't clear about and managing your own feelings.

I can imagine that as you read this definition of emotional intelligence you might have been nodding or thinking about how you experience emotions in your work. You might have recognized how emotional intelligence plays a role in what happens in schools and team development. Once you start noticing the role that emotions play in our work—whether in building teams or teaching children—you may feel like you can't stop seeing them everywhere. Why didn't that meeting go as well as you'd hoped? Perhaps because so many staff members are angry about the new curriculum and aren't managing their emotional responses. Why didn't the person you coach follow through on the work she'd agreed to do? Perhaps because she doesn't trust you and may not be conscious of that.

The good news is that emotional intelligence is a set of *learned abilities*—we can learn these skills and become more emotionally intelligent. High emotional intelligence is found behind many indicators of success—from personal relationships to professional success. Some researchers suggest that EI is the strongest predictor of successful job performance and that 90% of top performers are high in emotional intelligence—in all fields, at all levels, in every region of the world (Bradberry and Greaves, 2009). This makes sense because emotional intelligence is the foundation of building trusting relationships, interpersonal communication, flexibility, time management, empathy, decision making, collaboration, presentation skills, assertiveness, regulating stress, managing anger, dealing with unexpected change, and resilience. And this is why in a book about building teams we're starting with this skill set.

Recent discoveries about the brain suggest that we can develop emotional intelligence. It was long thought that a brain didn't change, but in fact the brain grows new neural connections as it develops skills, a quality called neuroplasticity. For thousands of years, the limbic system kept our species alive. When our nomadic ancestors were out collecting nuts and berries and heard a rustle in the bushes, their limbic system responded in a way that made them flee or fight—appropriate responses when the noise might have been a predator. The human brain now needs to adapt to a context in which we don't need to panic so quickly at perceived danger. We aren't served by a flood of adrenaline into our systems or by an urge to fight or take flight when an eighth grader rolls her eyes at us. Neuroplasticity means that we can develop habits that allow us to recognize our emotions and respond to them in appropriate ways. In Appendix F you'll find recommended resources for further exploration of these ideas.

Emotional intelligence isn't about suppressing, controlling, or even eliminating emotions. It's about recognizing a full range of emotions when they arise and making choices about how to respond. Emotional intelligence allows us to feel empowered and to act in integrity, to experience joy, to build strong connections with others, and to create communities of resilient educators and children.

Layer on Personality

Emotional intelligence is a skill that can be developed, and there's convincing evidence that for a leader, the more, the better. Personality is another component of who we are as a leader, but, in contrast to our emotions, it is something to understand rather than to develop. Awareness of personality gives us insight into what we feel, how we respond, and how to manage our own emotions and those of others; therefore, this knowledge can contribute to increasing our emotional intelligence.

Personality is an individual's unique patterned body of habits, traits, attitudes, and thoughts. Within the field of psychology, there are different approaches to describing personalities. I favor the Myers-Briggs Type Indicator (MBTI), which is based on Jungian psychology and is the easiest to understand. The MBTI is prevalent in the

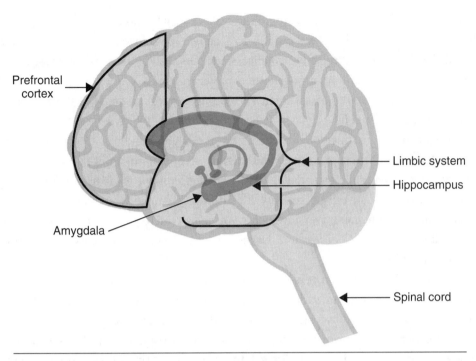

Figure 2.1. The Brain

public and private sectors, and people often first encounter it in career counseling (Briggs Myers 1995).

Personality traits include a tendency toward introversion or extroversion—how you get energy. Introverts replenish their energy reserves from time alone or in small groups, whereas extroverts feel energized from large groups. Introverts tend to want quiet time to process, enjoy working independently, and prefer to work with one partner or the same partners over a period of time. Extroverts often like brainstorming in teams, want to frequently mix up the configuration of groups and pairs, and often turn and talk during quiet reflection times. With just these few examples, I imagine you can see how knowledge about your and team members' personalities could be useful.

Personality also contributes to how you make sense of information—do you focus on concrete, actual data? Or do you prefer to use your intuition and interpret what you see or hear? Our approaches to decision making also differ according to personality.

Some people prefer to first look at logic and reasoning, whereas others make decisions based primarily on feelings and emotions. Finally, the way we deal with the outside world also differs according to personality. Some personalities prefer their outer world to be very structured and orderly, yet others prefer spontaneity and flexibility. If you've never taken a personality assessment, I encourage you to do so. (See the resources recommended in Appendix F.)

Understanding your personality can help you recognize and play to your strengths and preferences and accept yourself and identify areas for growth. It's also reassuring to discover that some habit you have had forever (e.g., creating to-do lists, color-coding your calendars) is just your personality. It's empowering to understand your tendency toward introversion or extroversion so that you can attend to your energy levels. We all have a finite amount of energy, and the more we can control how we use it, the more effective we'll be.

Understanding your own personality boosts the self-awareness component of your emotional intelligence, and understanding the personalities of team members boosts your social awareness and social management. If you know, for example, that six of the eight members of your team are extroverts, then you can organize meetings to accommodate their needs, and you can also ask the extroverts at times to accommodate the needs of the introverts. You will also be able to better differentiate learning opportunities with information about how others process information, how they make sense of data, and what kinds of data are most compelling to them. Understanding is invaluable as it is a gateway for empathy.

Thinking back on my leadership of the humanities team, I recognize how my lack of awareness about my personality impacted my emotions and made me a less effective leader. For example, I prefer my outer world to be very structured and orderly—I love color-coded calendars, to-do lists, and schedules made far in advance. I'm not able to produce my best work when I'm asked at the last minute to design and deliver PD (as I was often asked to do). Those requests produced a cascade of emotions of which I was unaware and of which I didn't manage well. Furthermore, as an introvert, my energy plummets when I interact with dozens of new people for many days. As I remember my first weeks at Wilson Middle School, I see how I was often exhausted because I did not attend to my own needs.

I wonder what might have happened had I known about what it means to be an introvert and had I developed relationships with the staff in one-on-one situations. I wonder what would have happened had I not been pushed immediately into a front-and-center place of the room and instead been able to professionally express my feelings and communicate my needs. I wonder what would have happened had I said to myself, "I feel anxious and put on the spot right now because I've been asked to deliver the back-to-school PD and have only one day to plan. My personality preference is to have a much longer time to think, plan, and prepare, and because I'm an introvert I also prefer to build relationships in smaller settings. I know that building relationships needs to be my top priority as I join this staff." I suspect that this kind of awareness would have helped me make decisions in those moments and would have helped me manage my emotions.

Consider Ability

To do any complex task well, we need skill, will, knowledge, capacity, and emotional intelligence. Together, these elements constitute ability, and they are inextricably connect to feed into each other: it's hard to have skill if you don't have knowledge; it's hard to have will if you don't have skill; and emotional intelligence is both a skill set and a capacity. These are useful buckets to think about because when we're struggling to implement something there's likely to be a gap in one of these areas.

Leading a team requires a skill set in which very few of us have ever been trained. Being able to identify your gaps can boost your emotional intelligence because you might recognize that the root of some of your uncomfortable feelings (such as insecurity) might be just a learning gap. Learning gaps can be closed, they are not a reflection of who we are, and they don't mean we're not meant to be a leader. An awareness of our abilities helps us understand and manage feelings.

I've created a tool for you to use to reflect on yourself as a facilitator. The Facilitator Core Competencies (Appendix A) will help you assess your skill, knowledge, emotional intelligence, will and capacity. Had I been given this tool during my first year as a humanities team lead, I may have felt overwhelmed and also relieved. I felt like I was stumbling through the leadership role, unclear on the skill set I needed and unsure of where to start learning. I would have rated myself low on almost every indicator, but I would have also felt like I had a map to start plotting my learning journey. I hope this tool will help you appreciate the complexity of being a facilitator, and I hope it will guide you to recognize your strengths and identify areas for growth. You might use it to set goals for your development and track your progress over time.

My intention in this book is to build your skill in and knowledge of the items identified on the Facilitator Core Competencies, but I am aware of the limitations. Even though reading increases knowledge, you'll also need practice and feedback. You'll benefit from discussing these ideas with others—talking is a primary way we process information. We also make meaning by writing, so I want to encourage you to capture your written reflections on the prompts offered throughout this book. Reflection is a primary vehicle for cultivating emotional intelligence because the process itself leads to the formation of new neural pathways.

Cultivate Cultural Competence

Cultural competence is both a skill and knowledge set. It means having an awareness of one's own cultural identity and the ability to understand and appreciate people of other identities and to work effectively with them. Our *cultural self* is formed in great part by our gender, age, race and ethnicity, socioeconomic status, class background, and sexual orientation. It can also be influenced by the region we grew up in and by our affiliation to religious traditions. These cultural identifiers form who we are as leaders and affect how we show up in leadership roles and how we are received as leaders.

For example, when I taught a group of new immigrants from Yemen, I recognized that my interactions with their parents would differ in some ways from how I interacted with other parents. When I met the father of one of my students, a very traditional Muslim man, I did not shake his hand: I had been advised that because I was a woman, physical contact would be inappropriate. I also scheduled my parent–teacher conference with him in a public place, recognizing that he may feel uncomfortable being alone with me, as a woman, in a classroom. I wanted him to feel at ease coming to his daughter's school and meeting with her teacher, and I knew that I needed to be aware of some of his social customs. Because I'd had very little interaction with Muslim immigrants and had no knowledge about Yemen, I had to do some research. I asked my students for advice (they were wise teachers), and I also consulted colleagues who'd had more experience working with Muslim immigrants.

When we are not conscious of how our identities affect who we are as leaders, we may view our ways as the best ways and make assumptions based on these values about how we should lead, communicate, make decisions, or manage conflict. To understand others and to appreciate their cultures, we need to be able to see our own cultures with some objectivity and recognize that they are social constructs. If you can't name your own culture and how it manifests, you can't code switch—which is the ability to shift your communication patterns when working with people from other cultures.

One year, I coached a young new principal from the Midwest who had never lived in a diverse urban area like Oakland, California. Almost from the outset, her communication with her mostly veteran staff was challenged by the pop culture references she made, the tools she used for communication, and the language she used. Her staff also complained that she was indirect, that they wanted her to just say what she thought, and that they distrusted her "niceness." This well-intentioned principal lacked awareness of how her ways of relating to others were culturally constructed: they were appropriate in her suburban community back home but not in Oakland. She also didn't recognize that her lack of awareness was diminishing the impact she could have.

Knowing who you are as a leader involves a lot of exploration—into your emotional landscape, your personality styles, your skills and abilities, and the cultural construction of self. This knowledge is essential when leading a team: It's from this knowledge that we can make a tremendous range of decisions, and it's from this knowledge that we can access transformational potential.

REFLECT: Cultural Competency

1. Of the various identity markers, is there one that feels most central to who you are? Your gender, ethnicity, religion, sexual orientation, age, or something else? Why is this so?

2. What does it mean to you to be a man or woman?

3. What does it mean to you to from the ethnic group to which you identify?

4. How do you think your class background affects who you are as a leader in the community you work in?

5. How do you think your race or ethnicity affect who you are as a leader in the community you work in?

6. How do you think your political leanings affect who you are as a leader?

7. How do you think your gender affects who you are as a leader? As a team member?

8. What feelings come up for you when reflecting on your cultural self-awareness?

9. Are there groups of people whom you find challenging to work with because of their cultural identities? Because they are a particular gender, ethnicity, age? What feels most challenging when working with them?

10. Are there groups of people you'd like to increase your understanding of? What thoughts do you have about how you could go about doing this?

EXPLORING THE TERRAIN OF LEADERSHIP

Let's expand this discussion of who we are as leaders further into the social and political realm. A reflection on who you are as a leader includes looking at the experiences that fed the beliefs you hold about leadership, authority, and power. This reflection can build self-knowledge and emotional intelligence as we recognize that our leadership identities are a construct—they were informed by our families of origin, and our culture and society. With this comes the awareness that identities aren't fixed and can be shifted. We can choose who we want to be as leaders.

Reflect on Home and Family

Who held power in your family when you were growing up? What kind of power was that? What was it based on? What were you taught about authority? What granted someone authority? How did those in authority positions manage conflict or express disagreements?

The power dynamics in our families of origin deeply influence how we relate to those with positional authority at work. Call to mind someone who has what you perceive as power over you—perhaps your supervisor, manager, or principal. Think about the way you relate to this person: Do you get anxious if you receive an email from the person asking for a meeting? Do you feel comfortable sharing your concerns or doubts? Are there ways you relate to him or her that are similar to how you related to an authority figure in your childhood? What feelings come up for you when reflecting on these questions?

Our formative experiences have ways of sneaking up and taking over while we aren't looking. If you were raised in a home where your father ruled by fear and you were taught to do what you were told, not to talk back, and never question his authority, you've internalized some messages about power. You may consciously or unconsciously act in response to what you experienced in your early years. Of course, this experience doesn't determine who you will be as a leader—you have tremendous control over that—but you'll need to cultivate awareness of your experience in an authoritative leadership model.

Ask yourself these questions:

- In what ways am I replicating the authority models from the home I was raised in? What might be the impact on others of replicating these?

- Are there ways I'm consciously being a different kind of leader from what I experienced as a child?
- Do I ever think, "I sound just like my mother/father right now?" Does that evoke positive or negative feelings?

Who we are professionally is rarely isolated from who we are personally. We are complex beings, and every aspect of our lives—both past and present—intersects. I coached a principal once who had been raised in a very strict military family. He frequently told me, "I'm not yet ready to go to therapy and process what I lived through as a kid, but I'm really clear that I can't treat my staff the way my dad treated our family." This was useful information for me as a coach, and although I never probed into what he'd experienced I was able to help him make connections between his leadership actions and his childhood experiences. As he cultivated that awareness, he was able to take more intentional action as a leader.

Define Good Leadership

Who we are as team facilitators is also informed by models of leadership in our society. Reflect on these questions:

- Who is a leader you admire?
- Who are the leaders in your community, city and country?
- What kind of leadership do they demonstrate?
- How did they come to be leaders? Can you relate to them?
- What do you think makes a good leader?
- What kind of leader do you aspire to be?

Very few societies have shared agreements about what constitutes *good* leadership. Depending on your beliefs and values, a good leader might listen to all voices and take them into account when making a decision; or a good leader might consult with a few trusted advisors and then make a decision; or a good leader might make a decision alone based on his or her expert knowledge and experience. Team leaders can benefit from exploring the big philosophical questions that surround the definition of good leadership. When we are aware of our core values, beliefs, dispositions, preferences, and histories, we can make conscious choices about our leadership stance.

Institutions also struggle to define the core competencies of good leadership. I have seen very few schools or districts that delineate these criteria—not for site administrators, superintendents, coaches, or teacher leaders. This becomes problematic when stakeholders have different needs and expectations and operate from assumptions that their needs and expectations are shared. A principal, for example, might lead in response to what she understands her school community's needs are. Her supervisor, however, might have a different perception of how she should lead. When stakeholders are not on the same page, they place different values on a leader's actions. In this case, because the supervisor holds positional authority the principal may be obliged to follow her boss's mandates and may feel that she has to compromise her values. The root cause of this kind of conflict is that there's no definition of or agreement on good leadership.

At Wilson Middle School, where I led the humanities team, among the staff there was a vast difference of opinion on the administration's leadership, which became most evident in conversations around discipline. Some teachers felt that students who shouted in the hallways or wore hoodies should receive an office referral. Others longed for the days when corporal punishment was acceptable and thought cursing was grounds for suspension. Others were alarmed by the high rates of office referrals and suspensions and argued that the problem lay in the teachers' response to student behavior. Most of the time, everyone was frustrated with the administrators, who wavered between camps trying to appease all. Staff struggled to get behind decisions that were made, and some even undermined those decisions. The principal's boss told him to act in one way; teachers had conflicting perceptions of the problem and solutions; parents also had strong opinions. What was missing was a clear definition of and agreement on what a principal in this school or in our district needed to value and do.

A lack of agreement about what constitutes effective leadership in a school creates a disequilibrium or discord that percolates through a team. For example, when one person dominates discussions, some members of the team might look to you—as the positional leader—to address the behavior. If you don't, then there's a risk that their confidence in you and respect for you will diminish because they hold a belief that as the leader it's your job to manage people on the team. However, it's also possible that another team member might believe that if someone dominates the discussion he also has authority to address the issue with the overtalker. He values a different model of leadership. So where would you stand in this? If you think that because you're the facilitator it's your job to deal with that dominant team member and then another team member intervenes, would you feel like he undermined your authority? Do you worry that others will see him as the leader and won't respect you? Or are you grateful for the shared leadership?

Within our schools and teams, we don't have to necessarily agree entirely on what good leadership is. However, we do need to know what we each value, and we need to make these values clear to each other. We start by cultivating the self-awareness that allows us to understand who we are, why we act as we do, and what we believe about leadership and authority. Then, to manage relationships, we need to share this self-awareness with those we lead, and we need to understand their values, beliefs, and needs. One way to do this is to share some of your responses to the prompts in this chapter about leadership and to invite team members to do the same. Share your thoughts on what good leadership is, and listen to their definitions. Let your team know why you lead in the way you do and also that you're willing to hear feedback on your leadership. We don't need to necessarily seek full consensus—understanding would go a long way.

Acknowledge Your Identity: What Is My Role?

Whether you are a teacher who is also a department head, a teacher who has become a coach, or a teacher or coach who has become an administrator, you've experienced an identity shift. You may have noticed some conflicting feelings. Perhaps you think that by becoming a coach you've moved over to the "other side" and are now seen as allying with the administrators. You may have become a coach precisely because you felt such strong affiliation with teachers and because you want to help them manage the overwhelming demands of the job. But maybe they've started seeing you differently now that you're not in front of a group of kids all day and now that you have regular meetings with the principal. Maybe you've also gained new insight into their teaching practices, which raise some unsettling questions in you.

This is all part of a very normal process that many of us go through when we become leaders. We may even be reluctant at first to call ourselves a leader, but if you are a coach, department head, team facilitator, coordinator, grade-level lead, or instructional facilitator, you are a leader. You can define leadership to align with your core values and vision.

There are subtle distinctions in terminology that are worth considering and that reflect how you see yourself in relationship to a team. You might call yourself a *facilitator* of a team or a *leader*. A *leader* is often imbued with more authority to make decisions about who is in the group, what happens in the group, and the direction it's headed; a leader attends to both process and product. A *facilitator* may have been asked or invited to work with the group to guide its process. Facilitators usually don't have decision-making power or say over the product or outcomes.

Most site- or district-based coaches who work with teams are facilitators, but some teachers consider anyone who partners with administrators or who comes from the central office as having authority—they may see you clearly as a leader. What's important is that you are clear on your role and what it means and that the members of your team are clear. In this book, I alternate between using *facilitator* and *leader* because many of us play both roles at different times.

> *Authority is always granted to people who are perceived as authoring their own words, their own actions, their own lives, rather than playing a scripted role at great remove from their own hearts.*
>
> PARKER PALMER, 1997

Reflect on Your Role

Consider a team you're currently facilitating or leading.

1. Who are you now in this team?

2. What roles have you previously played in the team? How has the shift in your role affected you? How do you think it's affected others?

3. What's your formal title—facilitator, coach, leader—in this team? Who determined this? What does this title mean to you?

4. What understanding do team members have about your role? How did they receive this message?

5. How does your formal title affect how you feel about your role in this team?

THE POTENTIAL OF TRANSFORMATIONAL LEADERSHIP

I want to be transparent about the leadership I believe would best meet the needs of the children in our schools and perhaps of the inhabitants of our earth: transformational leadership. It offers the potential to do more than put a bandage on our problems; it offers the ability to create fundamental, long-lasting change. According to Bass and Riggio (2005), the authors of the definitive volume on this model of leadership, there are four components of transformational leadership:

1. Intellectual stimulation: Transformational leaders challenge the status quo and encourage creativity among others.

2. Individualized consideration: To foster supportive relationships, transformational leaders develop open lines of communication so that others feel free to share ideas. This allows leaders to recognize the unique contributions of others.

3. Inspirational motivation: Transformational leaders have a clear vision that they are able to articulate. They generate passion and motivation in others to fulfill these goals.

4. Idealized influence: Transformational leaders serve as role models. Others emulate these leaders and internalize their ideas because they trust and respect their leaders. (Bass and Riggio 2005, 5-7)

Transformational leaders are energetic, enthusiastic, and passionate, and they inspire others to change expectations, perceptions, and motivations so that they can work toward common goals. You can probably predict that researchers have found that this style of leadership has a positive effect on a group, particularly in contrast to the other two most common leadership styles—transactional leadership and laissez-faire leadership. Transactional leaders use rewards and punishments to achieve compliance from others; they seek to maintain the status quo. Laissez-faire leaders hold a leadership position but don't provide leadership, leaving followers to fend for themselves (Bass and Riggio, 2005, 193-194).

I hope that this might provoke an exploration of models of leadership and of how you lead others, and I want to be transparent about my underlying values. I believe that the children and adults in our schools need transformational leaders who seek to build the capacity of all in the system, who strive to rupture the status quo, and who create learning communities that are far more just, equitable, and joyful than what currently exists.

Reflect on Leadership

1. Who held power in your family when you were growing up? What kind of power was that? What was it based on?

2. What were you taught about authority in your childhood home? What granted someone authority?

3. What did you learn as a child from other social institutions (e.g., a church, the military, school) that contributed to your understandings of leadership and authority?

4. In what ways might you be replicating the leadership or authority models you experienced as a child? What might be the impact of replicating those?

5. Are there ways you're consciously being a different kind of leader from what you experienced in your childhood home?

6. Who are the leaders in your community, city, and country? What kind of leadership do they demonstrate?

7. Can you relate to the leaders in your community? What do you have in common with them? How are they different from you?

8. Who is a leader you admire? From which leaders do you draw inspiration?

9. What do you think makes a good leader?

10. Why do you lead in the way you do?

11. What assumptions are you acting on as a leader about yourself and your team and the work to be done?

12. How does the system in which you are operating impact who you are as a leader?

13. How do you negotiate power dynamics as a leader? Where do you notice power playing a role in your leadership?

14. What kind of leader do you aspire to be? How do you want others to see you?

15. What kind of leader does your team need you to be?

16. What kind of leader does the community you serve need you to be?

SPOTTING THE TENTACLES OF POWER

If you aspire to be a transformational leader, you will benefit from reflecting on how power works within our historical, social, and economic systems. Power is an abstract concept, but it has concrete effects and, left unchecked, can undermine our intentions. The ability to spot how power is manifesting, who is holding power and how it's being held, and who doesn't have power is essential in transformational efforts. Power in group dynamics needs to be managed for our efforts to result in something different from what we already see and experience in our institutional settings.

To talk about power in the context of transformation, we need to start by talking about structural inequities because they go hand in hand. Authority, leadership, and power in schools have emerged from a history in which certain freedoms and privileges were granted to some groups over others—this is what defines a *structural inequity*. Structural inequities are intrinsic to the majority of our institutions—they are part of the fabric of our social, economic, and political systems, and they have their own current manifestations.

Let me offer an example. A cursory glance at the composition of top administrators in any school district will reflect the predominance of male leadership—in fact, less than 25% of superintendents in the United States are women. We know, of course, that this isn't because women lack the skills or are unable to perform the duties of a superintendent. Power has worked visibly and invisibly to keep women out of this position. Furthermore, it is not an anomaly that women or people of color are not found in the highest ranks of our school system. In fact, it is a product of our history. Privilege has been granted institutionally and informally in our society for hundreds of years based on gender, race and ethnicity, class, and sexual orientation. To interrupt inequitable power dynamics, we need to recognize how power has been constructed, in which structures, and who has benefited and been excluded. This kind of reflection and examination will be hard work, but it is part of transformation.

Understanding power means that you can walk into a room and recognize where you stand in relationship to this history, how you hold power in a group, and on what basis. If, for example, you are a male leader, then having an understanding of power means that you recognize how your gender has given your voice privilege and priority for many, many years—that this privilege was institutionalized in the right to vote, to attend colleges, to own property, to be published. The legacy of this institutionalization of privilege is that many people unconsciously grant others the right to speak, to make decisions, and to direct others because we have internalized unequal power structures. Given this awareness, as a male leader you may intentionally make decisions about when you speak, how often, how much, and how you create space for others to speak.

On many occasions, I've observed struggling teams so I could make recommendations for improvement. Although I notice the facilitator's technical moves—the agenda, protocols for discussion, and meeting opening—what captures my attention is how power manifests in the group. I see how a facilitator wields power in her selection of words, body language, and emotional tone. And I see how team members use power in their words, nonverbal communication, and emotional tenor. I see how control is exercised by the room set-up (e.g., team sits around a single, large table; team sits in individual desks facing the front of the room). My recommendation might be that the leader join the team and sit in a circle rather than stand in the front of the room, but I explain that this is because when he stands in front of the room he's communicating to his team that he has power over them: They literally have to look up to him. Perhaps he did this unconsciously—that's how power often works, quietly and insidiously—but in doing so he is establishing leadership based on dominance, one many human beings resist.

Transformational leaders need to intentionally interrupt power to create something different. Doing this takes the ability to spot the manifestation of power and skill because, for example, what exactly do we say when we notice that the same individuals (who mirror those who have had power for hundreds of years) continuously dominate conversations? Interrupting power also takes tremendous courage, and once you begin to see the undercurrents of power it can be scary to interrupt it.

"We have no morally persuasive power with those who can feel our underlying contempt for them."

DR. MARTIN LUTHER KING, JR.

If you are feeling just a little bit overwhelmed by what it takes to lead a team, I commend you on this awareness. Coaching teams is challenging because of this extensive, complex set of factors that influences who we are when we show up to a meeting. We bring our wild emotions and finicky brains, our fluctuating and fixed identities. We move into undefined expectations around leadership and differences of values and beliefs, and we exist inevitably in a historical and current system of power that can be hard to recognize at times. Figuring out who you are as a leader is hard, complicated work, but it's also the starting point if you want to exercise transformational leadership.

Reflect on Power Dynamics

Use these questions when reflecting on a team you facilitate, when observing a team, or when you are a process observer in a team.

1. How is the facilitator physically positioned in the room and with the team?
2. How are team members positioned in relationship to the facilitator and to each other?
3. Who speaks first in this team?
4. Who speaks the most in this team?
5. What or who gives someone the right to speak? How is a team member heard?
6. What is the impact on the group of those who don't speak?
7. Who makes decisions in this team? How are decisions made? Is it clear when decisions are being made?
8. Which emotions are demonstrated by the team leader? What impact do these emotions have on team members?
9. Which emotions are demonstrated by team members? What impact do these emotions have on the rest of the team and on the leader?
10. Who holds power in this team? What is that power based on?
11. In what ways does the holder of power and the kind of power that's being held reflect historical manifestations of power?
12. What patterns are there in this team in terms of who holds power? Do any of these patterns reflect historical manifestations of power?

EMOTIONS ARE CONTAGIOUS

Now that we've spiraled out into models of leadership and systems of power, let's loop back to our brains and emotions and reflect on how this knowledge informs our practice. In their book *Primal Leadership: Learning to Lead with Emotional Intelligence*, Goleman, Boyatzis, and McKee (2002) offer invaluable insights. They suggest that a leader's emotional intelligence is the key to success for any organization. Conversely, a toxic leader is poison to a workplace. Furthermore, they convincingly argue that emotional intelligence is the key to success of any organization. For hundreds of thousands of years, our nomadic ancestors survived in small bands if they understood each other, got along, and cooperated. They had to feel connected to each other and valued by each other. Today, educators and organizations thrive when leaders cultivate connections, understandings, and relationships between members of the community.

The finding that emotions are contagious is the bridge between the emotional intelligence of leaders and team development (Goleman, Boyatzis and McKee, 2002, p. 9). Think for a moment of someone in whose presence you did not feel good; perhaps the person left you feeling exhausted or sick. Now think about what that person's emotional state was when you were with him or her. Most likely, it was a negative one. Researchers explain that other people's emotions affect our brains, which affect other systems in our bodies (Hanson, 2009). For example, research in intensive care units has shown that the comforting presence of another person lowers a patient's blood pressure. One person can transmit signals that can alter the hormone levels, cardiovascular function, sleep rhythms, and even immune function inside the body of another. Other people's moods can change our physiologies and emotions—we can, indeed, catch feelings from someone else.

The percentage of time people feel positive emotions at work turns out to be one of the strongest predictors of satisfaction, and therefore, for instance, of how likely employees are to quit.

(GOLEMAN ET AL., 2002, P. 14)

Furthermore, neurologists report that groups tend to synchronize their feelings with each other and that a group's moods are largely independent of the actual stresses and struggles that the group members face (Hanson, 2009). This means that as a unit teams have their own levels of emotional intelligence. This level may or may not reflect the EI of the individuals within the group. Chapter 6 expands on this and offers strategies for building the EI of a team, but first let's continue to focus on you as a leader and how your EI affects those you lead.

Implications for Team Leaders

This research holds many implications for those of us who coach teams—about ourselves as leaders and about how we bring groups of people together. The following are some of the primary lessons that apply to coaching groups.

As the leader, your emotions matter the most. You have the maximum power to drive a group's emotions because everyone looks to you for emotional cues. This could feel daunting because it implies that you need to be aware of and able to manage your feelings, and it could be empowering because you can use your emotions to promote a team's development and productivity. First and foremost, we need to learn how to manage our own emotions. No amount of agenda templates, protocols, lists of norms, or decision-making strategies will shortcut this learning journey.

As the leader, you set the emotional standard. In a group, leaders tend to talk more than anyone else, and what they say is listened to more carefully. Team members also watch the leader more than anyone else, give more credence to whatever he or she says, and tend to see the leader's emotional reaction as the most valid one. As facilitators, our way of seeing things has special weight, and we often manage meaning for a group. We can model how to interpret and react emotionally to a given situation.

You can intentionally spread positive feelings. Your facial expressions, voice, and gestures convey your feelings. So the more open you are with positive feelings and the greater your skill at transmitting those emotions, the more readily those emotions will spread.

When people feel good, they work at their best. A primary responsibility for a leader is to help team members experience positive feelings—confidence, hope, inspiration, and connection. Positive emotional states are conditions for engaging in hard work. To cultivate these states in others, we have to manage our own feelings so that we're not bringing negative emotions such as chronic anger, anxiety, or a sense of futility into our work. This doesn't mean that everyone needs to feel happy all the time, but, beyond moderate stress levels, anxiety erodes mental abilities and the ability to accurately read the emotions of others, which as a result impairs social skills.

The more emotionally demanding the work, the more empathetic the leader needs to be. There are probably only a handful of professions in which the emotional demands are as high as they are for educators. Teachers and administrators have to make hundreds—possibly even thousands—of decisions each day that affect children. Decision making itself is emotionally taxing, in addition to the fact that many of these decisions are emotionally charged. The emotional experience of working in organizations that are in constant change is draining; working in communities in crisis can lead to secondary trauma for educators; working with people (children and teens) who express strong feelings is exhausting. We know this, yet sometimes leaders struggle to demonstrate empathy.

Leaders need to help a team build emotional intelligence. I frequently hear leaders express dismay over a staff member's lack of emotional intelligence. They recognize it as a primary problem in how a group is running or how the individual is doing, but they don't address it. Although some individuals have emotional intelligence gaps that far exceed what can be addressed in our domain of school and professional development, leaders can do a great deal to build a team's self-awareness and ways of relating to each other. Professional development for educators in building emotional intelligence might just be the highest leverage kind of PD possible. Chapter 6 continues this discussion.

> *"I've come to a frightening conclusion that I am the decisive element in the classroom. It's my personal approach that creates the climate. It's my daily mood that makes the weather."*
>
> HAIM GINOTT

Our way of being as a leader and our moods are firmly within our sphere of control when we show up to a team meeting. Leaders have a primary responsibility to know ourselves, to understand and manage our emotions, to be aware of our triggers and sore spots, to know our strengths, and to lead in a way that helps the group meet its goals. There are various ways to engage in this kind of exploration: through individual reflective practices such as reading and writing, by working with a coach or at times a therapist, and by engaging with others such as in a leadership professional learning community. To build an effective team you need to know yourself. There is no other place to start.

Reflect on Emotional Intelligence

1. Think about your experiences as a member of a team. What kinds of things impact how you've felt? In what ways have you responded to those feelings?

2. Which feelings do you most often experience when coaching or leading a team? How do you suspect those feelings impact the group?

3. How aware—or not—are you of those feelings? When are you most aware of your emotions?

4. In what kinds of situations are you less aware of your feelings?

5. How does it feel to consider that as the leader your emotions matter the most? What does this bring up for you?

6. In what ways do you cultivate positive feelings in the groups you coach? How does it feel to you to do this? What do you see as a result of doing so?

7. When have you noticed a connection between the quality of your work and the positive emotions you experienced? What were the factors that allowed you to feel good and do your best work?

8. What strategies do you use to manage your feelings, especially when you're feeling upset, frustrated, worried, or hopeless?

9. Recall a time, if possible, when you may have modeled how to react emotionally to a given situation. What was the emotional tenor of your reaction? How did that affect the group?

10. Of the four domains of emotional intelligence (self-awareness, self-management, social awareness, relationship management), in which do you feel most competent? In which area might it be most useful to expand your skills? How might you go about doing this?

11. How do you know when someone expresses empathy for you? How do you express empathy for others?

12. Is there someone on your team who may be experiencing more stress and who may need you to be more empathetic? What might that look and sound like?

Transformational Coaching Team, August 2012

It's the first morning of seven days of professional development and community building with the group of coaches I hired. We are sitting in a circle in my living room, eating a breakfast that I prepared. I formally open our meeting with introductions inviting everyone to share his or her name, his or her role in our team, and where he or she is coming from.

I say, "My name is Elena, and my job is to take care of you so that you can do your best work. To take care of you, I'll ask that you let me know what you need." I have thought about this for months: My job is to take care of them, to care for their learning needs. I see myself as primarily a coach (although I'm officially their manager) but also as a provider of a range of other needs that as human beings we all have, including the need for community and even for food. I will extend myself in any way I need to support them in their work, and I have concrete ideas for how to do this.

I've spent half a year exploring my fears about taking on this role. I've never successfully led a team. The stakes are high: We're receiving a huge federal grant and are expected to make big changes in our schools. In addition, we had a major unexpected leadership change that's rattled our program. Although I experience moments of insecurity, I have written up a vision for myself as a leader, I have a work plan and detailed professional development plan for this year, I've thought through big picture questions and details, and I'm excited. In each coach, I see great potential, unique qualities, and the possibility that we'll work well together. I really like these people.

I sense the nervousness in the room, and I know it will pass. I invite stories to be told: I offer various ways for people to share who they are and to speak from the heart and about what matters. I ensure that there's structure so that everyone has time to talk. I prompt reminders to listen to your own listening, for listening is something we'll practice over and over. I'm thoughtful to keep my own verbal participation to a minimum. I want to be a colleague, a thought partner, a coach of coaches. This is my team: I feel protective from the start and intent on avoiding the traps of hierarchy and rank. I want to create something new with this team that will meet our needs as learners and human beings so that we can contribute to meeting the needs of children.

CHAPTER 3

Creating a Culture of Trust

Humanities Team, 2008

Wilson Middle School had a reputation in the district. I knew it was struggling. When I toured prior to accepting the job, the principal took me to Bess's classroom. The lights were off in the room, an audio book played, and students read along. Bess sat at her desk at the back of the class, a baseball cap pulled low over her eyes. When I was introduced she barely lifted her head, made a small nodding gesture, and said nothing.

I had no trouble seeing what wasn't working at this school: The principal was overwhelmed and under supported; some teachers talked from the front of the room the entire time; others commandeered a strict and silent environment; and many classrooms were chaotic. Kids wandered the campus, clutching what they claimed were bathroom passes. The bulletin boards lining the walls bore a few scraps of student work—book reports and tests—but many were empty, lined with nothing but tattered butcher paper.

In my interview with the principal, I described the instructional practices we used in the school I was leaving where I had taught for 6 years—inquiry-driven, project-based, equity-centered practices. I thought I would just bring those approaches across town with me and plant them in this new school.

Truth telling now: I felt angry before I even began working at Wilson Middle, a place I didn't wanted to be associated with too closely, a school I never—in the two years that I worked there—referred to as my school. I didn't want to be a leader at this school, although I was asked to be one and be seen as one. I didn't trust that some—even perhaps most—of the teachers wanted to meet the needs of children, nor did I believe they knew how to do so.

It took me some years to figure out who I wanted to be as a leader and what my vision for myself and my work was, a journey prompted by my experiences leading the humanities team. I came to this awareness by working with a coach, engaging in a great deal of personal reflection, and talking with friends and colleagues. Articulating a vision for myself has proven to be a guide as I've navigated other challenging teams and contexts: I calibrate my actions to align with my vision, not a dysfunctional organization, not in response to the behaviors of individuals, and not in reaction to a fleeting feeling or thought. I know who I want to be and what I want to do in the world.

I aspire to build resilient communities that transform schools and teams that take up challenging work together, that discuss difficult issues and make hard decisions, whose members put aside their own personal needs, beliefs, and interests in service of the greater good. For us to build teams that are resilient and transformational, we need to intentionally create a culture of trust. There is no way to get around this truth. And to cultivate trust, we need to know ourselves as leaders. The work of team development is cyclical—the ability to build trust is predicated upon the ability to know yourself.

Trust is also built through the structures that we put in place to foster healthy relationships and to make decisions. If structures don't exist, the chance of creating a transformational community is lessened. We can strengthen trust by holding ourselves and our teams to implementing those structures and by reflecting on the implementation, making course adjustments as necessary, and being flexible and responsive.

WHY HUMAN BINGO DOESN'T BUILD TRUST

Midway through my career as a teacher, I helped start a new public school in Oakland called ASCEND. Larissa Adam was also a founding teacher and later became the principal. She had lived and worked in the community we served for almost a decade. I had observed her teaching and was in awe of the way she knew her students and organized instruction. As a leader, she was thoughtful and reflective and listened carefully to staff questions and concerns. She shared how her experience as a child inspired her to lead a school with strong arts integration. She walked the walk and talked the talk.

Trust is the feeling of confidence we have in another's character and competence (Covey, 2006). Character comprises integrity, which includes how honest we are and how aligned our actions are to what we say. It also encompasses intent: What is our agenda? Are we really here to help or serve another, or do we have hidden agendas? The confidence we have in another's competence will also build or decrease our trust. Does the other person have the skills, abilities, attitudes, and knowledge that we need? Can he produce the results he says he will? Distrust, therefore, is suspicion of integrity and capabilities.

Most of us have experienced what I'd call *traditional methods* for building trust in a convening group: getting to know you activities (perhaps including human bingo), staff social events, and maybe even a ropes course. But how do these activities build *confidence* in *character* and *competence* as educators? For example, when I taught third grade, these kinds of activities didn't build my *confidence* in the second-grade teachers whom I hoped would have the skill and commitment to prepare my future students for success. I appreciated that human bingo uncovered the fact that a colleague and I had the same favorite book—but this commonality didn't indicate how the teacher might respond if I raised a difficult issue with her. When activities are disconnected from building confidence in character and competence, many people feel unsatisfied by what they experience as superficial team building or dismiss these activities as a waste of time.

Knowing about each other's histories, backgrounds, values, beliefs, hopes and dreams, skills and abilities, and fears and concerns is important. This understanding helps cultivate empathy for each other and contextualize the behaviors of group members. One leadership move that builds trust is to facilitate a range of team-building activities, and a selection of my favorites are in Appendix C. But we must push beyond just learning about each other if we want to build deep trust in a team. As team leaders, we must ensure that team members know each other and build a community based on personal and professional appreciation.

"We can let the circumstances of our lives harden us so that we become increasingly resentful and afraid, or we can let them soften us, and make us kinder. You always have the choice."

THE DALAI LAMA

Cultivating trust might be the hardest thing about building teams. Michael Fullan (2014, p. 130) offers leaders a warning: "You can't talk your way into trust." You can only behave your way into it by naming, modeling, and monitoring your trustworthiness. You must name trust as a value and a norm that you will embrace and develop in your team, you need to model it in your day-to-day actions, and you need to monitor it in your own and others' behavior. Your team will need many opportunities to witness and appreciate each other's competence and to give each other feedback that can help increase their competence.

Developing trust isn't a linear, steady process. It will be tested and challenged, and trust will breakdown and need to be rebuilt. When the process is skillfully, attentively led, trust in leadership is strengthened, and confidence is built that the team can strengthen its way of working together and can become even more effective.

TRUST ISN'T BUILT IN A DAY, BUT WE CAN LAY BRICKS EVERY HOUR

Your primary role as a leader, especially while a team is in the early stages of development, is to build trust so that a safe learning space can exist within which educators can have meaningful, sometimes difficult conversations about student learning. Once trust has been established, your job is to maintain and deepen it. In essence, this entire book is about building trust—about learning the skills with which to create and hold these kinds of spaces. Trust in you and in team members will increase or decrease in moments of decision making and conflict and in every interaction and communication. Making decisions, managing conflict, and communicating are addressed in upcoming chapters and need to be layered onto the following leadership moves that build trust.

What follows are suggestions for leadership moves that build, maintain, repair, and strengthen trust. You could follow these sequentially or reference them as a guide when you feel trust is fragile. It might be that you've neglected one of these components of trust building or slacked off on using another. As you read these, I encourage you to reflect on which actions you are comfortable with taking, which feel like they'd be challenging, and which ones you'd hesitate to take.

1. Know Who You Are and Who You Want To Be

If I were coaching you as a team lead, the questions I'd most often ask are, "Who do you want to be?" and "Who does your team need you to be?"

Self-knowledge is the foundation upon which trust is established. Consciously or not, we trust leaders who know themselves. The strategies I offer for building trust in a team must rest on this foundation: that you know who you are as a leader within a sociopolitical historical context. Finally, you need to understand who you are as an emotional being—to understand your emotions, how you manage them, and how they impact others. This was discussed in Chapter 2.

Once you've done some reflection on who you are as a leader, you'll want to reflect on the discrepancies between your aspirations and how you currently show up. Many people say they don't trust leaders who seem fake. Inauthenticity results from a misalignment between who we want to be and our actions when we say one thing but do another. For example, I might say that I value shared leadership, but then I consistently dismiss the suggestions from those on my team. If I continue acting in this way with my team, their distrust in my character and competence will increase. We don't always act in alignment with our vision for ourselves, which means there's an opportunity for growth.

Reflect on Ways of Being

These reflective questions and activities can help you develop an awareness of your way of being.

1. Before a meeting, respond in writing to these questions:

   - Who do I want to be in this meeting?

   - How do I want to show up?

   - What will it look and sound like if I'm showing up the way I want to?

   - What evidence could I look and listen for that would indicate that I was showing up as my best leader self?

   - How do I want to feel during and after this meeting?

2. After the meeting, reflect on these questions:

   - How do I think I showed up?

   - How did I feel during the meeting?

   - How do I feel now?

   - When was I triggered? How did I respond in those moments?

   - What evidence did I see or hear that indicated that I was showing up as my best leader self?

3. Find a coach or a trusted colleague who can occasionally observe you and offer feedback. Be very specific and clear in what you ask for feedback on. For example, you might want feedback on your nonverbal cues and those of your teammates, or you might want a script of what you say.

4. Video or audio record yourself facilitating, and watch it alone or with a trusted colleague. Pay attention to your nonverbal cues, listen to the words you use and reflect on the potential impact of those words, and pay attention to how your teammates respond to what you say and do—notice their nonverbal communication.

5. Ask for written feedback from you team. Ask for their observation of how you show up. Share who you are trying to be with them, and ask them to let you know when they see that person showing up. For example, perhaps you want to be a leader who takes everyone's perspectives into account before making a decision. You could ask your team to call it to your attention if there are times when you move into a decision without hearing from everyone.

2. Know Each Other

I was coaching a principal who was debating activities for the first meeting of a new leadership team. "I'm trying to decide between Two Truths and a Lie and A Visual Journey Line," he explained. Because there are dozens of books and resources that describe activities team members can use to get to know each other, it's useful to consider how to make a choice. I guided the principal through the criteria I use when the purpose of an activity is for participants to get to know each other in deep and rich ways to further the work of the team.

First, I consider the levels of trust within the group and think about how to carefully nudge the members into closer relationship with each other. I know I can't push too hard or too fast, so I think about creating opportunities for people to move closer when they're ready. So I ask myself, how vulnerable will this activity make people? And how do I know whether team members are ready for this?

Second, I consider how the activity allows people to reveal who they are to each other. I look for activities that invite sharing but don't put tight constraints around what is shared. I select activities in which stories and ideas can be shared, and connections can be made.

Third, I aspire to offer a team a range of community-building activities that invite us to reveal who we are with each other. I'm always looking for activities in which we can create something together and express ourselves through art, music, drama, or movement. For some people these kinds of activities raise performance anxiety levels, so I consider how to give everyone comfortable access to the activity. I also know that activities reveal otherwise unseen aspects of ourselves and help teammates appreciate each other's less visible skills and qualities.

Fourth, I select activities that connect to what we will do during that meeting. I strive to offer community builders that open the kinds of mental and emotional spaces that will serve us during our meeting—that create a platform or get thoughts and feelings flowing in a direction that will help us meet our outcomes and fulfill our purpose for convening. I strive to create an obvious connection between the activity and the meeting's purpose.

Finally, I consider the potential emotional impact of the activity. Sometimes I seek activities that provoke laughter and lightness, and sometimes I want to generate a thoughtful, reflective mood in participants. I also know that we need to feel inspired at work, so I frequently offer activities and community builders that might leave members feeling hopeful and rejuvenated.

After reflecting on these criteria, the principal decided to use the activity, Two Truths and a Lie because he felt that people could make their own decision about how much they wanted to reveal, he thought it would allow teammates to share personal aspects of their lives that they felt comfortable sharing, and he suspected there would be laughter—which he felt was paramount for a first meeting with a new team.

3. Keep Your Commitments and Expect Others to Keep Theirs

When there's an agreement to do something (e.g., bring student work to a meeting or respond to an email request) and one or more members don't honor this agreement, trust can be eroded. There are a number of ways you can set a team up to honor its commitments starting by incorporating this as a norm (which is described in Chapter 5). You can also ensure when the agreement is made that everyone is onboard, then provide reminders to the team about their commitments, and then name the impact on the team if a commitment isn't held. This could sound like the following:

> So we've all agreed that next week we'll bring a sample of a student essay to look at together. Everyone is onboard with that right? (Pause, ensure that all heads are nodding.) I'll send out a reminder the day before, and perhaps when you receive that email you can select the student essay and tuck it into your PLC notebook so it'll be ready to go. But I also want to remind everyone that if you don't bring it, we won't be able to learn from you and your students and we need everyone's participation in this. One of our team agreements is to honor our commitments, so this is an opportunity to do so.

Facilitators can regularly and respectfully remind the team of their commitments to each other and to student learning. When team members honor these, they build trust in each other.

It's critically important that you honor the agreements that you make to a team and that you do what you say you're going to do. Remember that team members take their primary cues from you—all the time. So if you are impeccable in your honoring of agreements including responding to emails and requests in a timely manner, there's a greater likelihood that others will honor their agreements.

4. Be Transparent about Your Leadership Actions

You can increase trust in your team by boosting members' understanding of your leadership actions. When you say, "This is what I'm doing and this is why," you give team members an insight into your thinking and behavior. You might curtail doubts or suspicions. You also demonstrate self-awareness and thoughtful decision making. For example, let's say that there's been low engagement in a meeting you're leading. You might say, "It seems like this activity isn't really working for us right now. I'd like to suggest that we take a 5-minute break and then discuss what to do next. I'm not sure if it's because it's a hot afternoon and we're all tired or if it's something about the activity. How does that sound?" Or you could say, "I'm stuck. I'm not sure how to make this activity more engaging. Does anyone have an idea?"

You can also be transparent around decisions such as grouping. This can sound like, "I've been thinking about each of you a lot and what you each know and can offer our group. Today I'm going to ask that James work with Julie; Marta, could you work with Samuel? I hope that these groupings will allow you to continue learning from each other." Help your team understand why you do what you do.

By communicating your thinking and sharing your leadership actions, you can also enlist your teammates in a partnership with you. Sometimes we can forget that they are grown-ups, capable of helping to figure out some of the leadership challenges we're grappling with.

5. Clarify Agendas

We've probably all had experiences where we can tell that a leader has a hidden agenda that may have made us feel uneasy and distrustful. The broad context in education right now is not one of great trust—there are many systemic factors eroding the trust of educators including performance pay initiatives, teacher evaluations processes, changes in assessment methods and curriculum, and rapid turnover of staff. Given this context and the inevitable prior negative experiences of most adults with untrustworthy authority figures, we have to be diligent about making our agendas transparent.

To do that, we need to clarify our agendas. Sometimes this can be complicated because there are often competing agendas in our organizations. As a team lead, we might be asked by administrators to enact what are essentially *their* agendas and implement *their* initiatives. However, we may also know that team members are not onboard with these plans. And then as a team lead, we may have our own agendas, which may or may not align with the administration's or with our team members.

Transparency is tricky. As coaches, department heads, or team facilitators, we're often in between administrators and teachers. One implication therefore is that we need to be mindful about how transparent we are with administrators and teammates. Simply put, we have to filter some of what we say. One of the big mistakes I've seen team leads make, in an effort to build trust with their team, is to be *too* transparent—to share every twist and turn of her thoughts. This can make the team feel uncertain whether the lead can monitor her sharing when she's with the administration or it can foster divisions within the school. In these moments, team leads need to thoughtfully reflect on the potential and unintended impact of transparency.

Clear and transparent agendas are possible when the team has an articulated purpose. Teams are more likely to have clear and articulated purposes when the school has a clear mission and vision. These elements contribute to fostering trust in a team, and often, when trust is low or absent, systemic elements (e.g., the absence of a school mission) are at play.

There will be times when as facilitators we have to deal with competing agendas. For example, administrators may ask us to lead our team in using a new curriculum, and personally we may have reservations about it. We may also anticipate that others will not be enthusiastic about the curriculum. First, it helps to engage in conversations with administrators to understand where the request is coming from. Then share something like this with your team:

> This year we're going to be exploring the impact on student learning of using XYZ curriculum, and my role is to facilitate this. This request comes from our administrators—and I've had a chance to hear their perspective. I want to be up front with you: I have some reservations about this curriculum, but I'm willing to suspend those so that we can engage in this inquiry together. I'd like to ask that we see what happens if we put aside our personal opinions while we engage in this learning. I want you to know that right now I'm feeling some conflict in my opinions as a teacher and our administration's—I don't want you to be suspicious of my agenda—but I also know that conflict is natural and can be healthy, so I'm willing to explore it.

There's a fine line to navigate around being transparent about your agendas (and thoughts, opinions, feelings, beliefs)—because as the team lead you hold power that can influence others. You also need to maintain a positive relationship and partnership with administrators, so you have to be thoughtful about how you engage with them.

Here are a few ideas for how to articulate transparent agendas:

- Make sure you know what your agenda is before showing up with your team—your literal agenda and your underlying agenda—your unstated purpose, hope, or intention.

- Invite your team to question your motives. This can sound like, "I want to make sure that I'm cultivating trust in our team. If you ever feel like I'm harboring a hidden agenda or like there's a discrepancy between what I'm stating as our agenda and some other information you have—or even just your gut feeling—please say something. I'm doing my best to be transparent, and I need your partnership."

- Before a meeting or a moment in which your agenda might be questioned, respond to these questions: What *is* my agenda? How can I articulate it in a way that others will hear it? If I say it in this way, how will my team hear it? Are there any potential negative consequences to saying it that way? If I articulate it this way, how will administrators or supervisors hear it? Are there any potential negative consequences to saying it that way?

6. Always Ask for Feedback

To cultivate a culture of trust, you need to ask your team for feedback in various ways and at different times. The first thing you'll probably need to address are your own feelings about asking for and receiving feedback. It can be difficult to open yourself to feedback, especially if the team is challenging, but it must be done.

A key time to ask for feedback is at the end of meetings. I usually ask these questions:

1. What's a big learning you're taking from today?

2. Which activities worked best for you?

3. What didn't work for you?

4. What questions or concerns came up?

5. Is there anything else you want me to know about your experience today?

What's essential is that you ask for feedback in a way that truly communicates your willingness to hear it. This will come across mostly in your tone of voice and body language and less in the precise words you select. Furthermore, your team will build trust in your receptivity to the feedback based on what you do with it, which means that you may need to act on the feedback.

When I get feedback from a group that I'm working with regularly, I often summarize the feedback I receive when I next meet with them and sometimes share highlights. Without identifying who said what, I might say something like, "Last time someone commented that the time for reading the data report was too short. I appreciated that feedback and will be sure to check in to see if the time I've allotted works for everyone. I'm also really open to feedback in the moment, so don't be shy about telling me you need more time. I'll improve my facilitation skills with your feedback, so I really appreciate it."

Handwritten feedback usually becomes identifiable if you work with a small group, so I ask people to write their names on their feedback sheet. This also allows me to follow up with individuals if things come up that require a one-on-one conversation. I also believe that we want to strive for the kinds of teams where members feel comfortable saying whatever they need to say and identifying themselves.

However, when I coach a group over a long period of time, I also invite anonymous feedback through a digital platform a couple times a year. I want a team to have the freedom and opportunity to give me feedback anonymously. Particularly when there are power dynamics within a team (e.g., if you're a team's supervisor as well as team lead), it's critical that they can feel safe to share their experience of you as a leader.

Asking for and being responsive to feedback is an essential component of building trust. The more you invite it the more it opens the way for you to give others feedback. This has to be a two-way street—and as the leader you have to go first, modeling the asking and modeling your openness and responsiveness to feedback.

When I work with a new group—or even just a group that I'll spend only a day with—I always let them know within the first 10 minutes that I'll ask for their feedback at the end of the day (and I hand them the feedback form then so they can write things on it during our time). Sometimes I feel that a product of our dysfunctional education system is that people walk into a training or meeting room with one unconscious, predominant thought: Will my voice be heard here? Or will my needs, desires, thoughts, feelings be ignored, again? I hope to preempt these anxieties by communicating from the start: I want to hear from you. Your experience matters and I want to know about it. Here's when and how you'll share it with me.

7. Apologize and Say You Don't Know

Whenever you make a mistake, you have a wonderful opportunity to cultivate trust by taking responsibility for your mistake and apologizing. This is also a critical moment for you to model how you respond to conflict. Many people fear that when there's a breakdown in a relationship it won't be repairable. I want to encourage you to acknowledge and embrace mistakes you make so that you can have an opportunity to repair the relationship and model that we can survive conflict.

Here is written feedback I once received: "Today I felt like I was sharing an idea and I know I couldn't get the words out quickly, but you cut me off and said I needed to review the document you'd handed out." Critical feedback can prompt defensiveness. I've worked hard to acknowledge this reaction so that I can hear what the feedback is telling me and respond to it positively. This is challenging, but it pays great dividends. The next time this group convened, I took the opportunity to say, "Last time we met I got some feedback about my communication. I am so grateful that you were honest and brought my awareness to how I interacted with you at that moment. I apologize and want you all to know that I'm working on this. Please let me know if I do it again."

By apologizing and owning your areas for growth, you are modeling this for your team. This is an area in which you must lead for the team to follow. When there are power dynamics such as those that inevitably exist within a team, the leader must go first when it comes to modeling this kind of vulnerability.

To be human is to make mistakes, and we can't learn if we don't make mistakes. In a healthy team, we feel safe enough to take risks, and perhaps along the journey we make lots of mistakes. In a healthy team we acknowledge our mistakes, own them, take responsibility for them, and commit to improving.

8. Reflect Regularly on Team Process

One way for a team to improve how it works is by collectively reflecting on how it's doing, essentially, by giving each other feedback. When team members have to look at their own individual behavior and its impact on the group's functioning, their self-awareness can increase and behaviors can change. This allows for individual and mutual accountability and buy-in to the team's development.

There are various ways to do this. Exhibit 3.1 shows a quick way to get feedback from a team on how members are feeling. Depending on the feedback, the facilitator can share some portion of the data to help the team heighten awareness of how they work together and of how they could refine their teamwork.

Appendix B contains a process that takes more time, and it could be done two or three times a year. The data from this survey can also be shared with the team to provoke reflection, discussion, and decision making around how to improve the team's work. Whenever a facilitator engages a team in reflecting on how they work together, there's a greater likelihood of getting deeper buy-in from members, which helps the team to develop. These tools also help to communicate the message that your role is to *facilitate* a team—and that the team's true development is contingent on the full participation and engagement of everyone. When team members participate in these reflections, they are more likely to see their own responsibility for the health of the team. This kind of activity also helps people build trust in each other as each person recognizes his or her positive (or negative) contributions to a team.

Exhibit 3.1. Team Temperature Check

This tool can be used on an occasional basis (e.g., monthly for teams that meet weekly) so that team members can offer feedback. The facilitator can share this feedback with the team to spur discussion about how to improve their work together or can use it for personal reflection. Note that the facilitator should also respond to this and reflect on the statements.

Indicator	3 = Usually 2 = Sometimes 1 = Rarely
1. I show up as my best self to our team meetings.	
2. I look forward to our meetings.	
3. I feel that I can meaningfully contribute during our meetings.	
4. I feel that team members are respectful to each other.	
5. I feel that we all learn from each other.	
6. I feel that the facilitator or lead holds a safe space for learning and collaboration.	
7. I feel that our work together will serve our students.	
8. I feel that our work together stays focused on our purpose, goals, or projects.	
9. I leave our meetings feeling stretched, energized, or inspired.	
10. I feel that my feedback on our meetings is acknowledged.	
TOTAL	

Comments:

9. Foster a Culture of Listening

Our fear of not being heard applies to a context beyond just that of the facilitator. We want to know that the person in charge will listen to us but also that colleagues will listen. To build a culture of listening that can contribute to trust, you must start by modeling this value. This is hard, especially when you're in a leadership role in which you might be expected to talk the most. But as we continue to explore the role of a leader, you may rethink this assumption and consider when it's more important for you to listen than to talk.

Listening—truly open and nonjudgmental listening—builds trust. To be responsive to someone's needs, to create a safe learning space, you'll need to have listened to what the speaker needs. There's just no other way to gather that information. When decisions are to be made, people must feel listened to so they can believe that their opinions were truly considered. Whether it's in the whole group or in one-on-one meetings, you'll benefit tremendously by being an effective listener. Listening is further discussed in Chapter 7.

This tension—being heard, having a voice—exists within a larger context in our country and world, which we need to keep in mind. In the past and present, many people's voices, stories, opinions, and needs have been marginalized or outright suppressed—in particular, the voices of women, people of color, low-income people, and immigrants. As a facilitator, you need to know how you fit into this reality: Has your voice also been marginalized? Has it been privileged? These answers are often complex, and a lot of self-reflection on these questions is required to create trusting spaces where all voices are heard. Furthermore, you need to be aware of who is in the room and where each person fits within this historical reality. If you aspire to lead transformational endeavors, you need to be sure you're not replicating the status quo.

John was a principal I worked with who strove to create equitable schools. As a very tall, middle-aged, white man, he was aware of his privilege. He knew that his words were often received as the voice of authority, even when his intention wasn't to offer a determining opinion. When he met with his leadership team, made up of a very diverse group of teachers, he was upfront and direct about why he spoke when he did. He explained, "When we have discussions, I want to hear from all of you. Many of you have insights into the community we serve that I don't have. I will not speak first in these discussions, and I will speak very little. I may ask clarifying or probing questions, but I'll hold back on giving opinions. My voice has carried too much weight in our institutions and society. I want to create space for your voices."

When your team gathers, you'll want to offer structures for people to use so that they can truly listen to each other, and you'll need to attend to the group's dynamics to encourage and promote listening. I am a fan of protocols—of using structured routines for discussion—because when we don't use protocols, pair shares or group discussions are often not equitable and furthermore often default to the status quo of communication, which is fundamentally inequitable. I am fully aware that some people (usually a minority in a group) don't like protocols—they are often extroverts, highly verbal processors and sometimes belong to the aforementioned dominant groups. When they express their dislike for protocols, I acknowledge their feelings and explain why we'll continue to use them: "Protocols allow for equitable participation, and for us to do this work or learning together we need to ensure we have everyone's voice." I help them see the greater goal to which we are working and to see beyond their own needs, which is usually well received and understood. Protocols are further discussed in Chapter 10.

10. Surface Team Members' Strengths and Skills

Revisiting the definition of trust as confidence in another's character and competence, we might realize that to feel confident in a team member's competence we need to know which competencies he possesses. An effective team leader actively surfaces each person's unique skills, strengths, and abilities so that team members recognize and appreciate those competencies. This can be done in a few ways: team members can be invited to share their skills in various ways and can volunteer for tasks for which they believe they are qualified. This allows members to name their own strengths—but there are limitations with relying on individuals to do this. Some people are reluctant to share their strengths for many reasons—they're shy, insecure, or humble or simply don't see their own strengths.

A facilitator can also create ways for team members to name each other's strengths. For example, a high school math department is preparing to share their end of semester student data with the whole staff. One of the tasks to be accomplished is to prepare visual depictions and graphs of the data. When the department head asks the team, "Who might be able to do this?" everyone looks at the geometry teacher and one teacher says, "You are great at creating visuals. I've seen the posters in your room! Could you do this?"

Moments like these build trust in a team—and they happen because rather than the facilitator just asking the geometry teacher to do this task he or she invites the entire group to recognize each other's competence. If no one had volunteered or directly asked the geometry teacher, the facilitator (who may know which member possesses the skills for the task) could also say, "Geometry teacher, I have seen the posters in your room and know we'd all appreciate it if you could lend your skills to this task. What do you think?"

As a team lead, your job is to constantly highlight and name the strengths, skills, and competencies of team members and to provide opportunities for them to do so about each other and to recognize their own individual assets. To do this, you'll have to get to know each person so that you can be aware of their strengths. Furthermore, you'll need to create opportunities for them to contribute these strengths and skills. This implies something of a paradigm shift in our schools where we're so focused on looking at areas for growth, areas where we aren't yet performing, at our weaknesses and failures and shortcomings.

As team leaders we want to be cautious not to assign tasks to team members who we suspect or know lack the skills and competencies to perform those duties. We might think, "Oh, it would be great for the algebra teacher to take on this job of creating visuals because that's an area she really needs to work on," but this is a risk. Sometimes it may be our role to push the edges of our colleague's learning, but we must be mindful about when and how we do this because it's also our role to set people up for success. So perhaps we pair the algebra teacher with the geometry teacher, or perhaps if the teacher has volunteered we take that into account. But particularly when a team is in the forming and norming stage, we want to highlight strengths and invite people to shine, and thereby we cultivate trust.

11. Celebrate Successes

We also build trust in teams when we recognize and appreciate each other's contributions and when we celebrate individual and group successes. After the geometry teacher has prepared the visuals for the presentation, the team lead must acknowledge her contribution—perhaps at the whole school share as well as during a team meeting. Although the facilitator's acknowledgment is very important, it's equally important that team members appreciate each other. That's how we build trust between ourselves as leaders and our team members and how we build trust among team members.

Celebrating successes and appreciating each other can be routinized in team meetings. Providing just a few minutes at the beginning or end of a meeting for team members to verbally acknowledge each other can be very powerful and cultivates trust. Every time someone gives or receives an appreciation, our brains are literally getting emotionally healthier as they strengthen neural pathways that promote positive feelings.

12. Acknowledge Areas for Growth

Halfway through the first year of our existence as a Transformational Coaching Team, the coaches delivered a day of professional development to a large group of teachers. Some components went very well, but other pieces were disorganized and poorly delivered. At the same time that I engaged in a process of digging around to learn why the delivery was what it was, I also made it clear that our work products needed to be a much higher caliber. Only a few coaches were responsible for the weak PD session, and my conversation with them differed from what I said to the whole team because everyone was aware (even if they hadn't been present in the room) that some breakout sessions hadn't been a success.

To the whole team I said, "I realize that I made some assumptions about both what was expected for that PD session and what support you might need. I recognize that we need to calibrate our approaches to PD and that I need to be explicit about the quality that's expected. To do so, going forward, we'll have more time during our Friday meetings to plan for PD, and we'll also spend much more time giving each other feedback on PD plans. I'll also be sure to provide more feedback during the delivery of PD. I want to make clear that all PD going forward will be consistently high caliber."

In private, to one of the coaches, I said, "There's no excuse for not having a plan for that PD. You had 4 weeks to prepare. Your disorganization reflects poorly on our whole team. I made an assumption that you didn't need support in preparing, and I am not clear on why you weren't prepared. Could you help me understand this, and also could you help me understand what you need so that next time you deliver PD it's a great improvement?"

This wasn't easy for me, but I've learned how to share feedback so that it's not painful and so that it results in a change in behavior. I know that if you don't address incompetence, you risk losing the trust of your team. I acknowledge that this can be made harder by power dynamics: if you're a department head and considered to be equal to your colleagues, this can feel difficult. You can still say something like, "It seemed like you struggled during that PD session, and the feedback wasn't great. How would you like it to go next time? What can I do to help you?" What's equally important in these moments is that while you try to support an individual to build skills you skillfully make sure that the rest of the team knows that you recognize that one person (or more) has some learning to do. When they know that you know, they'll continue to trust you.

When a team member's low competence becomes apparent to the whole group, a leader needs to respond. This can be a fragile moment that can increase or decrease the trust of other team members. The team will watch you closely as a leader to see how you respond to someone who clearly can't do something well or doesn't do something they'd agreed to do. In those moments, even if you feel nervous, you have an opportunity to build trust by skillfully and thoughtfully saying something. Some parts might need to be said in private and some in public—because your team needs to know that you'll do something about even small demonstrations of incompetence.

13. Practice Appreciation

Appreciation is an undervalued source of fuel and inspiration in our schools. To shift a culture (especially if it's stuck in a negative zone), appreciation can be a powerful tool. One way of appreciating others is by simply acknowledging their existence. Taking the time to connect with others in a genuine and authentic way communicates your appreciation for them as a human being. It's those moments in the hallway on a Monday morning that really count when (although you have a lot to do) you open the door to a teacher's classroom and ask how her weekend was. You make eye contact and use her name. You wish her a good day. Psychologists say that the frequency of small, positive interactions between people is essential to the health of a relationship (see John Gottman's work). This is true for teachers and students, for couples, and for anyone in a community. The magic ratio, they say, of positive to negative interactions is 5:1—we need five small, positive interactions for every one negative interaction for our relationships to withstand the inevitable ups and downs they'll go through. Lots of neutral interactions are also fine, but we need a large dose of positive interactions with each other. We can fight our neurological structures, or we can smile at each other more, ask, "How are you?" and take the 5 minutes to attentively listen.

When appreciating others, sometimes it helps to be specific, naming the action or behavior that you appreciate. Sometimes our appreciations are for no apparent reason and are the individual's unique qualities. Let others know their positive impact on you, the qualities about them that you appreciate and how those qualities have enhanced your life. If you're offering an appreciation in person, even if it's in a team meeting, look at the individual directly, talk to her in the first person, and let the rest of the group just listen. Most important—say what you mean and mean what you say.

Appreciations are a powerful ritual to incorporate into team meetings. Some groups prefer to do them at the beginning of a meeting, which creates a positive tone for the subsequent work. I tend to favor doing them at the end of a meeting—this leaves people feeling good as they walk out the door. Receiving appreciations can feel uncomfortable to some people at first. I usually suggest that people just say thank you when they receive an appreciation and to let it sink it. Sometimes we'll want to downplay an appreciation from someone else or reflexively appreciate them back, but I encourage people to accept the appreciation and take a deep breath.

There are also many other times when a leader can appreciate team members and other ways to do so aside from verbally. It helps to ask people how they like to be acknowledged. I worked with one principal who asked her staff how they liked to be appreciated. She was surprised by the responses: one teacher said she liked notes because she could reread them when she felt discouraged. Another teacher said she loved being mentioned in the weekly newsletter. Another staff member said he dreaded being publically appreciated and that it made him unbearably uncomfortable. And another said her favorite expression of appreciation was dark chocolate. "I had no idea that Samuel hated it when I appreciate him in meetings," the principal said. "He's so quiet I just thought I should shine the light on him." As she read through the survey responses, she kept nodding her head, "I can do this," she said to me. "I can appreciate them the way they want. No problem." She created a table, listed each person and his or her preferred appreciation, and spent the rest of the year delivering acknowledgments in the way her staff wanted.

14. Appreciate Yourself

Here's a hard truth: You can't truly appreciate others until you can appreciate yourself. This can be extremely challenging, and many of us know that we are our own worst critics. However, if we are going to create transformational communities, we're going to have to work on this. If you are a coach or leader who is really self-critical but you extend appreciations to others, at some point people will distrust those appreciations. After all, you're a human being, too, and as a member of a learning community you get to make mistakes and also need to recognize your successes. You need to model the mind-sets you hope to instill in others, and self-appreciation is a part of this. The good news is that we can build our ability to be kind and compassionate to ourselves and to practice self-appreciation.

Many people are raised with values around humility and conflate self-appreciation with bragging. There's a simple distinction between being arrogant and appreciating yourself. If what you're thinking or feeling about yourself in a positive way has anything to do with feeling better than someone else, it's not self-appreciation. Comparing yourself with others, competing, or thinking you're better than others is arrogance, which is a mask for fear and insecurity. But genuine self-appreciation is an expression of gratitude and recognition for something you've done and for you who are. Self-appreciation is about taking care of yourself, using positive self-talk, accepting compliments with gratitude, and celebrating your success.

Self-appreciation is also about forgiving ourselves for the mistakes we make. We need to remind ourselves that failure is okay, that we can learn from our mistakes, and that we need to continue to take risks. I've worked with many coaches who are committed to holding this kind of a growth mind-set for children and teachers—but struggle to do so for themselves.

This will sound paradoxical, but the only way we can make the personal transformational changes that will ultimately serve our children and world is by accepting ourselves just as we are. We have to begin where we are. This doesn't mean that we are

> *"Laughing is the shortest distance between two people."*
>
> VICTOR BORGE

resigned or that we won't work to change some way that we're behaving or being, but it means we accept ourselves while also committing to continued learning and growth.

15. Play and Have Fun

Stuart Brown (2009) is the author of a book called *Play: How It Shapes the Brain, Opens the Imagination and Invigorates the Soul.* He defines play as an activity with "apparent purposeless" and with something that's fun and in which we lose ourselves. But there's a paradox because, as Brown offers the scientific research on play, we learn that play is also a way to become more innovative, to refine certain skills, and to increase our happiness. Play might also have an evolutionary survival value. It helps sculpt our brains to help us learn and make us more resilient, and it's a way that we bond with others.

When we laugh and play with others, we strength our connections. We see different aspects of each other and skills and traits that might never show up in our professional settings. We appreciate each other's full humanity. If your intention is to build resilient communities that do transformational work, then don't underestimate the power of play. Structure some fun and games—inside of your school building as well as outside of it. Play board games and charades, have water gun fights, go hiking together, and make music if there's a music teacher (or musically inclined person) among you.

USE HINDSIGHT TO STRENGTHEN FORESIGHT

As you read this chapter, perhaps you reflected on experiences when your trust in a leader increased or decreased. You may have had epiphanies when you realized why you'd never really felt safe in a particular team (maybe because the leader ignored incompetence, maybe she never acknowledged your strengths or contributions, maybe she never solicited feedback and seemed defensive about her leadership). You might have also had insights into why others have trusted, or not trusted, you as a colleague or leader.

And you may have even had moments of regret. When I reflect on my entry into leading the humanities team, I recognize how little intentional trust building I did. Reviewing this list of trust building moves, I'd have to admit that I took very few, or perhaps none, of these actions. I did not value what trust would allow us to do, I just wanted the teachers to change. I didn't have ideas for how to foster change, and I worked from some ineffective models of leadership that I'd been exposed to early in my life. I tried all kinds of coercive methods to make people change, but none of them worked. After a while, I recognized that this approach was in conflict with some of my core values.

But I didn't only have a will gap; I also recognize that I didn't know what to do. I didn't know which bricks to lay to create a culture of trust, and I didn't recognize how long it would take. The shift from who I was and what I did as a leader with the humanities team and who I was and what I did with the transformational coaching team was made through reflection. It's this ongoing learning process (which still hasn't ceased for me—like everyone, I still have big areas for growth) that has led to the refinement of my skills. There's no point in hindsight being 20/20 if we don't use it to look ahead.

Transformational Coaching Team, 2012

It was a few months after we'd started working together. Our weekly professional development meetings had been rigorous, so I decided that we needed to have some fun. After lunch, I pulled out Pictionary, and we quickly lost ourselves in the game. I love playing games, and I can be very silly—but I'd never been silly at work, with my team. There I maintained a professional stance that most people experience as pretty serious.

At some point I was drawing on the white board, and although I was doing my best my team couldn't identify the image and their guesses were completely off. I kept scribbling and emphatically circling and stabbing the dry erase marker on the

---

board, but they didn't get it. When the word I was trying to draw was revealed, we all broke into the kind of laughter where your eyes water and strange sounds come out of you.

For Dave, this moment changed something. On multiple occasions over the following year and a half he referenced seeing me laughing that afternoon as a pivotal moment. Something shifted in the way he saw me and in his relationship to me as his manager. I suspect that it was because when my face was contorted in laughter I looked open and relaxed. I felt like myself in that moment, not like a team lead or supervisor, and I suspect that he may have seen that—the role removed, the humanity more apparent than anything else.

CHAPTER 4

Defining Purpose, Process, and Product

Humanities Team, 2008

The written feedback from our team meetings included these comments, each made by a different person:

- "I found the first brainstorming activity to be very useful."

- "That brainstorming was a waste of time."

- "Could we start 30 minutes later so I can have a longer lunch?"

- "I think we need to use this time to plan grammar lessons."

- "Do we have to meet? I don't think this is in our contract."

The meetings were tense, we didn't get anything done of value, and none of us—myself included—could explain with any clarity why we had to meet. Meetings were a thing we had to do—an attendance sheet to submit, an endurance test.

So I created a work plan and determined goals for the team. When I presented it to teachers, their response to the work plan was encapsulated in statements such as, "There's *no way* we can meet these goals!" and "These goals are ridiculous." I got defensive and angry. We didn't meet our goals that year. Meetings continued to feel unfocused.

Recall a meeting that you attended as a participant that did not leave you in a good mood. What was your primary complaint about it? When I ask this question, the most common responses I hear are, "It was a waste of time," "We didn't get anything done," and "I don't know why we had to meet."

I aspire to hold meetings that are focused, meaningful, and productive and that feed the heart, mind, and spirit. I want to make sure we get things done, and I want people to leave feeling energized and rejuvenated. I strive to find the balance between production and nourishment, and I know that one cannot exist without the other. When I imagine how I want participants to feel about meetings I lead, I envision them saying this to a colleague: "I can't wait until our team meeting on Friday."

For a meeting to be focused, meaningful, and productive, the team needs to have a clear purpose, processes to get things done, and something that they're working on. This chapter explores how to set goals with a team, articulate a team's mission and vision, determine core values, and get focused.

Reflect on Purpose

1. Ask members of a team to write down why they think their team exists and then read the answers aloud to the group.

2. Consider:

   - How aligned are the responses?

   - Where are there big discrepancies in understandings?

   - Which responses match your understanding of the team's purpose?

THE NECESSITY OF A REASON FOR BEING

Think about a team you are a part of now. Can you succinctly state *why* that team exists? Perhaps you lead a department- or grade-level team. How would you describe that team's reason for being? Maybe you can conjure up a vague explanation for the existence of teams such as departments or grade levels, but leaders need a clear understanding of a team's reason for being. This is what allows us to design agendas and construct activities that answer that enduring question: Why do I have to be here? A leader's responsibility is to ensure that members are so clear about their reason for being at a meeting and for why the team exists that this question never crosses their mind.

Teams exist to uphold an organization's mission, to fulfill its vision, and to meet its goals. For a team to do this, it needs a clear and articulated reason for existing—an explicit articulation of the connection between the team's work and the organization's big picture goals.

So how do you figure out why a team exists? If you created and convened the team, you probably know why it exists although you may still need to articulate your reasoning. I've heard leaders convene groups like a culture and climate team because "we need some staff members to address these issues." Although this may be true, this statement needs refining and further clarification for the team to be effective. If you were appointed to lead a team such as a department- or grade-level team, then you might not be clear on why it exists. Ask the person who appointed you what the team's purpose is. Then ask the others on the team.

As you're working to identify the team's purpose, consider alignment in the organization. A team is a body within a larger structure such as a school or district. Surface the connections between what your team does and that larger entity and how your team's efforts serve the organization's mission and goals. This alignment is critical to secure commitment and buy-in from team members, and it gives the team a reason for existing. If we produce transformational change in schools, we need to work strategically and be mission aligned in all groups that work within larger units. Articulating purpose in relationship to other parts in the system is a critical action step for leaders.

Keeping Students at the Center

Throughout conversations about team purpose, students' social, emotional, and academic needs must stay front and center. Student needs can sometimes get lost and buried beneath great ideas, strong personalities, adult needs, and competing agendas, but a leader needs to consistently remind team members that our purpose is to improve the experiences and outcomes for all children. The question to return to is this: How are our students' social, emotional, and academic learning needs at the center of our teamwork?

Table 4.1. Determining Actions for Team Development

Situation	Next Steps
I know why the team exists. I convened it.	1. Articulate the why: Write it down. Also explain how this team's work supports the larger mission and goals. 2. Explain the why to others and listen to their questions. Revise the why if necessary. 3. Get buy-in from other team members. You may need to do some elements of the mission and vision process, or you might be able to move into how the team will work together.
I was appointed to lead this team. I'm not sure why it exists.	1. Talk to the person who appointed you and ask why he or she thinks it exists. 2. Map other teams in the organization and consider how their work serves the mission. 3. If you determine that the team can play a role to meet the organization's mission and goals, then engage the team in the mission and vision process. 4. If you determine that the team doesn't need to exist (perhaps its work is redundant), share your reasoning with the person who appointed you.
This team structure has existed for a long time, but no one really knows what it's supposed to do.	1. Engage your team in the mission and vision process.

Furthermore, many schools and organizations feel a moral obligation to address the opportunity gap (often called the achievement gap). The opportunity gap is the disparity in access to quality schools and the resources needed for all children to be academically successful. Opportunity and achievement gaps in the United States (as well as in many other countries) are based on race, class, language, and other social differences. Teams in equity-driven organizations may also want to reflect on this question: How is our team working toward creating equitable schools?

Let's consider a high school English department that's debating its focus for the following year. Perhaps one teacher advocates that he does what he's always done in the spring: teach literary analysis with a focus on the great classics. "After all," she argues, "that's what we do here at Great Western High; it's what we're known for. We've taught *Beowulf* every year since my grandfather was a student here." Perhaps she can make an argument about why students need the classics ("To be successful in college, they'll need exposure to these texts and skills."), but this decision may not be the best to serve all students. Other texts may be more relevant to students, texts that more closely reflect the challenges they grapple with and the communities they come from. Furthermore, this focus may not match up with the academic needs of students.

A team leader can ask: What current student data do we have that indicates this is what we should focus on? And how will that focus help our school meet its goals and fulfill its mission? If the leader of the English department at Great Western High posed these questions to his team, perhaps another teacher could offer this:

> I analyzed last year's high school exit exam and saw that the area that our students struggled in the most was writing. Specifically, they couldn't back up their arguments with text-based evidence. When I disaggregated the data by levels of English proficiency, I saw that only 13% of our English learners passed this component of the exam. Digging deeper into their results, I found that 78% of these students struggled with organizing their ideas. I propose that we focus on argumentative writing and organization of ideas.

As your team determines its purpose and identifies what it will do together, you'll want to listen for what's motivating people to go in the direction they're exploring. These questions are useful to pose while in this stage of development: Which student needs are we addressing? And what evidence do we have that our students have that need?

Questions to Keep Students at the Center

- How are our students' social, emotional, and academic learning needs at the center of our teamwork?
- How is our team working toward creating equitable schools?
- What current student data do we have to indicate that this is what we should focus on?
- How will *this* focus help our school meet its goals and fulfill its mission?
- Which student needs are we addressing?
- What evidence is there to indicate that our students have those needs?

Determining Mission and Vision

> A *mission* helps us establish priorities and guides decisions. Our mission is our fundamental purpose.
>
> A *vision* provides a compelling future. It is a basis for assessing the current reality and it provides a sense of direction.

High-functioning schools and organizations are guided by mission and vision statements that inform the behaviors of all members. Even though perhaps every stakeholder can't recite the precise verbiage of the statements, everyone knows what his or her school is about and what his or her big goals and intentions are. This knowledge plays a key role in decision making, prioritizing, and aligning school culture. Those of us who have been in schools where there's a clear mission and vision know how grounding this is; those of us who have also been in schools where these are absent know how lost and aimless we can feel.

Teams also need their own mission and vision statements so that members know where they're headed. There's great value in having the statements and using them, and there's equal value in the process of creating the mission and vision with a team. The process involves discussing what a group intends to do and why it exists. When this process is well facilitated, it can build buy-in to the work that will be done and can yield long-lasting benefits. Exhibit 4.1 is the mission and vision statements from the transformational coaching team I led.

Exhibit 4.1. Transformational Coaching Team's Mission and Vision

Our Mission:

Our coaching team's mission is to develop teachers and leaders who can serve the whole child, create equitable classrooms and schools, and provide students with learning experiences so they will graduate and be college and career ready.

Our Vision:

Teachers and administrators in our schools will report that coaching was essential in supporting them to improve their instructional practices, implement a new curriculum, develop trusting relationships with colleagues, refine their reflective capacities, build their emotional resiliency, and improve student outcomes.

Our clients will report that coaches built effective teams that examined instruction, curriculum, and assessments and led teams to make changes to practices to transform the experiences and outcomes for students.

Teachers and administrators will all say that coaches relentlessly surfaced and interrupted inequities.

Coaches will feel effective, empowered, and proud of their work. They will describe a year of rigorous learning (for themselves) and will express that they felt supported in their work by their manager and by the team of coaches. They will be able to trace their work as coaches to improved student outcomes.

Everyone who participates in our coaching program will have positive feelings about it and will be able to trace its impact on student learning.

When a team is not yet formed and you can plan for each stage of its development, then follow the agenda shown in Exhibit 4.2. In some cases, you might need to determine the mission and vision for a team yourself. You'll still need to engage team members in a process so that they understand these and buy in to them.

Exhibit 4.2. Determining a Team's Mission and Vision

Time	Topic/Activity
5–10 min.	Provide the district/organization and school's mission and vision statements, if available. Invite reflection: • I see … • I think … • I wonder … If good examples are available, share mission and vision statements from other similar teams. Ask reflection questions: • I see … • I think … • I wonder …

(continued)

Defining Purpose, Process, and Product   **69**

Time	Topic/Activity
5 min.	Provide a definition of mission and vision (see previous definitions). Discuss how having a mission and vision can help a team.
15–30 min.	Ask participants to write and then talk in pairs and then in a whole group about the following questions: • Within our team, which component of our school, district, or organization's vision can we work toward? • Within our team, which component of our school, district, or organization's mission can we uphold? • What specifically can our team do to move our school, district, or organization forward on its mission? • Which student needs are we aware of that our team can respond to? (Also, if relevant, which teacher needs are we aware of that our team can respond to?) • What data do we have from and about students that could help us determine our team's mission and vision? • Why do we think this team exists? • What is the most important work we think this team could engage in that would be of service to children?
10–15 min.	First in pairs ask participants to brainstorm keywords and phrases that reflect what they think should be the team's mission (its fundamental purpose) and its vision (a compelling future). It's useful to have lots of chart paper and markers available for this section.
10–15 min.	Have pairs join other pairs and then groups of four join other groups of four (and so on) to share their brainstorms. As groups join up, they share ideas and look for repetition of ideas and additional important ideas that might need to be included but aren't repeated. The goal of this activity is to combine ideas and condense the brainstorms.
5–10 min.	With the whole group, look at the words, phrases, and ideas that stand out. Invite discussion.
5–15 min.	Use a decision-making process (see Chapter 8) to agree on the keywords, phrases, and ideas—not the exact wording.

Time	Topic/Activity
5 min.	Explain next steps: • Ask for two team members to volunteer to wordsmith the ideas, phrases, and words into a mission and vision statement. • Determine when this will happen and when the team will come back to look at their work and make a final decision. Inform that team that the final decision will also be made together (and let them know exactly what kind of decision-making process will be used). The process of agreeing on the draft brought by the wordsmiths can take anywhere from 10 minutes to an hour. Close the meeting.
60–105 min. total	

If you lead a team that's already in existence (e.g., a grade level or department team), it can be useful to revisit the team's mission and vision. If these don't exist, then consider a process to determine a mission and vision. Ideally the mission and vision are communicated in short statements and frequently referenced. When a member of a functioning team is asked why his or her team exists, he or she can offer a succinct response that aligns to the responses of all other teammates.

> *"Perhaps the secret of living well is not in having all the answers but in pursuing unanswerable questions in good company."*
>
> RACHEL NAOMI REMEN

IT'S ALL ABOUT HOW WE WORK TOGETHER

Highly effective teams know what we're working on, why we're working together (what our team's mission and vision is), and how we'll work together. How we work together includes the following components: our team's core values, norms or community agreements, team member roles and responsibilities, decision-making agreements, and communication agreements. (Community agreements and decision making each requires its own chapters; see Chapters 5 and 8.) Many teams benefit from discussing their mission and vision before naming their core values, but in some cases—such as a team that is already formed and might have some ineffective ways of working together—starting with core values and norms can be helpful.

Core values are the collective commitments that guide our behavior.

Core Values

Core values are a precursor to norms or community agreements. They express the commitments of the team members, commitments that then direct behavior (norms articulate behavior). Core values are an answer to these two questions: Which beliefs and behaviors will allow us to fulfill our team's mission and realize our vision? What do we stand for?

A conversation about a team's core values can begin with individuals identifying their own core values. On my website you'll find an activity to guide a group through this process. This is a meaningful way for team members to get to know each other, after which they can proceed to articulating their team's core values. Then you can use a process similar to the one described for determining a team's mission and vision to determine core values with a team.

As with the mission and vision process, it is the conversations that unfold that are important. These conversations build commitment, understanding, and trust. Although this takes time, the discussions contribute to cementing a solid foundation for the hard work to come. Team members usually enjoy articulating their core values as it offers them an opportunity to speak about what really matters to them. Exhibit 4.3 offers the core values that the transformational coaching team developed when we started working together.

Exhibit 4.3. Transformational Coaching Team's Core Values

Our commitments as transformational coaches:

1. We are guided by the principles of adult learning so that we can meet our clients where they are and can further their learning.
2. We build trusting relationships with our clients because we know that people learn best in the presence of compassion and love. We know that there is no coaching without trust.

3. We apply a growth mind-set, and we take the long view. We recognize that practicing transformational coaching and changing behaviors, beliefs, and being will take time.

4. We apply a systems-thinking approach to support our clients and their schools in change because we believe that the whole is greater than the sum of its part.

5. We believe that people work better in resilient, trusting communities than they do alone, and we intentionally build these communities. We work to bring people together and bridge the gaps that have divided educators.

6. We manage our own emotions and develop our skills to interrupt systemic oppression. We are advocates for children as well as the adults with whom we work.

7. We embrace our role as leaders at the sites we work at, and we acknowledge that we are looked at as leaders. Because of this, we recognize the need for us to be mindful of our words and actions and maintain the highest levels of integrity about our work at all times.

8. We value our own time and space for learning and recognize our need for support. We commit to taking care of each other and taking care of ourselves.

Team Member Roles and Responsibilities

Roles and responsibilities are part of how we'll work together and contribute to a team's efficiency. Roles usually don't need to be co-constructed (Exhibit 4.4), but teams need to determine which roles they use. More important, team members need to know and understand what the roles entail. For example, the note-taking process used by one person might differ significantly from that used by another. Agreements need to be made about which components of the role need to be standard—for example, whether the note taker records only decisions and next steps or will capture each member's comments.

Roles can rotate each time a group meets or be consistently held by one individual. Sometimes a team discovers that one member is an outstanding recorder and agrees that this individual should always be the recorder. In some ways, this makes sense as it plays on the strengths of members. However, recorders often have a harder time participating in discussions and activities because they're thinking about taking notes. Another reason to rotate is to give members different perspectives on how the group is functioning and to ensure that work is equally distributed. As with so many moments in team building, what's essential is that the process of determining role rotation is thoughtful, intentional, and invites input from all team members. Every moment in team development is an opportunity to increase buy-in to the team. What's tricky to figure out is the balance between getting input and getting something done. Explore this tension with the knowledge that at times you might fall heavy on one side or the other, but as you learn about your team and yourself as a leader you'll find a good balance.

Exhibit 4.4. Team Member Roles and Responsibilities[1]

The Facilitator

Purpose: To help the group achieve meeting objectives during the given time frame.

Facilitator's Role and Responsibilities:

- Create or co-create the agenda, or preview the agenda ahead of time. Facilitator must be clear on the objectives or outcomes.
- Listen actively to all participants and periodically summarize as needed.
- Check for shared understanding in group.
- Keep the group focused on the topic.
- Refer to the objectives of the meeting to keep the group focused on the outcome.
- Identify the components of the agenda: for example, discussion, brainstorm, decision making, announcement.
- Determine whether the agenda needs to be altered based on the needs of the group and checks for consensus on making those adjustments.
- Remind the group of the agreed upon norms when necessary.
- Manage unproductive conflict and power dynamics.
- Keep a list of people waiting to speak and facilitate the order of discussion.
- At the end of a section or of the meeting, review decisions and commitments made during the meeting, review items postponed for future meetings, and ask for process observations.

Tips:

- The facilitator role can also be shared between two people. For example, one facilitator can keep track of speakers, to-do items, and commitments that individuals make.

- A co-facilitator is also useful when there's a decision to be made about the components of the agenda because the two facilitators can confer and make a shared decision.

The Timekeeper

Purpose: To monitor the group's adherence to the times laid out on the agenda.

Timekeeper's Role and Responsibilities:

- Establish an agreement with the facilitator about how to communicate—verbally or nonverbally.
- Let the group know when time is running out or has expired for each agenda item.
- Work with the facilitator to renegotiate time frames as needed.

The Recorder

Purpose: To document the meeting.

Role and Responsibilities:

- Records major decisions and action items without adding opinions.
- Takes more detailed notes of a discussion if requested by the facilitator or group.
- Checks with participants as needed to ensure accurate recording.
- Distributes typed notes to the group within a specified time period.
- Archives all agendas, handouts, and notes in an agreed upon location.

Tips:

- Make sure the recorder knows whether the expectation is that everything said during the meeting is written down or only the main decisions and next steps.

The Process Observer or Process Checker

Purpose: To help the group gain more awareness of its group dynamics so that it can accomplish its goals.

Role and Responsibilities:

Community agreements: The process observer pays attention to how the group honors its community agreements. The process observer can do this by affirming behaviors that are consistent with the norms and naming behaviors that don't uphold the norms.

Participation: The process observer can track who talks, how long people talk, who doesn't talk, and any patterns in participation that might be important, such as female team members participating more than male members. The process observer can also record the nature of each person's participation, for example, whether the contribution was a question, an opinion, a clarification, an assertion, a criticism, or an attempt to facilitate or problem solve.

Decision making: The process observer can note how decisions are made (whether by the facilitator's discretion, by the demands of one person or a small group, or by group agreement). The process observer might also simply name when decisions are being made—often a group is not cognizant of decisions being made.

Tone: The process observer might also pay attention to the general tone of conversations (if this is something the group is working on) and offer specific examples to support an observation. For example, the process observer might pay attention to moments when the team is collaborative or antagonistic.

Operating Guidelines:

- The process observer can offer observations on how the team upheld the norms during the meeting or at the end of it. How and when the process observer will make observations should be communicated at the outset of the meeting.
- The process checker can use a rubric, if the team has one, to note how the group works together.

A Process Check <u>Is</u>:	A Process Check <u>Is Not</u>:
1. Evidence based—observations are about specific behaviors. 2. A way to name behaviors in relation to shared agreements. 3. A time to reveal patterns of participation. 4. An opportunity to raise challenging and sometimes hard questions to the group connected to shared purpose and agreements. 5. A moment for the group to listen openly.	1. A time for blame or judgment. 2. A time to challenge specific individuals in the group or the team leader. 3. Focused on meeting content. 4. Time to present proposals.

Examples of Process Check Prompts:

1. A norm we seem to be holding well is …
2. A norm we seem to struggle with is …
3. Some patterns of communication that I noticed were …
4. Some of the non-verbal communication that I noticed was …

5. Frustration seemed to increase when ... and decrease when ...
6. People seemed more engaged when ... and less engaged when ...
7. Our ability to make decisions seemed to increase when ... and decrease when ...
8. We seemed to get stuck when ...

Tips:

- It can be useful to have a second process checker who supports the primary process checker, catches things that might slip past him or her, and who pays attention to the process checker's participation.
- Everyone in the team can be invited also to pay attention to process and to offer his or her insights at any time.

[1]Modified and used by permission from the National Equity Project.

Communication Agreements

Clear and shared communication structures, processes, and expectations are critical to how a team works together. In this section, we'll consider communication agreements that are purely technical—that can be quickly and fairly easily determined. For example, an agreement such as, "Work email will not be sent to each other after 8:00 p.m. on weeknights," is a technical agreement. Chapter 7 expands on communication.

When you're forming a team, discuss your hopes and expectations for communication. Team members often hold different assumptions about seemingly straightforward components of communication agreements. For example, I would never call a colleague after 10:00 p.m. because I assume she'd be asleep and might have the phone by her bed. I wouldn't want to risk waking her up, so I would wait to relay an important message until the next morning. However, someone else might assume that a colleague may have her phone turned off and would want to receive an important message as soon as she woke up. She might believe that calling a colleague at any time of night is acceptable, especially if she has an important message. Taking the time to iron out these agreements can prevent misunderstandings and potential conflict.

Questions to discuss and make decisions about include the following:

1. What is the purpose for using email?
2. Within what period of time do we expect team members to respond to email?

3. How often do we agree to check our work email?

4. Are there any parameters we want to set for using email, phone calls, or text messages?

5. Do team members have a preference for how they receive communication (e.g., email, voicemail, text messages, in person)?

6. Are there any other agreements we want to make about communicating with other teams, colleagues, or administrators?

Communication agreements need to be revisited occasionally and may need modification. Be sure to address the little things as they come up. Exhibit 4.5 offers an example of a team's communication agreements.

Exhibit 4.5. Example of a Team's Communication Agreements

- Email is used for communicating logistical information, sharing resources, and providing reminders. It is not used for airing grievances, talking about students or colleagues, or dealing with conflict of any kind. Those issues are to be raised in person either with the team or with a specific individual.
- We will respond to each others' emails as soon as possible and within 48 weekday hours of receiving the email.
- We agree to check our work email on a daily basis.
- Emails and text messages should be brief and to the point—otherwise the content probably merits a conversation or team discussion.
- We will use Google Drive for our shared documents and will check with each other before giving anyone else access to our files.
- Notes from our team meetings will be edited and posted on Google Drive within 24 hours of the end of our meeting.
- When one of us communicates with our administrators about our team's work, we'll copy the whole team on the email or report back on the communication if it was in person at our next team meeting.
- We will not call or text each other after 8:00 p.m. on weekdays or before 7:00 a.m. or on the weekends unless it's an emergency; we respect each other's time with family.

WHAT ARE WE GOING TO DO TOGETHER?

Goals mark our progress. They help us establish priorities and determine whether our team is making a difference in the work of the larger organization. Ideally we create SMARTE goals: strategic and specific; measurable; attainable; results based; time bound; and equitable.

A *work plan* outlines steps to reach goals. It identifies the strategic actions that the team will take and the benchmark indicators that will show evidence of progress toward goals.

A work plan includes goals, strategic actions, and benchmark indicators and is used to guide the team's activities during a period of time. This document directs what happens whenever the team convenes, and the team uses it to monitor progress. A work plan is also a tool for communication within the team and to groups or individuals outside of it. In a high school, for example, each department might have a work plan. In monthly check-ins with the principal, the department heads report on their team's progress toward goals using the work plan to reference their actions. For anyone who monitors and supports teams in a school or organization, work plans are crucial tools. Ideally, within a large organization or district, every team and individual works from a plan that is tied to and in support of the organization's strategic plan.

There are various ways to determine a team's goals and work plan. In some cases, the school's leader decides what a team will do or may engage others in the process of creating it. For example, a principal might write the leadership team's work plan alone, might get input from the team, or might co-construct it with the team. What's important is to know why you're making the decisions you're making and to have considered the impact of this decision on the group. There are times when it's wholly appropriate for you to create the plan yourself, and your team will appreciate you for doing so. There are other times when your team may feel excluded from key decision-making moments if they play no role in developing the work plan.

Team Goals

There are two ways to think about directing a team's efforts: toward goals or toward an area for inquiry. Many teams set goals, ideally SMARTE goals. Exhibit 4.6 is the goals that guided the transformational coach team for 1 year.

Exhibit 4.6. Transformational Coaching Team Goals, 2013–14

Teacher performance, as measured by the teaching evaluation rubric. By June:

1. On Element 3.4A of the rubric, 100% of teachers will make one column of growth;
2. On Element 1.2A, 80% of teachers will make one column of growth, or consistently score at a three (out of four) or higher;
3. On Element 2.3A, 95% of teachers consistently score at a three (out of four) or higher.

Client satisfaction: By June, at least 90% of those participating in this coaching program will agree or strongly agree with the following statements on our end-of-year survey:

1. I feel that my coach has helped me improve my professional practice.
2. I feel that coaching has been a positive experience.

Teacher retention: At the end of this school year, we will retain at least 85% of effective teachers.

Student learning: Our work is in support of the following student learning goals. We will take these into account when evaluating the success of our work.

Reading: 100% of students will make 150 points of growth on the reading assessment.

Writing: 100% of students will make one level of growth on the writing assessment.

Student experience: Our work is in support of the following student experience goals. We will take these into account when evaluating the success of our work.

- Reduce the suspension rates of African American and Latino males by 20%.
- Reduce chronic absence by 5%.

These might be determined by the team lead alone or with input from others, or they might be fully co-constructed with a team. For example, department leads might determine goals for their team in the school's leadership team. This can ensure that department goals will align to school goals and to those that other teams set. It can be challenging if a department thinks that goals were externally imposed, that is, handed down from above. A team needs to feel some ownership of its goals, or it can be hard to mobilize energy toward meeting them. The process around goal setting is one that facilitators need to thoughtfully engage in, considering the possible consequences of their decisions and balancing the need to get buy-in from a team with the need to get things done.

Goals often trigger strong feelings in educators because in many places they haven't been used well. Many of us have experienced the destructive side of goals when unsatisfactory test scores have led to punitive consequences. So many goals have been set (by districts, schools, and individuals) that have felt unattainable from the start, and in some places the failure to meet those goals has led to public humiliation of teachers and leaders. Furthermore, many of us have had the experience of setting professional goals at the start of the year, which were then filed into a dusty binder in the office of an administrator and forgotten about until an end of year evaluation. Leaders need to consider how goals have been used in their context previously when working to gain buy-in on a goal-setting process.

Goals have the potential to be wonderfully motivating. When used effectively, when there's buy-in to realistic, meaningful goals, they help us focus and prioritize, get energized and aligned, and help us see that we can make big changes—one step at a time. If you've worked in contexts where they haven't been used well, reclaim your right to use goals as empowering devices.

A Note on Using Urgency

How do you get people to act? How do you light a fire under them so that they'll change? As a leader, I have wanted others to see what I perceived as the urgency in a situation and hoped that they'd become motivated to act as a result. I've also experienced someone else trying to show me her version of an urgent situation and trying to get me to act. Instilling a sense of urgency in others can be critical in fostering change, but it must be used with caution because it can also diminish motivation to enact change.

John Kotter, a change management expert, argues that big changes need to be initiated with a strong sense of urgency (Kotter, 2008). Leaders galvanize conversations about mission, vision, and goals by addressing the urgency of the work. Naming the urgency in our education context can be a powerful way to increase investment of all involved in a change effort. In our case, the urgency is often the lives of children and a moral obligation to ensure that kids receive the education they need and deserve.

Kotter (2008) also offers words of caution when using urgency. He explains that once changes begin, our efforts must quickly focus. Without focus, urgency makes things worse and results in what Kotter calls "a false sense of frenetic urgency" rather than a "true sense of urgency." (Kotter 2008, p. 3) According to Kotter, this kind of urgency is characterized by frenetic activity to cure a problem in which people run from one thing to another. This results in persistent failure, anxiety, frustration, and anger.

False urgency is probably familiar to many educators who have worked in reform initiatives. I've seen many schools and districts adopt program after program and begin initiative after initiative. In the aftermath of these whirlwinds, many educators are left exhausted from investing emotional energy and time into various initiatives only to have had them prematurely terminated and replaced with something else. And then the next time that the urgency of children's lives is then evoked, I've seen educators respond with cynicism and sadness.

You get people to act by believing that they want to act, by demonstrating your own commitment to a project, and by creating the conditions in which they can be effective. When sharing the urgency of a situation, guide them to recognize it and make connections to it. You don't need to force feed them statistics or grim stories—these are rarely inspiring. Help them see how others have made change, and help them connect to one child and to see the unique ways they might contribute to that young person's life. Help them set reasonable, short-term goals, and help them identify the action steps that will lead to meeting those goals. Use urgency in small doses—in large doses it's lethal and usually is not the key ingredient needed to get people to act.

Tips for Goal Setting

1. Set goals, even if there's anxiety about them. Reclaim goal setting and the experience of working toward goals as something that is energizing, motivating, and empowering.

2. Set yearlong goals, and then break them down into monthly or quarterly goals.

3. Set goals that are doable.

4. Revisit goals regularly and emphasize progress toward them.

5. If goals aren't reached, recognize external factors that prevented their accomplishment (there are usually many) and acknowledge the team's responsibility.

A Team Inquiry Project

For some teams, the structure of a work plan, goals, and benchmarks is not a good match for the content of their work. A team can still be very focused and productive without a work plan as long as some structure guides their time together. An inquiry project is an alternate way for a team to engage in learning and working together. This entails determining a focal area to investigate, creating inquiry questions, and engaging in action research. Engaging a team in an inquiry project (rather than anchoring a work plan in goals) is a subtle and powerful shift in identifying purpose. It energizes the part of us that is a lifelong learner, responds to the needs of adult learners, and creates a more inviting, open approach to teamwork. Especially for teams that have had negative experiences with working toward goals, it can be a transformational experience to engage in an inquiry project.

Leading an inquiry process (or in *action research*, as it is sometimes called) takes a specific skill and knowledge set. The best resource I've found is *The Art of Classroom Inquiry: A Handbook for Teacher Researchers* (Hubbard and Power, 2003). If you're curious about what an inquiry project might look like for your team, I encourage you to explore. It can be an exciting, energizing way for team to engage in learning.

Example of a Team Inquiry Project

A group of teachers working at a large high school came together as a professional learning community for a year to address the needs of their newcomer students—students who had just arrived in the United States from other countries. Many of these students had little formal education in their native countries, very few spoke any English, and most had tremendous social and emotional learning needs. The teachers, however, knew very little about newcomers, so rather than setting goals and creating a work plan they decided to spend a year doing an inquiry project.

After a series of discussions, they determined that the following questions would guide their learning:

1. What do we need to know about our newcomers to meet their needs?
2. What do our newcomers really need to know right now?
3. How can we surface their skills and strengths so that we are building on their assets?

4. What kind of social and emotional learning is a priority for our newcomers? How can we deliver this given their low levels of English?

The team generated an exhaustive action plan, which included selecting focal students, observing students, seeking out translators to interview students and family members, and partnering with the arts and music teachers to deliver instruction. Each of these actions was undertaken in a spirit of inquiry—which meant that teachers were constantly asking, "What happens if we teach a lesson on social skills through photography?" or "How do our relationships with students shift after we interview their family?" This approach—open, unattached to outcome, inquisitive—is the spirit of inquiry.

This team also set goals for its inquiry work around its research. For example, the team's goals included interviewing each of the 47 newcomer students it served, attempting four different kinds of nonverbal modes of instruction, conducting three surveys, and presenting its research to the staff at the end of the year.

As the teachers engaged in the inquiry project, they documented their findings, wrote reflective pieces, and shared their learning with each other. There was energy and rigor in this team that came from members' internal motivation and commitment, which I'm not sure would have existed had they been asked to create traditional goals for their work. The next year, the team created a traditional work plan that included student achievement goals. This plan was founded on a rich wealth of learning from their inquiry process and resulted in significant positive impact on the student experience. In addition to implementing a work plan, these teachers also chose to continue an inquiry project because they had felt so inspired and energized. Several teachers stated their decision to remain at their school and not seek jobs elsewhere because of the inquiry they'd done in their professional learning community.

Work Plans

Once a focus is determined, the team creates a plan to reach the goals or undertake the inquiry. A work plan names the specific things that teammates will do and the benchmarks that will be evidence of progress toward goals. The work plan is the team's driver, as it determines what happens at each meeting. Regular reflection (perhaps monthly) to identify progress toward goals and to make course corrections is important.

Given that members will have to implement what is determined, they need to give input into the work plan. In a team where there's high trust and buy-in, this process can be fast and easy. In a team that's struggling—either because it's just forming or it has some unproductive dynamics—this process can be complicated. If this is the case, it is useful to remember that the problem isn't the work plan—the problem is the underlying conflict and ineffective communication skills, in which case you might consider addressing those to some extent before trying to develop a work plan. Sometimes it's possible to take a timeout from teamwork to deal with the root causes of the dysfunction, and sometimes you can't. Exhibit 4.7 offers an example of a team's work plan. A blank template of this plan is available to download from my website (http://www.elenaaguilar.com).

A challenge with implementing work plans is to be flexible in response to what arises in schools and also to implement enough of the plan to see results. We often lose focus when the business of daily school happens and we shift into reactive mode, responding to the chaos, rather than proactively

> *Problems cannot be solved by the same level of thinking that created them.*
>
> ALBERT EINSTEIN

working toward goals that might address some of the underlying reasons for the chaos. We don't want to be a slave to the plan: we need to modify it at times based on what we learn and what's happening in our organizations, but we also can't abandon our plans as soon as something happens or a new shiny thing comes into our midst. Leaders need to be very thoughtful about decisions to stray from the plan or stick to it. We need to discuss these decisions with our teams and get their input. Sometimes we might make suggestions: to hold to the plan, to go forth and see what happens (sometimes plans fail because they were given up on too early), or to shift the plan (sometimes plans fail because they were adhered to rigidly in spite of other data that indicated a need to shift).

MAPPING OUT THE JOURNEY

Every team is different. Every team is a complicated unit with its own configuration of personalities, in its own unique place and time and with its own history and trajectory. For this reason, I can't offer a specific prescription for building a team or mending one that's not working. I can make suggestions—try doing this or try that—but you'll have to map out your own adventure. Although our journeys might look different, all teams need clear a purpose, members need to discuss how they'll travel together, and they need to work toward something concrete.

Sometimes when I'm coaching a leader and we're trying to figure out this map for a team's development, I grab a set of colorful markers and sketch out different routes on a whiteboard. I offer a visual—pick your adventure—and we talk through the various options: Should the team engage in a visioning process before or after identifying core values? When would be a good time to take a side-detour and spend some quality time getting to know each other? How does the team's composition affect how members might participate in a discussion about norms? There's one thing, however, that's on the whiteboard before anything else: the end goal, where the team is headed. Do not pass go without determining purpose.

What emerges in our conversation is the leader's theory of action around building a team. A theory of action is an explanation of why you'll do what you're going to do. It sounds like this:

> My team has been working together for a year, and we have some healthy ways of working together and some unhealthy ways. There are some strong personalities, and I have let a couple of them dominate discussions at times. We need to hit the reset button in our team before continuing together next year, and because of our history I'm going to start by facilitating a conversation about norms. If we have that discussion, then I think our communication dynamics will improve, which has to happen before we have other important conversations. After we determine norms, then we'll talk about our core values. I think this will be energizing and will help us get to know each other better. After that, we'll revisit our team's mission and vision. We discussed this briefly last year, but I don't know that we all share the same meaning.

Devising a theory of action is a key phase in team development. It's one that you do alone, or perhaps with the help of a colleague or coach, and it's the time when you think through why you'll do what you'll do to help your team develop. Write it out or sketch it somewhere, and give yourself the time to think through your options and decisions.

Checking the Health of Your Team

When a team is well established, members can individually complete the following statements and their responses match those of others in the team. You may need to engage your team in the activities described in Chapter 5 (around community agreements) and Chapter 8 (around decisions) before everyone can answer all of these.

Reflect on Purpose, Process, Product

1. Our team exists to … Our mission is …

2. Our team aspires to … Our vision is …

3. Our team's core values are …

4. Our team's community agreements are …

5. Our team makes decisions by …

6. Our team's communication agreements are …

7. In team meetings we use the roles of …

8. Our team's goals (or inquiry questions) are …

9. Our team's work plan is reviewed [at what frequency].

10. Our team knows if we're making progress on our mission and goals and toward our vision because …

Transformational Coaching Team, 2013

Because of the timeline for the grant that we were working under, I had to establish our team's goals long before our team first convened. I was nervous about presenting these goals to team members because I didn't know how they'd respond, given that they hadn't played any part in determining them. Prior to the meeting where I shared them, I told myself, "Just listen to their responses—listen for the emotions under the words, give them space to think and make meaning, and don't try to fix it. Don't get defensive—these are the right goals. They might just need time and space to process."

At the opening of our meeting, I shared my plan: "After you read the goals, I'm going to give you time to process individually, then to talk with a partner, and then to discuss with the whole team. I'm going to just listen to your reflections and capture them in my notes. I'm going to hold off on answering questions or responding to specific concerns until after you all have shared your thoughts and responded to each other—probably for about 15–20 minutes. I feel confident that these are the right goals for our team."

Here's what some coaches said after reading the goals:

1. "Having 100% of teachers meet their goal doesn't seem reasonable or realistic."
2. "What happens if we don't meet these goals?"
3. "How can I control how teachers feel about my coaching?"
4. "Who is going to measure these and how often?"
5. "I don't like it that our goals are tied to their performance goals."
6. "If we don't meet these goals, will that affect whether we're rehired next year?"

As they shared their concerns, I listened as coaches responded to each other's questions. One said, "I think setting a goal of 100% is fine—it's a goal." Another said, "I think I can have a huge impact into how teachers feel about my coaching—I'm okay with the client satisfaction goals." And another said, "I doubt that if we don't meet these goals it would affect our employment status. If anything affects whether we're rehired, it's probably going to be whether we reach our own professional growth goals that we set a couple weeks ago—not whether our team meets its goals."

The conversation shifted into the underlying feelings without any nudging from me (although this is where I would have directed it to go). "I'm just feeling anxious about doing a good job," one coach said. "I know that our team is under intense scrutiny because of the grant. I don't want to let anyone down." Another coach added, "And our schools are struggling in so many ways. These goals feel huge to me, and I want to meet them but am nervous about how much impact we can actually have." Someone else said, "It's the final goal around reducing suspension that hit home for me. I really want to meet it—but I'm scared that I don't know how."

After some 15 minutes of whole-group discussion, I asked coaches to turn to a partner and identify their remaining questions. To everyone's surprise, few questions remained. I reiterated my stance on goals: "These are goals, which means that we strive for them and stay focused on them. It means that my job is to create the conditions so that you can meet them—including to provide the professional development so that you can contribute, for example, to reducing suspension rates. Whether or not these goals are met does not play a role in your continued employment. There are far too many variables that will affect whether we meet them. If we don't meet our goals, then we'll spend some time reflecting on why we didn't—and what needs to shift, be that the goal itself or our practices. And if we do meet our goals, then we'll also spend time reflecting on what allowed us to meet them—and what needs to shift. Goals help us learn, and our central work in this team is to learn."

Throughout the year as we assessed our progress toward meeting our goals, coaches experienced increased confidence in their skill sets and in being guided by goals. We didn't meet all of our goals, but we learned a great deal about a whole lot—including the conditions necessary for meeting ambitious goals. And one condition, I acknowledged, is that the leader presents goals in a way that leads to buy-in, that the leader can manage her own feelings while others process theirs so that we don't get all wrapped up in the emotional experience of goals. Sometimes as I reflected on how this team was developing, I could see the points along the path at which we could have gone in different (less effective) directions. I could see how if I had responded defensively in those initial moments when I'd presented the goals I might have sent us in a different direction. What I recognized was that often it was my ability to hold off, to be quiet, to wait before responding, to allow others to work things out by themselves that was critical. And again and again, I returned to the truth that who you are as a leader has the greatest influence on a team.

Exhibit 4.7. Team Work Plan Example

GRADE-LEVEL TEAM WORK PLAN
   Rise Up Elementary School's Fifth Grade Team
   2014–2015

Annual District or School Goals

1. 95% of students will make at least a 20% growth in reading on our school-created reading assessment *(Top focus for 2014–15)*.
2. 95% of students will use evidence from a text to support written arguments.
3. 95% of students will feel welcomed, appreciated, and cared for by the adults at school, as reported on our student survey.
4. 95% of students will feel connected to their peers and that they have at least one friend at school, as reported on our student survey.

Team Mission	Team Vision	Team Community Agreements
Our team exists to create a safe and nurturing community for our students so that they can take risks, be vulnerable learners, and reach their student achievement goals.	We aspire to create a safe space for our own learning as teachers where we can support and challenge each other, push each other to do our very best for our students, and celebrate our successes. With this foundation, we aspire to provide exceptionally caring and rigorous instruction for our fifth graders this year.	• Be fully present in mind and body • Challenge assumptions, our own and others • Tell the truth without blame or judgment • Be unattached to outcome

Team Core Values

1. We hold a growth mind-set for each other, our colleagues, our students, and their families. We know that everyone can learn.
2. We value relationships and spend time cultivating them because everything springs from relationships based on respect and care.
3. We practice looking at the whole and its parts at the same time. We remember that we are all connected, a part of many systems, and that we are more effective if we practice this kind of seeing.
4. We know that we work better in resilient, trusting communities, and we strive to build these with each other and with our students and their communities.
5. We acknowledge that our emotions are a part of our work. We work to understand them and manage them in ourselves and in others.
6. We know that our own backgrounds and experiences shape our beliefs and actions; we pay attention to who we are and who we serve so that we can interrupt systemic oppression of all kinds.
7. We value productive conflict and know that disagreements about ideas can lead to insights that will help us better serve our students. We embrace these opportunities and learn from them.

Team Decision-Making Agreements

We aspire to make the majority of our decisions through consensus, but we recognize that sometimes this may not be possible. In these cases, we will make decisions using a voting process. If this is not possible and we are unable to make a decision, we will use a majority voting process.

Team Goals

SMARTE Goal 1

- To support our top focus school goal and specifically our most struggling readers, (so that they meet their growth goal) by June 2015, we will use at least 20 different reading comprehension structures and strategies in our classes, we will use four different assessment tools and will analyze the results from these tools, and we will apply these approaches to at least five different genres of text.

	Strategic Actions	Benchmark Indicators
July—August	• Attend professional development on reading comprehension for struggling readers and English learners. • Create unit plans for the first quarter that incorporate our learning into all content areas. • Outline yearlong scope and sequence of reading comprehension strategies and texts. • Determine which assessments to use, create some if necessary, and calendar assessments.	• Unit pans • Yearlong scope and sequence • Assessments selected, created, and calendared
September	• Administer preassessments. • Analyze preassessments with team and set individual student growth goals. • Introduce first set of reading comprehension strategies to students and practice with one genre of text (fiction). • Share student work from this first set with team and analyze together.	• Preassessments analyzed • Student work analyzed
October	• Conduct in-depth assessments and interviews with focal students; share these with team. • Observe each other's focal students and share feedback and observations. • Plan a science text reading comprehension lesson together. • Video record ourselves teaching this lesson and share videos with team.	• Assessments and interviews of focal students gathered and shared • Collaboratively planned lesson • Video recordings of teaching shared with team

(continued)

	Strategic Actions	Benchmark Indicators
November	• Administer end-of-quarter reading assessments and analyze results together. • Introduce second set of reading comprehension strategies with third genre (biography). • Share and analyze focal student work from biography lessons.	• End-of-quarter assessment results analyzed • End-of-quarter assessments show a positive trend toward growth for 95% of students • Focal student work shared and analyzed

SMARTE Goal 2

- To support our school's third and fourth goal, by June 2015, we will ensure that at least 95% of the students in our grade-level feel welcomed, appreciated, and cared for by at least one teacher; and we will ensure that at least 95% of our students feel they have at least one friend in their grade level.
  - This is an action goal for ourselves as teachers.

	Strategic Actions	Benchmark Indicators
July—August	• Plan lessons for the first 6 weeks of school to implement the Caring School Community program. • Visit each child's home and conduct informal interviews with family members. • Plan for October overnight trip.	• Lessons planned. • Visits completed. • Overnight trip planned.
September	• Match fifth graders with their kindergarten and eighth grade buddy and launch buddy program. • Conduct whole-class and individual preassessments to gauge students' feelings about school, each other, and their teachers. • Based on the data collected this month, select focal students for the semester. • Hold several cross-grade level events and ensure that students build community with each other and with other adults.	• Buddy program launched. • Interviews completed. • Focal students selected. • Grade-level events held.

	Strategic Actions	**Benchmark Indicators**
October	• Implement "Month of Compassion" unit; observe each other's focal students during at least one lesson. • Arrange service-learning events for November. • Lead overnight trip; each teacher will spend a minimum of 1 hour with her focal student and at least 1 hour with another teacher's focal student to get to know them better.	• Unit implemented and observation of students accomplished. • Service-learning events planned. • Overnight trip goals accomplished.
November	• Conduct end-of-quarter survey and analyze results. • Conduct service-learning activities.	• Survey results show positive trend. • Revise action plans based on survey results if necessary—in particular for focal students. • Service learning activities produce evidence of students' expanding compassion for each other and all living beings.

CHAPTER 5

Laying a Foundation for Trust

Humanities Team, 2008

"I don't like the way you said that," Margaret said. "I feel like you're bossing us around, and I don't think that's your job."

We were 5 minutes into our department meeting, and I'd just shared only the objectives. I took a deep breath and said, "I am not sure I understand. Can you clarify?"

"You don't appreciate how hard our jobs are," Margaret said. "I get here at 7:00 a.m. and leave at 6:00 p.m. Then I go home and grade papers. And now you're telling us we need to make learning targets for every lesson?"

"That wasn't my decision," I said. "That was our principal's. Today we are going to talk about what makes a good learning target, and the objective is that everyone creates three learning targets for their lessons next week."

Margaret didn't respond. I thought we could proceed with the meeting, but then she spoke up. "So you've assumed that we don't know how to write learning targets. Why would you think that? And how can we be expected to write learning targets when we're already working 15 hours a day?"

> I sighed. Every meeting seemed to go like this—around and around in circles, distrust percolating up and obstructing our learning. And it didn't emanate only from Margaret. "I think we need to talk about how we're going to behave in team meetings," I said, my tone heavy with frustration.
>
> "Oh, so now you're telling me I'm not behaving well? Are you going to give me an office referral?" Margaret stood and picked up her stack of papers. "I'm sorry," she said. "All of a sudden I'm not feeling well, and I need to leave. I'll submit an absence form. Have a good meeting," she said as she walked out of the room.

COMMUNITY AGREEMENTS BUILD CULTURE

"Culture eats strategy for breakfast."

PETER DUCKER

If you don't already have Peter Ducker's wise words posted somewhere you can see it every day, I encourage you to do so. Through the long work of building teams, these words remind me where to focus my energy. I would suggest this addition: we need to remember that we can *use strategy* to create culture—that in fact, if we don't approach the building of culture strategically, intentionally and somewhat methodically, we may not achieve it. Healthy cultures aren't just built by themselves; they are also formed by leaders who mold, design, and construct.

Community agreements, or norms, can be a foundation for positive culture. They are essentially a system to sustain emotionally intelligent practices. Norms can cultivate trust and safety. They exist to prevent unhealthy conflict from mushrooming, to guide our behavior, and, most important, to help us do whatever it is we've decided to do as a team.

Whenever I hear about or observe a team that's struggling, the first question I ask is, "What are your group's norms?" If the facilitator or a team member hesitates trying to recall the norms, I suspect this lack of agreement about how to treat each other is at the root of the problem. Without community agreements, everything else we apply to remedy a team's dysfunction will flounder.

Many educators have had negative experiences with creating norms or just haven't experienced them as meaningful tools. If you're feeling even the slightest bit annoyed that I've given norms a whole chapter, please bear with me. Perhaps you've joined the ranks of educators concerned about the time spent creating norms, or perhaps you've felt frustrated by how infrequently norms you've made are used. It's not the fault of the norms that they ended up banished to paper that was never referenced again. To build resilient communities, we must ensure that norms are written well and that they are used well: they must be both living and useful.

A GOOD NORM IS NOT HARD TO FIND

Effective norms help team members achieve their goals and, as such, need to reflect both a group's and individual needs. For example, I might engage in a norms conversation considering what I need to be my best self in this group—and I might decide that I need to be unattached to outcome. However, after discussion with my teammates, I realize that my personal norm might not be the most useful for me as a part of this particular group. Perhaps our group needs a norm such as, "Be solutions oriented." Norms must blend personal and collective needs to meet the team's goals. If your personal favorite norm doesn't make it into your team's norms, you might reflect on whether the norm is really a core value or a key way of being to which you aspire. For myself, being unattached to outcome is central to my ability to be a good team member and leader. If it's not on a list of team norms, it's still always on the forefront of my mind as a way I aspire to be.

In organizations where there's low trust, team members might suggest norms that they want to see demonstrated by another individual. For example, I might really need Carlos to stop talking so much; I've been in groups with him, and he always dominates the conversation. So I might propose, "Monitor airtime." However, even though Carlos's prior verbal dominance might suggest that we need to prevent this from happening in our new group, it's also not necessarily going to be the case. An overly dominant team member can be managed by an effective facilitator—so there is a chance that Carlos might be different in this group. And it might be more effective for me to have a private conversation with Carlos and express what I've noticed and how I feel about his participation in group discussions.

Norms are effective when a team determines them together and when their meaning is clear to all members. Settling on the best language is tricky because if a phrase is too general, such as "Respect each other," interpretations can vary and you might not see the behavior that you feel reflects respect. "Listen to understand" is another somewhat abstract norm because it's hard to get inside of someone else's head and evaluate whether he or she is indeed *listening* to *understand*. However, this can be a powerful norm if a group identifies what might be evidence that someone is listening to understand. The time spent making meaning together of norms can improve how a team functions.

The most common challenge with norms is that a group selects too many. When this happens, it can suggest that the group is struggling with decision making and trust. For norms to be useful, they must be memorable. And for them to be memorable, there must be no more than seven—although I think five is ideal.

Procedural norms and behavioral norms are both useful to establish. As you can see in Exhibit 5.1, procedural norms describe some of the technical agreements between team members. Behavioral norms describe the emotionally intelligent ways that we will interact with each other. Norms are most often activated and referenced during meetings, but their usage is not exclusive to team meetings. They are most useful when they also apply to anytime we interact with each other, whether that's in the hallways, during yard duty, or at a staff meeting.

Exhibit 5.1. Part 1. Examples of Norms

Facilitator's Procedural Responsibilities	Facilitator's Procedural Requests
<ul><li>Email agenda and anything that will need to be read that's over two pages at least 48 hours ahead of meeting time.</li><li>Invite feedback at every meeting and share a summary at the next meeting.</li><li>Articulate the purpose of all activities and connect them to our mission.</li></ul>	<ul><li>If you know you'll be absent for a meeting, let me know as soon as you know.</li><li>If you are coming but will be late, text me.</li><li>Communicate directly with me and as fast as possible if you have any issues coming up in this learning space.</li><li>Respond to emails (when requested) within 24 hours (during the weekdays) of receiving them.</li></ul>

A facilitator's roles and responsibilities are not norms for all team members. For example, "Have agendas that meet different learning needs" isn't a community agreement—it's a facilitator's job. If desired, *procedural* facilitator norms can be determined with a team. This serves as reminder of mutual accountability and can subtly address the power dynamics between the facilitator and the team. For an example of Community Agreements, see Exhibit 5.1, Part 2, later in this chapter.

Whenever possible, it's best to phrase norms in the positive since they are aspirational descriptions of behavior and since we want to focus on what we're trying to do. Some teams, at certain stages of development and in response to particular group dynamics, might need direct language to remind them of how they wanted to interact with each other. The humanities team was one such team, and we created directive norms such as, "Don't interrupt." After about a year, this team replaced, "Don't interrupt," with, "Listen to understand."

> *"The only thing of real importance that leaders do is to create and manage culture."*
>
> EDGAR SCHEIN

GETTING FROM HERE TO NORMS

As a facilitator, the most important thing for you to know when planning for writing norms in your team is that there's likely to be some tension. Tension can arise from disagreements about use of time (i.e., some feel that the process takes too long, and others want more time) or in discussions of what the norms should be. You'll need to work on managing your own discomfort because it's really hard to meet everyone's needs—even though you may aspire to do so. As you engage a team in determining norms, give yourself opportunities to notice and reflect on the feelings that come up for you. They can help you learn a great deal about how you deal with conflict, decision making, and leadership.

Time

The time required for this process depends on the number of team members, their history together, how long they anticipate working together, how often they'll meet, and the focus of their work. For example, a team of 10 who will write the district strategic plan and will meet weekly for 6 hours for 1 year needs more time to develop norms. This will likely be challenging work that involves a great deal of decision making. A group of six teachers who meet for 2 hours once a month might be able to articulate its norms faster. Basically, the more time together and the more complex the tasks will be, the more time will be needed for creating norms. In addition, if the group worked together before and has had unproductive conflict, the process will involve much more than just identifying a set of norms: it will require conversations that address previous ways of interacting. (Chapter 12 provides more information on this.)

Let the group know that although you have a time frame for the norming process it may take longer. You might say, "I've allocated 1 hour for our norm-setting process today. If we need more time we can take up to an hour of next week's meeting. I want to make sure this process is thorough and meaningful, and I'll facilitate as best I can to keep us on track and moving forward." In my experience, a norming process can take from 1 to 3 hours.

Steps

Exhibit 5.2 shows an agenda I used with a group to create norms. This team was composed of eight teachers, two of whom were new. There was some discussion and debate, but not too much. The process was completed within the 2-hour agenda. I hope that this agenda clarifies the steps and talking points for developing norms.

The process of creating norms can be fast and easy or long and challenging. To make sure that everyone stays engaged, you'll want to pay close attention to nonverbal communication and to solicit feedback along the way. When the majority of the group seems ready to move on, you may need to push ahead with the agenda.

If the norming process occurs near the beginning of your time working with a team, your facilitation skills may be keenly observed. You'll want to ensure that this experience builds the team's trust in your capacity to facilitate and be responsive to all needs.

Time for discussion during the formation of norms can set the stage for effective collaboration. As teammates share stories, they learn about each other and process feelings. You can—and probably should—plan for these moments to happen.

Exhibit 5.2. Example of Agenda for Norm Building

Math Department PLC

RISE UP ACADEMY

August 7, 2014 8:00 a.m. to 10:15 a.m. **FACILITATOR'S AGENDA**

Intended Outcomes

Participants will:

- Develop and agree on our community agreements for our department for this year

Agenda

Time	What	Why	How
			Materials
8:00 (20)	**Opening** • Welcome (3^1) • Agenda review (5) ✓ Frame our process today by referencing the discussion we had last week about what it would take for our team to feel safe and trusting with each other. • Grounding: Ball toss game (10)	To understand what we'll do today and bring our best selves to this team. To connect with each other and build community.	Pair share Written reflection Whole-group game Agenda

8:20 (25)	**Generating Our Norms**
	• Make sure to keep reminding the group why we're doing this, how these norms will help us work effectively together, to learn from each other, and to meet our students' needs. Emphasize this a lot!
	• Surfacing previous experiences (4)
	  ✓ Say: With a partner, share any experiences you've had with creating norms in a team.
	  ✓ Let them know after 2 minutes have passed to switch to next person.
	• Hopes for our today (3)
	  ✓ Say: With the same partner, now share your hopes for our process here today.
		To identify the community agreements that will be most useful to our group.	Pair share
			Individual writing
			
			Note cards
			Examples of Community agreements
			Highlighter pens

(continued)

Time	What	Why	How
			Materials
	• Brainstorming (9) ✓ Say: On your note card, list the behaviors you'd like to see others demonstrating in our team. Also list those that you know will be most important for you to demonstrate to be your best self here. 3 minutes to brainstorm. ✓ Hand out examples of community agreements. Say: Read these over and highlight those that you feel might be really useful for our group. Also, notice if there's language used that you really like and that might reflect one of your ideas. We'll take 3 minutes to quietly read and note. ✓ Say: Now, from the list you created and the one you just read, put a star by the FIVE [what] that are most important to you. We'll take a minute or two to do that. • Brainstorm share (6) ✓ Say: Now turn to a different partner and share the five that you just identified as most important for our group to follow. Explain why you selected those. You'll each have 3 minutes to talk, and I'll tell you when it's time to switch.		

Time	What	Why	How
			Materials

8:45 (20–40)	**Clarifying and Classifying Our Norms**
	• Select five and share (12)
	  ✓ Say: Select up to five of the norms that you brainstormed or chose from the examples, and write each one individually on a sticky note. You'll have a chance to explain your meaning soon, but for right now you just need to capture your idea. [Show an exemplar.] (1)
	  ✓ Have everyone get up and put his or her sticky notes on the chart paper in a way so that they can all be read. Invite everyone to just stand back and read what's been posted. It's OK if they start talking to each other about what they see. (10)
	• Clarify (2–15)
	  ✓ Say: Are there any terms or phrases on any of these sticky notes that you would like clarity on? Is there a norm that you'd like the author to explain? We want to make sure we understand what we've generated."
		To make sure we all understand the meaning behind the norms that have been generated.	Whole-group discussion
			
			Sticky notes
			Chart paper

(continued)

Time	What	Why	How
			Materials
	✓ NOTE: This conversation may need to be longer or shorter depending on what is generated. This is a moment to be a very watchful facilitator to ensure that there's equity of participation, that people can explain their ideas without going on too long or being silenced, and that everyone is engaged in the discussion. The group should be standing or sitting in a way so that everyone can see each other. This can be a really important part of the process as team members describe what they need from the group and perhaps share previous experiences or hopes. • Organize our brainstorm (5–10) ✓ Say: Let's see what happens if we try to organize and group these [xxxs?]. If you're already seeing patterns and groupings, then I welcome you to start moving the sticky notes around. You're also welcome to stand back and just watch—I'm sure we'll have plenty of hands helping. Our goal is to group these into 5–10 categories that could become our norms, even though we'll narrow them down to between five and seven categories in the end.		

Time	What	Why	How
			Materials

Approx. 9:05–9:25 (6–20)	**Finalizing Our List**
	• Narrowed list that we can all live with (4–10)
	  ✓ Rewrite the 5–10 norms that have been grouped previously in a list.
	  ✓ Say: Is there any norm here that you can't live with, that you'd be strongly opposed to having as a group norm?
	  ✓ If there is, ask for explanation. If necessary, attempt to revise or eliminate norms until everyone is comfortable with the list of between 5 and 10.
	• Voting (6–10)
	  ✓ Give everyone five stickers, and tell everyone to stick one next to each of his or her top five most important norms.
	  ✓ Once the top five have been identified, ask for a thumb vote: Thumb up if you are good with these; thumb sideways if you're okay with it and can live with it; thumb down if you can't live with the final decision. This can happen if there's a norm that someone really feels the group needs but it didn't get into the top five. Ask anyone with a thumb down to explain his or her reasoning, and then check the whole group to see if anyone else's thumb has been swayed. Attempt to seek consensus, but also balance the need to maintain everyone's engagement.
		To agree on and articulate our team's norms.	Individual voting
			
			Chart paper
			Stickers

(continued)

Time	What	Why	How
			Materials
	✓ If consensus can't be reached, ask the group to move forward with trying out the top five to seven norms and promising to return to them in 6 weeks to see how they've been working. ✓ IF IT'S BEEN A LONG TIME, TAKE A 10-MINUTE BREAK.		
Approx. 9:15–9:45	**Making Meaning of Our Norms** • Write each finalized norm on the top of a sheet of chart paper, and post around the room. Invite everyone to walk around with a marker and write the meaning he or she makes of that norm—and what it would look like or sound like if that norm was being held. (8–12) • Ask for quiet, but let all participants know that they can communicate in writing—they can comment on each other's notes, star what others have written, ask questions. Make sure to emphasize the purpose of this activity. • Ask that everyone contribute to each poster because we want to have everyone's voice in this conversation. • After everyone has circulated to each poster, debrief together. Say: What do you notice in our comments? Is there anything here that anyone thinks we should talk about together? Anything that needs clarification? (8–12)	To ensure that our norms will be meaningful and useful.	Chalk talk Whole-group discussion Markers Chart paper

Time	What	Why	How
			Materials
Approx. 9:30–10:00	**Closing** • Next steps: How will we ensure that our norms are living, meaningful things? ✓ Say: At our next meeting, we'll spend about 20 minutes discussing how we can make sure that our norms are really helpful and which structures we can use to uphold them. • Reflection (5) ✓ Say: With a partner, share your reflections on this process today. How did you experience it? How did it feel? You'll each have 2 minutes, and I'll let you know when to switch. • Feedback (5) ✓ Say: I really value your feedback on our time today. Please be honest and let me know if you'd like to follow up individually with me. • Appreciations (5) ✓ Say: I want to hold a few minutes for us to appreciate each other. ✓ If this feels authentic, say: I want to start with thanking each of you for your honesty, full participation, and investment in our team. ✓ Say: I know that the work we did today will really help us take risks with each other this year and push each other to refine our teaching practice— and therefore, it'll help our kids. Would anyone else like to express an appreciation?	To reflect on our process and build our community.	Pair share Individual reflection Whole group Feedback form

[1]Number of minutes for this section. I often add a minute or two here and there to account for transition time.

Exhibit 5.1. Part 2. Examples of Norms, Community Agreements

Procedural Norms	Behavioral Norms
<ul><li>Start and end on time</li><li>Announce comings and goings at the start of the meeting</li><li>Computers open only during appropriate work time</li><li>Cell phones on silent or vibrate and ideally out of sight during meeting times</li></ul>	<ul><li>Be fully present mentally and physically</li><li>Keep kids at the center</li><li>Tell the truth without blame or judgment</li><li>Assume positive intent</li><li>Pay attention to heart and meaning</li><li>Be open to possibilities</li><li>Be unattached to outcome</li><li>Welcome and manage discomfort</li><li>Challenge our own and others' assumptions</li><li>Be willing to push each other's thinking</li><li>Look at every issue from multiple perspectives</li><li>Be responsible for the way we say things; say them so people can hear them</li><li>Follow-through on agreements</li><li>Monitor airtime</li><li>Actively participate</li><li>Invite and welcome the contributions of every member and listen to each other</li><li>Take risks and be vulnerable learners</li><li>Air disagreements during the meeting if they involve everyone; air disagreements with individuals as soon as possible after a meeting</li><li>Don't interrupt each other</li><li>Acknowledge ideas and contributions even if you disagree with them</li><li>Listen to understand</li><li>Speak directly to people about issues; no gossiping, ever!</li><li>Agree to disagree</li><li>Be solutions oriented</li><li>Hold an assets-based and growth mind-set for adults as well as students</li><li>Take an inquiry stance when things get hard</li><li>Listen for and draw attention to successes</li><li>Maintain confidentiality about everything we talk about—if you're not sure if you can share, check.</li></ul>

Know that sometimes powerful discussions emerge from such planning, and sometimes they don't. When you hear, see, and feel the connections among participants solidifying and you observe the group's understanding of its values and norms increasing, don't rush the process. Give people the time to talk. This is when the foundation for a healthy team is laid.

MAKE YOUR NORMS SERVE YOU

Once a team has generated norms, you can take several additional steps to make these agreements become meaningful tools for team development.

Clarify What the Norms Mean

First, the facilitator leads a conversation around what the norms mean. Ideally, the norm creation process included multiple opportunities for participants to discuss the behaviors captured by the norms, so this conversation will have already been begun. However, because these discussions may have happened in pairs or small groups, the whole team may not have shared meanings about the community agreements.

This process can happen in several ways. Another meeting can be devoted to discussing what the norms look and sound like in action, or this conversation can be divided up so that each time the team convenes there's time to discuss one norm. After discussions, a team might decide that at a meeting they'll focus on holding one specific norm. This practice helps a group align around what a community agreement means. A team might also want to create a document like the one shown in Exhibit 5.3.

Exhibit 5.3. What Do Our Norms Mean?

Assume Positive Intent

- Ask yourself what intentions you're assuming about what someone else is doing or saying; be aware of your assumptions.
- Give the speaker the benefit of the doubt that he or she is not trying to hurt you.
- Activate your compassion for the speaker.
- If you're hurt, seek clarification from the speaker.

Be Solutions Oriented

- Think about how we can move forward to solve the problem.
- If you offer a criticism, also offer a solution or different way of approaching the idea.
- Share ideas—don't be shy about contributing your own.

Be Unattached to Outcome

- Before we land on a decision, make sure we've thoroughly considered it from all angles and that we've identified the root causes of the problem.
- Be responsive and flexible in the moment.
- Always hold an inquiry stance and be open to surprises.
- Also be careful that our lack of attachment doesn't mean lack of commitment; don't be afraid also to take risks.
- Remember that because we have a limited knowledge set and given that we don't know everything, we can't be attached to an outcome.

Stay on Topic; Be Fully Present; Actively Participate

- Be seated with the group when the meeting starts.
- Monitor your own airtime, and remind others to monitor themselves.
- Pay attention to what kinds of contributions you make (e.g., opinions, suggestions, ideas, agreements), and try to vary these.
- Give time for everyone to speak, and don't interrupt each other.
- No side conversations—not in whispers or in writing.
- Focus on the speaker, and make eye contact.
- No cell phone activity, that is, no texting unless it's an emergency.

Speak Your Truth without Blame or Judgment

- Take responsibility for what you say—communicate in a way that others can hear.
- Consider when and where you need to speak your truth, and be mindful of the impact that this can have. But don't hold back on speaking your truths.
- Be hard on ideas and soft on people.
- When others speak their truths, listen to understand.
- If you have a conflict with one person, deal directly with that person.
- Ask for help (from a conflict mediator) if you need support.

Make the Norms Visible

First of all, norms should always be visible during team meetings. I think they're most effective when they are close to our eyes, so I always include them on an agenda. However, they could also be displayed in the room where you meet.

Several routines can give norms life. During the opening of a meeting, invite people to review the norms and select one that they want to be particularly mindful of holding that day. This determination might be based on how they are feeling coming into the room. For example, after a busy and chaotic day, a teacher might want to focus on "Be present." A team might also decide collectively to focus on a particular norm. For example, if a hard decision is going to be made that day, they might select "Listen to understand" as a way to guide their interactions with each other.

When I begin meetings, I ask the participants to read the norms and select one to focus on. Then I ask participants to share their chosen norms with partners and explain why they chose it. This routine takes only 2–3 minutes and allows people to think about how they want to show up in a meeting.

At the end of the meeting, I ask people to reflect on how they held their norm: "Did your norm float into your awareness at any time during our meeting? Did you notice any moments when it felt hard to hold your norm? Did you notice any moments when you felt like you were holding your norm well?" After a moment of individual reflection, I invite members to share their thoughts with their partner. This provides a kind of soft accountability for holding norms, and it gives them meaning. This also takes only a couple of minutes.

Create Structures for Accountability

Given that norms are behavioral aspirations, it is common for there to be breakdowns in how they're lived. Because we can anticipate that there will be lapses, we can establish structures to use at the first signs of stress, and we can make sure that these structures support learning and thus strengthen our team.

A process observer is probably the most important role in a team. This person pays attention to the group's dynamics and notices behaviors in relation to the team's norms. There's a learning curve when incorporating a process observer into a team: it takes a while for everyone to really understand the role and feel comfortable using the skill set required. (See Chapter 4 for more on roles in teams.)

Very soon after a team has the "What do our norms mean?" conversation, members need to discuss the process observer. To invest in the norms, participants need and want to know how they'll be held. Remember that many educators have participated in creating norms that were never seen or heard from again or that were never upheld. Share the document describing the role of the process observer (in Chapter 4) and engage the team in discussion it.

Ultimately you're responsible for how effective the process observer is, so this is also a moment in which your leadership might be scrutinized. Team members will be extra sensitive the first time a process checker is used to the process observer's efficacy. So when the process observer role makes its debut, make sure that the person playing it is clear on the requirements for the role, is confident in these requirements, and can execute them well. You might carefully select the process observer for the first few meetings (rather than asking for volunteers or randomly assigning the roles) and offer him or her some one-on-one coaching to prepare for holding the role.

I like to alternate between having appointed process observers and having everyone play this role when I facilitate teams. When everyone is invited to play the process observer, anyone can intervene at any moment or can offer reflections at the end of the meeting on what he or she noticed about how the norms were upheld.

If you designate a single process observer, and he or she doesn't name a behavior that upholds or violates the norms, it is important that you, as facilitator, do so. This can happen either during or at the end of a meeting. Maintaining your team's trust depends on your playing this role. It also gives you a chance to model what the job of a process observer sounds like. For example, perhaps during a discussion about upcoming student conferences you hear a great deal of evidence of one of your community agreements, "Listening to understand." All you need to do is say something like, "In our meeting today, I heard a great deal of evidence that we were upholding our agreement to listen to understand." Teams need affirmation when they're working well. If the discussion becomes contentious, you can say, "It might be helpful for us to recall our agreement to listen to understand. Let's see what happens if we continue our discussion practicing this norm." That's the role of a process observer. It can feel uncomfortable to do this—it usually involves interrupting the flow of a conversation—but it's important. And if the team has committed to using a process observer in discussions, then it's also what's expected.

Constantly wearing the lens of process observer allows you to be aware of how the members are relating to each other and of the underlying currents of communication, emotion, and energy. This is one of the hardest and most tiring aspects of leading teams, but it's essential if you want to create healthy, resilient, trusting spaces in which adults can learn and work.

When Should We Revise Our Norms?

When a team is first using norms, midyear and end-of-year reflections are a good idea. This conversation can be part of a meeting or its entirety. Start by inviting members to reflect on the questions in Exhibit 5.4, and then facilitate a discussion about their reflection.

Exhibit 5.4. Reflection Questions on Our Norms

1. How do you feel our norms are working for us as a team?
2. When have you seen evidence that they've been helpful for us to get our work done?
3. Are there any norms that you feel we have a harder time upholding?
4. Are there any norms that you feel we don't have a shared agreement about their meaning?
5. Have you noticed anything in our ways of working together that suggests that we might need to add a norm? If so, what might that be? Or what behavior might need to be addressed?
6. What ideas do you have about how we can make our norms more meaningful or useful?

When new members join, a team needs to pause and return to the norms. Although a new member doesn't mean you need to start over with norms, you do need to make sure that new person understands the norms you've already created with your team and the expectations for holding them. This new member, however, also has to make meaning of the norms and buy into them, or he may not be inclined to adopt them. A facilitator needs to attend to this while also balancing the team's need to move ahead with their work and not spend too much time revisiting previous conversations.

Even if a team's membership stays intact, it's a good routine to start each school year by getting grounded in norms. As teammates work together over time, these moments create a space to acknowledge the trust that has grown, their own personal growth, and the positive feelings of being on an emotionally healthy team. The work of getting along with each other is the hardest part of being on a team; it is essential to celebrate those accomplishments and to continue to refine our relationships.

SETTING INTENTIONS:
A COUNTERPART TO NORMS

During the opening of professional development sessions, I invite participants to set an intention for their learning time. This simple practice takes very little time and can help us learn in a much deeper and more authentic way.

Intention setting comes right after welcoming the group, previewing the agenda, and reviewing the community agreements. Here's what I say when I introduce intentions:

> Given where we're doing today in our learning, and given whatever is on your mind, I want to invite you to set an intention. An intention describes an aspiration for how you might think, feel, and engage with others or engage in your learning. An intention can be, "I want to be fully present," "I want to take risks," "I want to connect with others," or "I want to ask hard questions." An intention could even be, "I don't want to be grumpy"; that's been mine on a few occasions. An intention reflects whatever might be most helpful for you, right now, to get the most from today.

I also explain why setting intentions is useful. I say:

> When you set an intention, you are more likely to make choices that help you to fulfill it. You might forget all about your intention today. However, some part of your mind remembers it, and unconsciously you may make choices that help you live your intention.

Sometimes I share this quote by Daniel Siegel (2007) from *The Mindful Brain*: "Intentions create an integrated state of priming, a gearing up of our neural system to be in the mode of that specific intention: we can be readying to receive, to sense, to focus, to behave in a certain manner" (p. 177). Sometimes it's important to note that neuroscience justifies this activity—it tells us that setting intentions primes our minds to notice the actions, opportunities, people, and things that can help us be our best selves. Those who might be unenthusiastic about intentions often get engaged when I produce the science behind what can otherwise feel a little fluffy.

After this explanation, I invite participants to write their intention on their agenda so that they can find it later. This accomplishes two things: it makes setting an intention somewhat mandatory (everyone else is writing), and it lets people know that we'll return to the intention. I also invite people to turn to a partner and share their intention. I say, "Declaring your intention to another person creates a gentle account-ability for ourselves. Our partner won't keep track of whether we're holding it, but because we've told someone else, we'll be more mindful of it."

Then I share my intention with the whole group. I do this to be softly accountable to them and also to model the ways we can set an intention. Sometimes I share that my intention is to enjoy the learning time or to listen to new insights. It's an opportunity for me to show up as a colleague, a learner, and a human being.

If I work with a group more than once, I ask them to identify what it'll look or sound like if they're holding their intention. "For example," I explain, "If your inten-tion is to be present, perhaps that means you will check your phone or email only during the break; if your intention is to take risks, then maybe you'll contribute to the whole-group discussion." I want to nudge people toward the actions that will demon-strate their intention.

It's important to reflect on intentions. If it's a short meeting (an hour or two) I'll include something like this in the closing section of the agenda:

> Pull out your agenda, and recall the intention you set. Were you aware of it at any point? Did it help you in any way? This isn't an opportunity to beat yourself up—if you forgot all about it or didn't hold it, that's OK. Just take a moment to reflect on how it worked for you.

Sometime—but not always—I invite people to share their reflection with their part-ner. If I'm with a group all day, I might say this as the participants are returning to their tables after lunch:

> As you're settling back in, recall your intention. Does that still feel like the best one for the afternoon, or is there another intention that might be more helpful? As you settle down, settle yourself back into your intention.

The longer you work with a group and engage in this intention setting routine, the easier and deeper it gets and the more comfortable people feel with it.

A BELOVED COMMUNITY

Sadly, I've observed teams where norms were as used as a form of social control. The facilitator used them to silence divergent opinions, and team members hurled them at each other like spears: "One of our norms is to 'speak your truth,' and that's what

I'm doing. So if you don't like what I'm saying, that's too bad." This is a corruption of community agreements.

In contrast, one of the most powerful examples of norms that I've seen was in a team that included a couple teachers who had attended a retreat by the Center for Courage and Renewal, the organization founded by Parker J. Palmer. This team's norms, based on the circle of trust that is a centerpiece of Palmer's work, were the following:

Be present as fully as possible: Be here with your doubts, fears, and failings and with your convictions, joys, and successes, with your listening and with your speaking.

Give and receive welcome: We support each other's learning by giving and receiving hospitality, kindness, and care. We need this to feel safe to learn.

Speak *your truth in ways that respect other people's truth*: Our views of reality may differ, but speaking one's truth does not mean interpreting, correcting, or debating what others say.

When the going gets rough, turn to wonder: Set aside judgment to listen to others and to yourself more deeply. If you feel judgmental or defensive, ask yourself, "I wonder what brought her to this belief?" "I wonder what he's feeling right now?" "I wonder what my reaction teaches me about myself?"

Respond to others with honest, open questions: Instead of trying to fix each other, ask questions to help hear each other into deeper speech.

Observe deep confidentiality: Nothing said in our team will ever be repeated to other people without each other's consent.

These norms offered this team a way of being with each other that had transformational potential. The team included an eclectic group of individuals, the kind of composition that some of us would suspect would lead to conflict and discord. However, the meetings I observed over several months were lively, honest discussions of teaching and learning. On one occasion, a teacher I'll call Brian shared a video of himself teaching. After viewing the video, one teacher said, "Look, I don't really know how to phrase this, and I'm here with my doubts, fears, and convictions right now. I'm wondering about that interaction with the girl in the front. I felt like your tone was hard, but I don't know if that's just my experience or what she felt. I'm really curious how you think she might have felt or what your reflections are on that interaction."

When this was said, I braced myself. This is the kind of feedback that can make some defensive. Yet there didn't seem to be any tension in the room—in fact, the facilitator's response was, "We're turning to wonder!" followed by enthusiastic affirmations from the team. Brian leaned toward the other teacher who had made the comment and said, "I'm listening. I want to hear more about what you observed. I have always had a hard time with that student, and I'm open to your insight because I trust you. Tell me more."

The conversation that ensued went in many directions. The teachers discussed how race and class affected their relationships with students, their fatigue at the end of a week, the new curriculum that exposed tremendous gaps in their students' skills, and the vulnerability they felt bringing video footage to their team. They also identified some instructional strategies they wanted to implement in their classrooms, and Brian outlined a plan to work with his challenging student—work that started with an effort to understand how she had felt during the interaction captured on video.

At the end of this meeting, I commented on how this team interacted with each other and asked them to what they attributed the seeming health of their team. Their responses unanimously named their community agreements. "It took us a while to really understand and internalize these," one teacher said, "but it's made all the difference in how we learn together. They're the glue for how we work."

Another shared this: "Our aspirations in this team go beyond improving our teaching practices and student learning. We want that, of course, but we are also committed to building a beloved community, as described by Dr. Martin Luther King, Jr. We know that the way we talk and listen to each other in these meetings can help create this community. We've agreed that if we want to work for this on a grand scale, we need to make it happen here, every week, during our meetings."

Dr. King's vision of a beloved community, as explained by the King Center, was a "global vision in which all people can share in the wealth of the earth. In the Beloved Community, poverty, hunger and homelessness will not be tolerated because international standards of human decency will not allow it. Racism and all forms of discrimination, bigotry and prejudice will be replaced by an all-inclusive spirit of sisterhood and brotherhood … Love and trust will triumph over fear and hatred" (http://www .thekingcenter.org). What might be possible if we were to construct our norms with such a vision in mind? If our teams aspired to construct, with every meeting, a new way of working and living together? What kinds of norms would we have then? If norms are articulated and identified as a tool for transformation, they will serve that end.

Transformational Coaching Team, 2014

We'd written our norms on chart paper, which hung near the oval table where we met weekly. Then, 6 months into working together, during an activity that required the use of large chart papers, the norms were covered up—we needed the wall space. By that time we had discussed our team dynamics and had reflected on our community agreements. We no longer used a formal process observer at every meeting—process observation seemed to happen organically and in the moment, by many team members. Week after week passed, and the chart paper with norms remained covered up.

Occasionally I'd worry that we should be using our norms more; after all, I'm a vocal and passionate advocate for them. I would raise this concern with the team and inquire in various ways if anyone felt that we needed to more actively use our norms. I usually got a unanimous shoulder shrug and an, "I don't think we need them," from each person.

A couple times we picked apart our assumptions behind an idea. For example, we tossed around the notion of equal airtime. How could we ensure equitable access to speaking in a group discussion while not pressuring people to speak? We had strong verbal processors in our team and others who preferred to make sense of their thoughts in other ways. How would we know when someone's lack of participation indicated a problem or when someone was taking up too much airtime and might be silencing another?

I shared that when I'm in a group I often need to listen and think for a while before saying anything. However, if people are in a lively discussion and I do have something to share, I feel very uncomfortable interrupting them and I appreciate if a facilitator invites me in, saying something like, "Elena, we haven't heard from you in a while. Do you want to share something?" Even though I might have something to share, it's also important that I know I can say, "No, thanks. Just listening and thinking," and don't feel put on the spot.

It wasn't the list of agreements that was critical to our functioning or the routines around upholding them; it was these moments of conversation when we spoke with an awareness of our own emotions (owning them, managing them), and each shared what he or she needed to be a part of a healthy community. Equally important, we each listened to what others needed. My role in making this happen, I recognized, was simple: hold space on an agenda for it, model my own vulnerability and share my experience, make sure everyone could contribute (if they wanted to), and validate each person's truth. This was what mattered, not the list of norms. During these moments I could sense the trust increasing between team members, almost as if each honest statement wove us closer together.

Our list of norms had mattered at one point—it had helped initially to create healthy interpersonal dynamics. But as we had absorbed the norms into our ways of being as a team, we realized that they had served their purpose. Norms are scaffolding for building a healthy community, and when the community is robust you can take down the scaffold; otherwise, it can be unnecessary clutter. Changes to the health of the community—a new teammate, a breakdown in communication, an unexpected challenge from outside—can require that we reexamine a way of working together or strengthen a weak spot. We might temporarily need to bring more awareness to a behavior in our team, and we can temporarily reconstruct our norms until we return to a wholesome state. Norms exist to serve us, to enable us to become strong teams. When a tool no longer serves its purpose, we might pick up a different one, or we might just toss them aside.

CHAPTER 6

Developing the Emotional Intelligence of a Team

Humanities Team, 2009

Megan and Cassandra usually got along well with each other and were a positive presence in team meetings. But on that day, something in our conversation about assessment triggered each teacher, and somehow the conversation spun out of control. Their faces tightened, and their words became choppy and tense. Megan folded her arms across her chest; Cassandra rolled her eyes. Other members of the team seemed to recline into spectator position, looking from the combatants to me, perhaps wondering what I'd do. Fearing the conflict would erupt in an unhealthy way, I decided to try something new.

"Okay, you two," I said with authority in my voice as well as a hint of levity. "Time out. I'm noticing some strong feelings coming up. I want to just name that it feels tense in here." I took a deep (audible and visible) breath and then continued. "We don't need to address this tension right now. I just want to name it."

Cassandra's shoulders dropped. She looked at me. "Thank you," she said. "Wow, I don't even know how that happened, but, yes, that was feeling tense." Megan seemed a little less appreciative of my facilitator move, but she smiled at Cassandra and said, "Yeah, that was weird. Let's come back to this at some other point, okay?"

The conflict dissipated almost as quickly as it had escalated. At the end of the meeting the two teachers decided to head off for coffee together and continue a conversation about standardized testing. "Thanks for snapping us out of it," Megan said as we wrapped up. I walked away feeling delighted with this new tool for managing team dynamics. It was one of the first successes I felt with this team.

WHAT IS THE EMOTIONAL INTELLIGENCE OF A TEAM?

"Between stimulus and response, there is a space. In that space is our power to choose our response. In our response lies our growth and our freedom."

VIKTOR FRANKL

In Chapter 2, I discussed the importance of a leader's emotional intelligence (EI), which I hope prompted you to explore your own EI. Although researchers have found that extraordinary leaders have high EI, they've also found that *collective emotional intelligence* is what sets performing teams apart from average teams (Druskat and Wolff, 2001). A team's emotional intelligence might be the most important predictor of what it will to do together, what conversations will sound like, and how members will feel about going to meetings. Just because a team is composed of individuals with strong emotional intelligence doesn't mean that the team itself will have high EI. Groups take on their own character.

Acknowledge Feelings and Manage Their Expression

In an emotionally intelligent group, members express feelings, are aware of each other's moods and how those moods affect the group, and have strategies for dealing with each other's moods. Emotions are both managed and acknowledged—space is held for members to experience feelings. A leader of an emotionally intelligent group needs two skill sets then: the ability to hold space for feelings, and the ability to manage them in a group. Human beings have feelings; teachers and others who work in and with schools and children have many feelings. We need to learn ways to welcome and explore those feelings in community with each other.

In a team with high emotional intelligence, a team member might recognize someone else's feelings during a meeting and say something like, "Karina, you seem really distracted today and maybe sad. We're missing out on your insights in our conversation today. That's okay, but I'm wondering if there's anything we can do to support you?" Recognizing a team member's emotional state, naming the impact it has on the group, and empathizing and offering support is a way to cultivate an emotionally intelligent team. Karina could demonstrate her own emotional intelligence by responding with something like, "I appreciate that. I'm dealing with some difficult family issues right now, and I'm engaging as best I can. However, I probably won't be able to participate much more than I have been."

Such an interaction between two team members takes less than 1 minute. It prevents other team members from wondering, "What's wrong with Karina? Is she bored or distracted? Did I say something to annoy her?" It creates understanding empathy for Karina and appreciation for the fact that she showed up. Like positive emotions, negative emotions are contagious, and we can resist their deleterious influence when we know what someone is feeling.

Emotionally intelligent teams have ways of managing the moods of one member and of the team as a whole. This management doesn't necessarily come from the leader—in fact, an indicator of an emotionally intelligent team is that any member accepts authority to address moods, communication dynamics, and interactions between members. Much of the time, the way teammates manage these interactions feels comfortable and appropriate. In an emotionally intelligent team, members welcome insights, observations, and suggestions for improving their work and team dynamics. When one person starts talking too much, another might lightheartedly say, "OK, James! We've got it. You love this idea and hope we start working on it right away. I appreciate your enthusiasm and want to make sure we hear from others, so zip it for a while!" And in an emotionally intelligent team, James would laugh, motion the zipping of his mouth, and sit back to listen to others.

Facilitators and members of teams with high levels of EI are attuned to the tone, mood, and energy of a group. Someone might just name what she notices, for example, saying, "It seems like our conversation has gotten stuck in blaming others, and it's bringing our mood down," or, "Our group dynamic feels off today." Or maybe someone says, "Our conversation doesn't feel good to me right now. Is anyone else experiencing this?" Sometimes this is followed by a suggestion, "Do others agree that we should shift the conversation into what's within our sphere of control?" Or "Maybe we need a 10-minute break to take a walk and get some air. What do others think?" The ability, skill, and comfort to address the emotional tenor in a group reflects a level of EI in that team.

In an emotionally intelligent team, one team member can say this to another who always arrives late for meetings: "We really need you here—physically and mentally—when we start. We value your contributions, and it's hard for us to make progress on our work when you're not here." The impact of the team member's tardiness is communicated, the request is respectfully made, and power dynamics have shifted because it is no longer the leader's charge to make the latecomer arrive on time. The team member who was confronted on tardiness can say, "I'm sorry. I don't want to negatively impact our team. I'll work on it." In teams with high EI, the emotional elephants are named when they make their appearance; they aren't allowed to occupy the center of the room month after month or year after year.

Can you see that in an emotionally intelligent team the undercurrents of resentment, annoyance, frustration, and disappointment that exist in so many teams might not exist? Can you see how it is less likely that one person will dominate a conversation? Can you see how quieter members might express thoughts they're apprehensive about sharing? Can you see how teachers could share student work, videos of themselves teaching, and engage in difficult conversations about their practice? Can you see how conversations about race, class, and privilege might be possible?

Building emotionally intelligent teams might be the most important work we do as facilitators. Exhibit 6.1 offers some indicators of a team's emotional intelligence. As you read them, consider different teams that you've been in as well as those you've led to help you get perspective on the levels of EI in that team.

Exhibit 6.1. Indicators of a Team's Emotional Intelligence

Indicators of Low EI:

- Team members don't look at each other when they're talking. A speaker might look at one other member or at the team leader.
- Team members allow themselves to be distracted by technology, each other, and other things.
- Team members interrupt each other in discussions.
- When someone shares an idea or perspective, the first response from another member is a disagreement, skeptical question, or challenge.
- Questions about the processes used in meeting are constantly raised.

- Individuals raise potentially contentious topics that might be important to address but are not relevant or appropriate at that time.
- Team members put each other down or attack each other.
- People speak their truth to attack someone else.
- One person can hijack the meeting—because of her opinion, confusion, disagreement, or emotional state.
- There's a lot of blaming others (e.g., parents, administration, the district).
- Conversations often focus on the sphere outside of our control or influence.
- Personal beliefs are espoused as truths, for example, "Our students can't do that."
- Team members don't follow the guidelines for activities. For example, in a silent reflection activity, there's talking, getting up to leave the room, or engaging in some other distracted activity.

Indicators of Strong EI:
- When a team member is talking, he makes eye contact with all others.
- Team members paraphrase each other's ideas.
- When a new idea is put on the table, there's curiosity and questions about it.
- You hear comments such as:
  - "I've shared a lot already. I'm going to sit back and listen to others on this topic."
  - "I'd really like to hear your perspective on this, _____. We haven't heard much from you today."
  - "That activity triggered something for me and I'm experiencing a lot of feelings." And you might hear someone else say, "Thanks for sharing that. It helps me understand your comments in that conversation."
  - "I'm having a hard day and I'm not feeling great this afternoon. I'm working on shifting this, and I don't want you to wonder why I'm less engaged today."
- Team members express empathy for each other and for others outside of their team.
- Conversations focus on seeking solutions.
- Team members monitor their verbal participation.
- Team members address when others seem to be having emotions. This can sound like, "I'm wondering what's going on for you right now, _____. You seem upset."
- Team members offer feedback in the moment on their process. This can sound like, "I feel like we might have rushed through that discussion too fast to surface everyone's ideas. Do others feel that way?"
- Team members offer feedback at the end of meetings on their process. This can sound like, "I appreciated our conversation at the start of our meeting. That was really helpful for me

to get clarity. I wish we'd had more time to articulate our next steps. Is that something that others would like to spend time on next time?"

- Humor is used appropriately to lighten situations and to call awareness to a group or individual's mood.
- People find things to be optimistic about.
- Team members appreciate each other for their contributions to the team, their action.

HOW DO I CREATE AN EMOTIONALLY INTELLIGENT TEAM?

"Group emotional intelligence isn't a question of dealing with a necessary evil—catching emotions as they bubble up and promptly suppressing them. Far from it. It's about bringing emotions deliberately to the surface and understanding how they affect the team's work. It's also about behaving in ways that build relationships both inside and outside the team and that strengthen the team's ability to face challenges. Emotional intelligence means exploring, embracing, and ultimately relying on emotion in work that is, at the end of the day, deeply human."—Druskat and Wolff (2008)

Building an emotionally intelligent team takes skill and knowledge on the facilitator's part and lots of time. An advantage in launching a team is that you can do a lot of intentional EI boosting up front. This time spent on establishing a foundation for a healthy team is worth it—think of it as an investment that will pay off when team members begin having hard conversations with each other about student learning and when these conversations result in changes in practices that positively affect children. Committing time and energy up front is much easier than trying to shift or reverse unproductive dynamics once they sprout up. A leader needs to know how to build emotionally intelligent ways of interacting and how to shift ineffective behaviors.

Building Behaviors
An emotionally intelligent team requires two things: norms and routines that support healthy behaviors, and a facilitator who encourages behaviors that increase the

ability to respond constructively in emotionally uncomfortable situations. If a team doesn't have norms, then your first task is to facilitate their creation and ensure that they are upheld (see Chapter 5). Remember that some norms strengthen the ability to respond effectively to emotional challenges and some norms don't. For example, "Be on time" doesn't directly address the emotional challenge we face when someone is habitually late. A norm that might be more useful in that situation is, "Speak directly to people about issues." The best norms create resources for working with emotions, foster an affirmative environment, and encourage proactive problem solving.

Leaders also need to establish routines that foster an emotional climate that is accepting of risk taking, listening, and celebration. Routines create buckets for healthy emotional behaviors; they become a structural assurance that emotions will be attended to. For example, a routine like a check-in at the beginning of a meeting lets people know that there's a place where they'll be able to share an emotional state if they want. This routine can take just a few minutes and can be done in whole-group whip around, dyad (see Appendix E), or pair share. Either way, it ensures that there's a place for teammates to connect with and listen to each other and allows people to build empathy for each other. Closing meetings with a space for appreciations is another structure that promotes a positive emotional climate. A leader needs to form, guide, and massage a team's emotional experiences so that members are oriented toward healthy and resilient ways of interacting.

Norms such as those discussed in Chapter 5 are a foundation for building teams with strong EI, but they are not enough—not even if you use them religiously and have a process observer. The great majority of groups go through a difficult stage as part of their team development. This storming phase is important as people open up and challenge each other and their ways of working together. The ability for a team to move through this stage has a great deal to do with the group's emotional intelligence and the facilitator's ability to support the process. When teams storm, facilitators can guide the group to reflect on how they function and strengthen their ways of communicating and relating to each other.

> *For me, forgiveness and compassion are always linked: how do we hold people accountable for wrongdoing and yet at the same time remain in touch with their humanity enough to believe in their capacity to be transformed?*
>
> BELL HOOKS

Uprooting Behaviors

Teams can also develop counterproductive ways of behaving that undermine agreed upon norms and erode the emotional intelligence of a team. Unspoken norms are behaviors that a group has unknowingly condoned. For example, an unspoken norm can be that it's acceptable to talk badly about our administration, or that we don't confront a teammate who rarely does what she says she'll do, or that we can wander in to team meetings a few minutes late. Another unspoken norm that I've seen a lot in school-based teams is that it's okay to complain about the district. These kinds of unspoken norms create emotional tones that are not energizing or collaborative. They don't boost EI. They don't build effective teams.

If unproductive or detrimental unspoken norms aren't shifted, they undermine a team's stated norms. As a leader, we can start by naming the unspoken norms and sharing your observations. For example, you might say, "I notice that whenever we talk about this curriculum our conversation turns into a litany of complaints about the district. It seems like this makes us feel disempowered and angry. What is the impact on our team if we stay in this conversation?" What's essential is that team members recognize the negative impact—if they don't, they are unlikely to change their behavior. Although they may claim that they need to vent (much unhealthy behavior is justified as necessary venting), there is no evidence that venting is productive. In fact, social psychologists and neurologists have found that venting makes people feel hopeless, it strengthens us versus them mentalities, and it solidifies neural pathways that make us depressed.

Although I'd like to suggest that you nip venting in the bud when it happens, that won't work. The group needs to recognize and acknowledge the negative impact it is having on the group for it to self-regulate and shift its behavior toward problem solving. Once the team has recognized the negative influence of complaints, you can move quickly to support a shift. Remember, to solve problems you need to acknowledge what is within your sphere of influence and control and minimize the amount of energy you spend engaged in activities (e.g., venting) that are outside of your sphere of influence. Suggesting that a team stop complaining about the district isn't the same thing as asking them to passively submit to top-down demands. A suggestion to stop complaining about the district is a suggestion to direct that energy to something productive—which might involve doing something to influence district decisions or offering feedback on decisions.

A leader's role in developing a team's EI is to guide energy and emotion. You can do this when you establish structures to help group members see how they work together. A process check is one such structure, as effective process checkers help bring awareness to how group members interact. Let's go back to the challenge of a dominant team member. A process observer who is concerned about this might report the following at the end of a meeting: "Today, I noticed that Bob, you participated a total of 14 times. Twelve of those times you were sharing an opinion, and two times you asked a question. Cecilia, you participated three times, and each time it was to affirm what someone else said. These were the observations that stood out to me. What did others notice about our participation patterns? How do you think these participation patters might impact our work together?"

As the leader, you hope that someone else might respond to these questions, but if no one does you need to comment. You might say, "Bob, I wonder if you felt like we weren't hearing your opinions and that's why you kept sharing them? Cecilia, your perspective as a new staff member here is really valuable, and I think our group would benefit from hearing your ideas more. What do others think?" And then you'd hope that other members would chime in and share their reflections. If no one else makes any proposals, you can say something like, "I wonder if next time we meet, for us to have a discussion in which everyone's voice gets equal airtime, we could try to do a couple things: We'll use paraphrasing to ensure that each person who speaks feels heard, and then we'll actively attend to participation. Bob—would it be okay if I remind you when you've had your share of airtime? That would allow others like Cecilia to speak up more. She's said that she has a hard time interjecting in a conversation when others are passionately expressing their ideas. What do you think? And Cecilia, would it be okay if I directly invite your participation?"

You can also address behavior as you observe it ("Bob, you shared that opinion already. How about if you hold off until everyone else has shared now?"), and invite the team to bring awareness about their interactions ("What do you guys notice about how we're communicating with each other?"). At first, it can feel very uncomfortable as a facilitator and for the team to call out behavior. As those feelings pass, the group's awareness of their patterns of communication increases, and they may be grateful for the direct intervention when they're not acting in a productive way. A key role for a leader is to heighten awareness of behavior, invite reflection on it, explore the implications of how people are engaging, and offer ways for the group to reflect on itself.

The majority of the suggestions offered in this book can, when used thoughtfully, boost a team's emotional intelligence (Exhibit 6.2). Many facilitators unconsciously make moves that build EI all the time. I imagine you can add to the ways listed in Exhibit 6.2, and I encourage you to do so.

Exhibit 6.2. Forty-Four Ways to Build The Emotional Intelligence of a Team

To Create Team Awareness of Feelings …

Between Individuals	As a Group
1. Include time at every meeting and longer chunks of time during the year for members to get to know each other.	1. Engage in appreciations at the end of meetings. Appreciate the group.
2. Include many opportunities for team members to tell each other stories about who they are.	2. Acknowledge and discuss group moods. Say, "It feels tense in this meeting today. Would it be helpful for us to talk about what's going on?"
3. Check in at the beginning of meetings so that people can share how they are feeling.	
4. Use poetry, metaphor, music, and art to give individuals entry points into sharing their feelings.	3. Regularly and systematically examine team effectiveness and group dynamics.
5. Share what you're thinking and feeling. Model language for talking about feelings.	4. Use a process checker—ideally one who reports at the end of a meeting and who can speak up at any point during it.
6. Acknowledge emotions when you recognize them. Say, "It looks like you're feeling frustrated today—is that true?" or "I hear that you're angry."	
7. Acknowledge nonverbal cues that might indicate emotions. Say, "Joe, I noticed that when Jane asked you that question you leaned back, crossed your arms, and frowned. How are you feeling about her question?"	5. Ask for feedback on your leadership.
	6. Offer feedback to your team.
	7. In general or at specific times, ask the group to use active listening.
8. Appreciate when individuals appropriately share how they're feeling. Say, "Thanks for letting us know that you're upset about yesterday's PD."	8. Develop a comfort with silence and allow for pauses at times during discussions.
9. Include intention setting at the beginning of meetings and reflect on these at the end.	9. Share participants' feedback on meetings (anonymously) with team to raise awareness and empathy for each other.
10. Invite participation from quieter members.	
11. Let quieter and more dominant members know the impact of their participation. Say, "Jane, we appreciate your comments and they are helpful. I also recognize that you are not as much of a verbal processor as others." Or, "Joe, we appreciate your comments and they are helpful. I wonder if others might speak up more if you held back at times."	10. Begin a meeting with 3 quiet minutes or five deep breaths.
	11. Create rituals (e.g., shake it all out) for managing stress when it comes up.
12. Acknowledge your part in any tension and apologize.	12. As needed, stop a discussion and ask participants to take five deep breaths and do a feeling scan.

To Help a Team Manage Feelings ...

Between Individuals	As a Group
1. Surface tensions if you sense them—either with the whole group or between individuals. Say, "I am noticing that you two disagree on that idea and it feels tense. What could we do about that?"	1. Take breaks if or when you feel the group needs a break. Invite team members to ask for breaks.
2. Give individuals options. Say, "I hear that you're really frustrated by what happened yesterday. Do you feel like you can still productively engage in our team meeting today? Is there something we can do to help?"	2. Make time to discuss difficult issues and the emotions that surround them.
3. Create norms or community agreements that support emotionally intelligent behaviors.	3. Find fun ways to acknowledge and relieve stress and tension.
4. Use norms or community agreements religiously.	4. Express acceptance of members' emotions.
5. Have a process checker who will call out unproductive behavior.	5. Express optimism that a team can manage a challenge.
6. Offer emotional support to members if they need it.	6. Focus on what you can control.
7. Validate members' contributions. Appreciate individuals.	7. Remind the group of their mission and vision.
8. Protect members from being attacked, put down, or ignored.	8. Remind the group of how it has solved problems before.
9. Follow up in private with individuals who attack, put down, or ignore others.	9. Focus on problem solving, not blaming.
10. Respect individuality and differences.	10. Acknowledge positive emotions and celebrations.

MANAGING UNEXPECTED CHANGE

I can't remember a single year of the 19 that I spent working in a large school district when an unexpected change didn't leave me feeling unsettled. Whether it was a favorite colleague quitting, or my teaching assignment changing a week before school started, or learning that the entire department I worked in was being shut down, constant change was a part of life in the district. Managing change is really about managing the emotions that come up in us and in others. Most leaders don't have a tool bag full of strategies to respond intentionally to unexpected change. Like many school leaders, I needed to learn some change management skills fast when I started coaching teams, and I found that helping a group manage change can be empowering.

M. J. Ryan's (2014) book *How to Survive Change You Didn't Ask For* is a great resource for just about anyone, but especially for those of us who work in volatile and ever-shifting schools and districts. I want to share some of Ryan's tips that are especially helpful when coaching—either an individual or a team—and I hope this will entice you to read the whole book. These tips are the ones I've found most useful when working with teams:

1. Focus on the solution, not the problem. It's okay to reflect on the shape of the problem but unproductive trying to figure out the history of the problem. Focus on what you're going to do about where you are.

2. Ask yourself: What am I free to choose right now?

3. Celebrate successes along the way, no matter how small. Give yourself credit for moving forward in a difficult situation.

4. When considering options, before you say something won't work, consider how it might work.

5. Get out and help someone. Focusing on someone else's problems helps us get perspective on what we're dealing with.

6. Find someone else in the same situation to help and pay attention to what you suggest they do. One of your best resources is the advice you give others. Follow your own suggestions.

7. Move! One of the best ways to counteract the stress of change is to move your body.

8. If you worry a lot, set aside a 15-minute worry time each day. When your mind starts worrying at other times of day, tell yourself it's not worry time, and do something to distract yourself.

9. Ask yourself what really matters here. That question will help you keep the change in proportion.

10. Focus on the positive qualities you have to make a change. The more we pay attention to the resources we have to cope, the better we will do.

I coached one team in a district that bounced through a sequence of volatile changes. After reading this list, team members made posters with symbols that represented these suggestions. They hung the posters in prominent places in their offices, turned them into note cards that they'd hand to each other at challenging moments, and referenced these ideas in tense meetings. When team members cut off venting colleagues and asked, "What really matters here?" I noticed a palpable relief in the group and a reorientation to what they could have influence on. As their ability to focus on solutions strengthened, they were able to have more impact on their schools and students—which was ultimately what they most wanted.

If you're working with a team that's struggling to manage change, give them this list (you can also download it from my website) and invite them to practice these behaviors. Teammates can prompt each other to reflect on "What really matters here?" or "What am I free to choose right now?" Invite

It was like this: You were happy, then you were sad, then happy again, then not.

JANE HIRSCHFIELD

them to celebrate every single success, especially the tiny ones. Invite them to take a walk. Sometimes I think people behave in unproductive ways (e.g., venting) out of habit: They just don't know what else to do, and they've done their unproductive things for so long. When you offer other ways of behaving, thinking, and feeling, there's great receptivity. Some people need a good deal of practice before there are substantial shifts in behavior, and sometimes you see quick change.

TAMING THE STRESS DEMONS

I first felt my face getting hot; I was sure I'd turned beet red. My palms started sweating. My mouth went dry. A colleague had asked me to stay after a meeting. We'd been butting heads every time our paths crossed, and she suggested we talk about our conflict. I'd felt these physical feelings before—most of us have. They are cues that we're feeling anxious, perhaps even afraid. What was different this time was that I recognized them quickly. "Ah," I said to myself, "conflict makes me nervous." I took a few deep breaths, relaxed my shoulders, and sat down for what was a very productive conversation.

Understanding anxiety and how to manage it is useful knowledge for those who lead teams. Let's start by reflecting on your own experience. Do you always know when you're feeling stressed or afraid? Can you tell right away, or sometimes do you realize you've been under stress hours or days later when you find yourself exhausted? Our physical response to stress can sometimes clue us in to our emotions. Rapid breathing, heart pounding and beating fast, dry mouth, sweaty or cold hands, shaky legs, and other symptoms can indicate stress. We can start to hone our emotional intelligence by paying attention to how our bodies feel and thus recognizing emotions such as stress more quickly.

Our physiological response to stress—often categorized as the fight, flight, or freeze response—is a legacy of the thousands of years that our ancestors spent in environments where they were potential prey. This response ensured the survival of our species for millennia. Although we are rarely in position to be prey anymore, our brains still register danger in the face of new stresses, and our bodies still react as our ancestors' bodies did. Quite often our brains register false alarms and overreact to perceived dangers. The problem is that each time our brain and body think danger, we experience a variety of biochemical responses including increased cortisol, which diminishes our ability for rational thinking.

Leaders need to recognize the impact that stress has on a team's ability to be effective. It can be futile to attempt to implement a deeply thought-out agenda full of meaningful structured activities if team members arrive so stressed out that their brains are closed to learning. When they come into the room with stress, their fight energies can be directed at you or another member—or they freeze or mentally flee, disengaging from the group. Consider how many of the meetings you facilitate or participate in happen after school, after participants have spent many hours teaching and managing the emotions and learning of other people.

There are simple, quick moves that facilitators can make to attend to challenging emotions in us and in others. One of the easiest ways to calm the body and quiet the mind is to breathe. Because breathing is something we do without thinking, we're often not conscious of how we're breathing, so starting with taking a few deep breaths can bring awareness and relaxation. In fact, just five deep breaths energize and relax us. Starting team meetings with five quiet breaths can help people transition into a learning space and calm down.

A team can easily learn and use some simple relaxation strategies. Guided imagery, progressive muscle relaxation, body scanning, and many mindfulness techniques are increasingly used in schools with children and are tremendously beneficial to adults as well.

When I open a meeting, I frequently offer people a few minutes to check in with each other or with the whole team (depending on the size of the group). Check-ins are a way for people to connect, debrief the day, and discharge stress. They are also an important transition routine, bridging whatever happened earlier with the meeting space. Check-ins can be simple. You can offer a prompt to discuss; I often use, "What's on your mind right now?" You can also frame the activity as one that transitions, grounds, and brings us into a learning space. This is how you subtly massage a group's emotions, guiding them toward being in the room in mind and heart.

Sometimes I know that team members have a lot on their minds, and I suspect that a brief check-in won't be enough to process what's going on for them. In these moments, I ask people to consider what they might be able to put aside for the time that we're together. I say, "I'm not suggesting that you let go of whatever you're bringing into the room; I'm just asking what you can set aside for the next two hours." I ask them to quickly write what they want to put aside, be it a hard afternoon with a group of students, a difficult parent interaction, worries about an upcoming evaluation, or a personal matter that's on their minds. I find that the simple act of acknowledging others' intense emotions can be healing: I offer relief in reminding them that issues set aside now can be addressed later, and I offer an invitation to be here now.

Transformational Coaching Team, 2014

The first Monday morning after winter break was wet and windy. One of the coaches hurried into our office a minute before our team meeting started. She didn't make eye contact with anyone, seemed frenzied as she grabbed her notebook and pen, angrily mumbled about her coffee cup getting wet from the rain, and sat down with a big sigh. My anxiety shot up: What was wrong with her? Why was she so upset? Would her distress affect the team? Then I told myself to let it go. "Proceed with the agenda. Let her be," I told myself. "She'll sort it out—and if not, then I can check in with her after."

I had designed this meeting's agenda anticipating that coaches might return to work with a range of feelings. I know that on the first day after winter break many educators can feel reenergized from their time off and can also feel some sadness and frustration at having to return to work. Before the coaches returned to their schools and teachers, I wanted to check in as a group, offer some space to acknowledge these emotions, and help everyone get reoriented toward our purpose and goals.

To start the meeting, I gave each person a piece of chart paper divided into four quadrants and asked them to write the following prompts in each box: (1) images that represent my winter break; (2) adjectives that describe how I'm feeling today; (3) goals, plans, or intentions for 2013; and (4) questions, concerns, or other thoughts about returning to work.

After these posters were created and shared, we moved into an activity intended to refine our vision of ourselves as coaches. I wanted coaches to think, again, about

---

who they wanted to be in their work. This trajectory of reflection—Where have I been? Where am I now? Where do I want to go?—was one I used often because it heightens our awareness of the choices we can make.

The final part of the morning focused on team development—in this case, the development of the school-based teams that each coach supported. I asked coaches to think about their department and grade-level teams and identify what they could do, as the leader, to strengthen the team. "What can you do at this week's team meeting that could bring teachers into more effective working relationships?" I asked. With this in mind, coaches planned for their meetings. In trios, they shared drafts of agendas and received feedback. We closed our morning by setting intentions for our work for the upcoming week.

By the end of our meeting, the coach who had arrived in a seemingly distressed mood seemed much less distressed. On her feedback form, she acknowledged feeling unsettled when she'd arrived in the morning and said it had passed. Perhaps dealing with emotions was easier than I'd thought.

When there was emotional discomfort in our team, here's what I told myself: I don't need to fix it or solve it. I might just need to give it some space. Honoring emotions was a growth area for me. I could manage other people's emotions (I could respond appropriately, with empathy), but I also found their emotions to sometimes be a barrier to getting things done.

Holding space for emotions—allowing them to be in the room—wasn't as hard as I anticipated. Sometimes all it took was the acknowledgment of an emotion (e.g., "I can see you're upset today") or a question (e.g., "Is there anything that we can do to help you right now?"). Sometimes I extended an invitation (e.g., "If you feel like it's too hard for you to be here right now, you always have permission to take care of yourself and come back when you're ready."). When necessary, I'd modify a meeting's agenda in response to emotions (e.g., "I'm sensing that there's more processing that needs to happen around this topic. I'm going to suggest that we do a dyad, or take a walk, or continue this discussion as a group."). These moments were always hard for me as a leader: Was I making the right choice? Would we keep moving toward our goals and outcomes if we took time to deal with feelings? But most of the time, addressing the feelings and allowing for some processing was not an obstruction—and sometimes, the feelings even transformed into a source of energy.

CHAPTER 7

Cultivating Healthy Communication

Humanities Team, 2008

"I have a question about working on rubrics that we'll probably never even use," Bess said. "I mean, we can't even get these kids to sit down in their chairs and hold a pen." She continued making a case for a discussion about student behavior, heading determinedly away from the plan I'd brought to work on rubrics. "Really," Bess said, "we should be talking about how to get these kids to walk in the hallways." Margaret chimed in, "I agree with Bess. That should be our priority for a discussion. Getting the boys to take their hoods off, to stop cussing, to stop running through the halls grabbing girls. Can you tell me when we're going to address these concerns?"

Bess and Margaret derailed meetings by asking questions that catapulted us far off course. It almost seemed as if they planned their synchronized questioning to forcibly shift our discussion away from their teaching practice and student learning and to argue the case that whatever it was that had been planned on the department agenda, or in the whole staff professional development, was the wrong thing to be doing.

In department meetings I tried controlling how much they spoke. One day I said, "You each get five pennies, and each time you speak you put a penny in the jar. When you're out of pennies, you don't get to participate anymore at our meeting today." This strategy simply resulted in lengthy soliloquies, their contributions now thicker with anger and frustration, their heels dug in even further. Glaring at them, I warned them silently that resistance was futile, and I drove onward to wear them down. We didn't discuss student writing on that day either.

In staff meetings, I tried the parking lot method. When someone raised a hand with a question, concern, or comment that was off topic, I'd ask her to please write it on the chart paper that was the parking lot. One after another, in almost constant succession, Bess and Margaret (as well as a handful of other teachers) moved back and forth between their tables and the wall with the parking lot. As page after page filled up, they sketched a parking garage around the posters. The parking lot came to physically, visually represent their ignored concerns, and was a new source of anger. "When will our parking lot questions be answered?" they'd demand.

Worn down, I finally went to the principal and insisted that he either attend our department meetings or remove Bess and Margaret from them. He denied my request, so it continued—this losing battle.

When I ask educators to name their top challenges working with teams, I most often hear, "How do you stop one person from dominating the conversation?" I've encountered this challenge many times—as a participant in a team and a leader. Initially, I blamed the individual—Why doesn't he stop talking? Can't he see how much airtime he's taking up? How can he be so disrespectful? As a member of a team with a dominator, I looked to the leader to do something about the overtalker. Then I got frustrated with the leader when she didn't do anything. As the facilitator of a team, I worried that it was my responsibility to do something, and I wasn't sure what to do.

I've come to understand that the problem in this situation is the way we look at the problem, the way we identify the challenge. The overtalker is a symptom of the team's explicit or implicit communication agreements, nestled within a larger social agreements about who has a right to speak. We can't develop healthy communication without exploring the root cause of the dominant team member's behavior and without analyzing the context in which he or she is using so much airtime.

Rather than exerting power over someone and creating more rules and consequences, some strategies for responding to a dominant team member have transformational potential. If we take an inquiry stance, we are more likely to identify those strategies. These questions can prompt reflection on the challenge of an overtalker:

- Why might that person talk so much? What does he need?
- How might we help her become aware of the impact that her talking has on the rest of us and on our work together?
- How does our broader social context support this person dominating conversations?
- How have we allowed one person to dominate the conversation?
- What does our team need to have good conversations?
- When have we discussed this and shared our needs?
- Have I been honest about expressing my needs?
- What would it take for us to have good conversations?
- Am I willing to take a risk and ask the questions that might shift how we communicate?

Simply by asking these questions, we're on new terrain.

Using these questions to reflect on the humanities team, I see Bess and Margaret's derailing questions in a new light: I acknowledge that they felt deep frustration because their concerns weren't heard in any formal structure, that they truly felt they couldn't engage in a discussion of their teaching practice while, in their perspective, things were out of control. I see that my response was to ignore those concerns and try and force them back onto the path I had set for our team.

I also recognize that I never raised this conversation dynamic directly with the team. While Bess and Margaret hijacked meetings, four other team members sat and watched and said almost nothing. I wonder what could have happened had I asked our team, "What does our team need to have good conversations?" and ensured that each person could speak. We had community agreements, but they weren't really working to promote good group conversations. In fact, Bess and Margaret evoked one of our agreements ("Speak your truth") every time they wanted to question the agenda. While they exploited this norm, other members rarely said anything, and I don't think I effectively invited them to do so.

Finally, I suspect that Bess and Margaret steered meeting discussions away from conversations about instruction because of their insecurities about their teaching practice. They had both taught for some years, and, based on my visits to their classrooms and what they shared in our meetings, they had significant gaps in their skill sets. On multiple occasions, one of the new teachers referenced a practice (e.g., using formative assessment or frontloading vocabulary), and Margaret's response indicated that she didn't understand. These two teachers had bounced around many schools in our district, not by their own choice, and I doubt they received good professional development. When I think about what I proposed on my ambitious agendas, I wonder if they recognized that their big gaps would be exposed. I wonder what might have happened if I'd designed agendas that would meet them where they were and that would scaffold up to a rigorous level.

What we say and how we say it usually reflect underlying emotions. Rather than trying to change the communication pattern—reduce overtalking, increase discussion—we can take a look at emotional intelligence, both an individual's EI and a team's. Conversations occur on three levels: there's what we're talking about (i.e., the content), then there's the other person's emotional response, and then there's your emotional response. If we want to have good conversations, we need to pay attention to all three levels.

When I recall conversations in the humanities team, the levels of emotions are now glaringly obvious. I was intensely frustrated with Bess and Margaret's behavior. They were frustrated with me and my agendas that didn't feel relevant. I spent so much energy trying to stifle their emotions, and I wonder what might have happened had I addressed this. I could have said something like, "I hear that you're really frustrated by student behavior. How about if we carve some time out of our agenda to problem solve together? I could also help you plan to bring these concerns to the school's administration. And then can we agree to spend the rest of our meeting time discussing what's on the agenda?" I suspect that such a response might have shifted the dynamics that otherwise felt like a battle.

A BLUEPRINT FOR TRANSFORMATIONAL CONVERSATIONS

How would you describe *a good conversation* between two people or within a team? What does it sound like to you?

The words you speak become the house you live in.

HAFIZ

For many of us, it might be easier to describe a *bad* conversation. We can quickly recall instances when communication didn't feel good or didn't result in what we hoped it would, conversations in which we've felt frustrated, angry, or hurt and from which we've eventually disengaged. The first step in moving beyond these kinds of conversations is to describe what we want to see, hear, and feel in conversations. Reflect by yourself and then engage your team in considering these questions.

Toward a Description of Good Conversations

Here's how I describe good conversations. In a good conversation, I feel heard. My listeners validate my thoughts, they don't interrupt me, and they don't leap to respond when I finish. I don't need others to agree with me or share their own story about a similar experience. I just need to know that they hear what I was saying. It's hard to describe how I know that they hear me, but I can tell often by nonverbal cues—they are making eye contact, they aren't fiddling or distracted, and they don't open their mouths as if about to interject something. I can also tell they are listening because I don't feel rushed to finish talking. If I pause, gaze off into the distance, and think for a moment, they don't jump in with a question, comment, or connection. They allow for silence. I feel like I've been listened to when I stop speaking and I hear, "I appreciate that perspective," or "I hear that you've put a lot of thought into that," or "It sounds like you were really frustrated." Usually the person's tone of voice communicates caring.

In a good conversation, I also hear curiosity, receptivity, and flexibility. I hear openness to understanding, I hear interest in varied perspectives, and I hear emotions acknowledged. I hear ideas shifting and morphing—I hear a willingness to be influenced by questions and contributions from others.

Good conversations don't always feel good, because in a good conversation I hear expansion—of one person's reflections, of a proposal, or of an idea. I hear participants building on each other's ideas, making new connections, digging deeper, pushing back on each other's ideas, and challenging each other. Good conversations aren't always comfortable. However, I sense that participants are aware of their emotional responses and have ways to manage them, and I see that the discomfort leads to greater insight and deeper work together. These difficult moments are not personalized: They are not attacks between or on individuals; they are challenges to thoughts, beliefs, and behaviors. Feedback is offered mindfully, without judgment and with the intention of building community, I might say, "Jaime, I'm wondering if you're feeling defensive as we give you feedback on your lesson plan. My intention is to support your growth as a teacher, and I hope I'm communicating that." And Jaime's response might be, "I was feeling defensive. Thanks for calling my attention to that. The feedback was hard to hear."

In our society, the voices of certain groups of people have long been considered more valuable and have been given myriad opportunities to be heard. In a good conversation, I don't see patterns of participation that reflect these inequitable power structures. I see women speak as often and as much as men, and I see women speak up *first*—not after all the men have spoken. I hear women speak with confidence, not qualifying, excusing, or diminishing their ideas with phrases like, "Well, I've only been here for two years, but in my perspective … " or "I'm sorry, I just want to say … " or "I don't know if this would be helpful but … "

The perspectives and experiences of people of color, immigrants, and working-class communities have also been undervalued and underrepresented in our political system, mass media, and school systems. Much has been decided about these groups without input from their members, without hearing what they think and need. In good conversations, I hear people from these social sectors speaking with confidence, knowing that their contributions are essential to the work of transforming schools. I see people from socially dominant groups stepping back so that those who have had less access to power can speak first. In good conversations, the unjust patterns of contribution to discourse aren't replicated; in fact, sometimes they are turned on their heads.

As the same time, in good conversations I see people speaking when they feel they have something to contribute, when they are moved to speak—and I see a group that respects that. Each team member doesn't necessarily need to speak for the exact same number of minutes as each of the others. A group's extroverts and verbal processors will likely talk more, and that's okay. Similarly, quieter members don't need to be put on the spot and asked to speak. A balance arises organically from a strong team culture. A team member or facilitator might notice that one member hasn't spoken in a discussion and might simply say, "Kendra?" And Kendra's response might be, "Thanks. I was thinking about … " or "Not right now," and her response is accepted.

In a good conversation, I can't predict who will speak first when the facilitator asks the group a question. I don't think, "Oh, of course Mark's hand will shoot up first." At the same time, in a good conversation a facilitator uses a range of strategies to invite participation: Sometimes she'll welcome responses from anyone (and hands will rise), and other times she'll ask a question and say, "Let's hear from everyone on this question. Kendra, would you mind starting, and we'll just go around the circle?"

What Do You Think Is Good Conversation?

What would you add to my description of a good conversation? To have good communication within a team, start by generating a definition, painting a vision, and articulating what it is you want to see, hear, and feel. What kind of communication do you hope for? What does your team need? What does the community that you serve—your students, your staff—need?

The questions in Exhibit 7.1 are a place to start in this exploration. I hope to help you take steps toward developing the kind of communication that can bring a group of people into trusting relationships in which they can improve their practice, collaborate to support the needs of all children, and create resilient communities.

If you want to change the culture you have to change the conversation.

SHOWKEIR AND SHOWKEIR (2008)

Exhibit 7.1. Reflection Questions on Communication

1. What do I notice about the conversations we have now? What dynamics do I see present?
2. How do I feel about the conversations we have now?
3. What do I want our team's conversations to look and sound like?
4. What purposes do our conversations need to have?
5. How do I want to feel during conversations?

6. What defines a good conversation for me?
7. What might I need to do differently to have the kinds of conversations we want to have?
8. Which skills will I need to cultivate to have different conversations?
9. What am I willing to do to have different conversations?
10. What's the first step I can make for our team to have different conversations?

CONSTRUCTING GOOD CONVERSATIONS

The etymology of the word *conversation* means "to keep company with" or "to turn about with." Interestingly, the word *discussion* means "to smash to pieces," which is an apt description of heated exchanges in which I've participated.

Within verbal discourse, there are a number of commonly occurring patterns. These can be categorized as follows:

- Debate

- Argument

- Advocacy wars

- One-upmanship

- I'm smarter than you are

- Polite talk

- Problem solving

- Empathic listening

- Inquiry and questioning to understand

- Perspective taking

Recall teams you've been a part of. Can you think of times when any of these became the dominant pattern of discourse? Some of these may not serve the purpose of a conversation—they don't generate trust, and they don't leave a team having learned something new. They can also have additional unintended consequences that undermine the team's purpose. For example, in teams in which debates are common, members adopt a defensive stance when they speak, anticipating that their ideas will be challenged and tested. People listen for weak parts of what others say, places to interject criticism or doubt. In other teams conversations become the stage on which members try to prove their worth, and a competitive atmosphere develops. Some patterns of communication on this short list foster a team's emotional intelligence, whereas others are a reflection of a low EI.

Process observers are invaluable in helping team members recognize their communication dynamics. With the group's agreement, a process observer can gather data on who talks, when, in what order, how much, and what kind of talk each person contributes. Groups can be surprised at what they discover looking at this kind of data and can be motivated to change their ways of relating to each other. Sketching webs of communication patterns is another method that a process observer can use. A visual web shows when people build on each other's ideas, who responds to whom, and whether there's a great deal of back and forth between the facilitator and individuals members. Whether with a chart of tally marks or a web of communication, graphic documentation can help a group see concretely how they relate to each other in conversation. Exhibit 7.2 is an authentic example of tracking patterns of participation. These data were collected at a leadership team meeting in which I was the process observer.

Exhibit 7.2. Patterns of Participation

Meeting: Site Leadership Team
Date and Time: March 16, 2013, 3:00–4:30 p.m.
Process Observer: Elena

Participant	Clarifying Question	Probing Question	Comment	Opinion	Notes	TOTAL
Thuy	II	II	II	I		7
Jim		I	IIIII IIII	IIIII IIII	Often the first to speak	14
Celina	II					2
Manuel	III	II	II	II	Interrupted Jim a couple times	9
Jackson		II		II		4
Arnoldo	I	III	I	III		8
Laela			IIII	IIIII		9

After this kind of data is collected, a group must have time to process it together, reflecting on the implications of their patterns of engagement as well as on any changes they'd like to make. Exhibit 7.3 is a portion of the transcript of the reflection conversation that the leadership team had after I collected their data. This conversation, of which you'll read only a snippet, resulted in some new agreements about group discussion that significantly shifted patterns of participation.

Exhibit 7.3. Reflections on Patterns of Participation

Elena: So what do you notice about this data?

Jim: I'm keeping my mouth shut in this discussion! (Some laughter from team members)

Manuel: I hope you all know that the reason I interrupted Jim was because I noticed that he was talking a lot and wanted to make space for others to talk, but maybe I shouldn't interrupt.

Celina: I feel uncomfortable with this because I feel like I'm not a good participant. I have a hard time in group discussions because I don't like interrupting, and I feel like as a new year teacher I just don't have as much to share.

Jackson: Celina, I'd love to hear more from you. In our lunch conversations I'm always impressed with your observations as someone new to our school. You have insights that those of us who have been here for a long time don't.

Laela: I didn't realize I share so many opinions. I need to think about what that means.

Celina: I think this is also cultural for me. As a girl in a big Mexican family, I was raised not to push back on what others say, not to share my opinions as vocally as some of you do. It wasn't considered respectful.

Jim: Is it okay if I say something?

Elena: Please do. But if you go on too long I might cut you off! (Laughter)

Jim: Ok, you have permission to do that too! Celina, your comment made me realize that my father always told me that I needed to speak up and say what I thought. I guess I've thought that this is how I can contribute to this group—to share my opinions and perspectives.

Manuel: That's helpful to hear, Jim. Sometimes I feel frustrated because I want to hear from everyone and I think that the women in this team don't talk as much as the men.

Thuy: That might be true. I know that this time, because Elena was taking notes, I was more conscious about when to speak and when to hold back. Maybe if we do this more often, it'll help us be more aware in the moment about our talking. Arnoldo, you haven't shared a reflection. What do you think?

Listening to Our Listening

Raising awareness of listening is also essential to improve conversations. Exhibit 7.4 describes ways we commonly listen—engaging your team in the activity described can lead to powerful learning.

Exhibit 7.4. How Do I Listen?

First read through the kinds of listening activities listed here. Ask someone to talk for a minute or two. Notice what kinds of listening activities your mind does, and check off the boxes as you notice your mind going into these places. Alternately, listen to someone talk, watch your mind wander, and then use this tool afterward to record your observations.

☐ Listening to find connections. Your mind thinks, "Oh, I remember when that happened to me too!"

☐ Listening to find a story of your own to share. Your mind thinks, "I can tell her about that time that I … "

☐ Listening but wanting to jump in and finish the speaker's sentence.

☐ Listening to find a point you agree or disagree with.

☐ Listening to find something you can ask a clarifying question about after because you want more information.

☐ Listening to understand the other person's perspective.

☐ Listening to ask a probing question to elicit the other person's thinking or build their reflective capacity.

☐ Listening to fix it—to find a way to help or solve a problem, to give advice.

☐ Listening and empathizing with the other person.

☐ Listening and judging the other person—finding fault with what they said or did, evaluating their thoughts.

☐ Listening to find something you can critique or offer a rebuttal.

☐ Listening and feeling impatient, wishing that the other person would stop talking.

☐ Faking listening. Being bored by what the other person is saying. Occasionally nodding or *ah-ha-ing* but spacing out.

☐ Listening and feeling excited, inspired, or moved by what the other person says.

☐ Listening for implicit meanings; listening between the lines.

After engaging in this exercise, debrief with these reflection prompts:

- What impact do these patterns of discourse have on the work we hope to do together?

- Given what we've uncovered, how might we best engage in conversation to fulfill our team's purpose?

- What other implications does this activity raise for our work together?

Conversations that are driven by inquiry will support transformational endeavors—we simply don't know everything we need to know and the only way we'll make progress is by being curious, seeking to understand each other's experiences and perspectives, and taking a shared approach to problem solving. This doesn't mean that there won't be conflict or that we won't need hard conversations. Indeed, we can be sure that we'll have to have some conflict in order to grow, but when conflict and hard conversations happen within a team that's working to build its emotional intelligence, the people move closer to each other and our community becomes stronger.

Teams can take a big step toward effective communication by naming what they want to hear and see in group conversations and what they don't want to hear and see. When one team I worked with was in a particularly stormy phase of development, members created the lists in Exhibit 7.5. At the opening of each meeting they reviewed their responses and each member selected a few of the positive attributes that she would focus on demonstrating. Sometimes the team asked the process observer to track what she noticed in terms of their communication and which of these elements they demonstrated. After several months of close focus on their communication by using this tool, this team's discussions improved dramatically. The team attributed its transition into the performing stage to this tool.

Exhibit 7.5. Behaviors That Foster and Undermine Effective Conversations

What Do We Want to Hear and See in Group Conversations?

- Active listening through paraphrasing and by asking follow-up clarifying and probing questions
- Active listening through nonverbal communication (making eye contact with each other, nodding)
- Questions and wonderings grounded in genuine inquiry
- Summarizing of each other's ideas
- Invitations to quieter members
- Making sure that everyone's voice is heard
- Probing questions that go below surface comments
- Clarifying questions that elicit more information
- Appreciations for what others say and do and for taking risks
- Productive conflict around ideas
- Respect for the opinions of others and valuing their input
- Problem solving
- Offering of ideas, suggestions, solutions, and next steps
- Empathy for each other and others outside of our team (including students, parents, and administrators)
- Flexibility and vulnerability
- Thoughtfulness around the language that is used and awareness of the impact that certain words can have
- Awareness of emotions when appropriate

What Don't We Want to Hear and See in Group Conversations?

- Going off topic and into long digressions
- Dominating the conversation by taking up too much airtime or trying to dictate the conversation
- Being sarcastic
- Disengaging and not participating
- Avoiding contentious topics

- Criticizing people and their ideas with negative comments
- Dismissing the ideas of others with "Yeah, buts"
- Taking pride in being a devil's advocate
- Being contrary and blocking team progress
- Boasting about personal skills or experience
- Pulling rank on each other
- Insulting team members or others outside of our team (including students, parents, and administrators)
- Gossiping about others
- Blaming others
- Complaining about things that are outside of our sphere of influence
- Using emotions to hijack a conversation
- Using language that is explosive and can trigger others as a way to bully the conversation
- Being distracted by other things (technology) or people

TWENTY WAYS TO IMPROVE YOUR TEAM'S COMMUNICATION

Here are some concrete ways that you can develop your team's communication habits and skills:

1. Raise awareness about discourse patterns and listening.

2. Practice active listening. Learn about and teach the group to use active listening, and incorporate 10 minutes of practice in each meeting. You can find a resource for this on my website (http://www.elenaaguilar.com).

3. Practice deep listening. The dyad structure (in Appendix E.4) is a way for people to hold space for each other and to practice their listening.

4. Make friends with silence. Silence, a necessary part of conversation, is often neglected. When a team is comfortable with the space that silence creates, they

will be less likely to fill quiet spaces in conversations, or they might ask for silence at times when they feel the group needs to process something.

5. Incorporate storytelling into meetings. Inviting members to share stories about their life and experiences builds empathy and is an opportune time to practice listening.

6. Explicitly teach and model productive language for challenging ideas and engaging in conflict. This is discussed in Chapter 12.

7. Explicitly teach and model questioning strategies that are nonjudgmental and anchored in curiosity. You can find lists of these questioning strategies on my website.

8. Explicitly teach about nonverbal cues, engage a team in raising awareness of the nonverbal messages they communicate, and model responding to nonverbal cues in your team.

9. Build shared meaning. All words are symbols and, as such, are abstractions, often meaning different things to different people. We need to inquire about the meaning that others hold in their words. Most discussions move so fast and we use words so loosely that it's hard to create shared meaning and people acquire vague or incorrect understandings. When you use or introduce a term (e.g., *transformation, backward planning, equity*), pause to clarify what you mean, ask others how they define the term, and ensure that you're all on the same page. When someone else uses a term that you suspect might be understood differently, ask the speaker to clarify his definition and invite others to share theirs.

10. Model and encourage self-awareness when conversations feel emotionally charged. Ask the team to stop, do an emotion scan, and take a few breaths. Mild discomfort in a conversation is fine and can be productive, but too much discomfort is unproductive.

11. Use discussion protocols strategically. Protocols can promote equitable oral participation, offering, for example, 3 minutes to each participation to share a reflection on an article. The National School Reform Faculty has an extensive bank of protocols that I draw from (http://www.nsrfharmony.org).

12. When opening a discussion, explicitly share the why and the how for the discussion. For example, say, "Today we'll discuss the advantages of extending our school

day. I want to hear from everyone, so we'll go around the room. You'll have about 2 minutes to share your thoughts, and if you go on too much longer I'll wave the yellow flag." This clarifies for the team the parameters for the discussion.

13. Use pair shares and trio discussions so that participants can process their ideas. When organized in pairs and trios, each person has more time to talk than in a whole group—and verbal processing is critical to learning.

14. Follow pair shares with small-group conversations that allow people to expand the thoughts that arose in the pair shares. Pair shares can often be effective, and sometimes, depending on the pair, conversations can be limited.

15. Engage a team in whole-group discussion to deepen shared meaning and understanding across the team. Teams do need whole-group discussion, but the amount of time for whole-group discussion needs to match the number of participants. For an open discussion in which everyone might participate, you need to estimate 5–7 minutes of time per person. However, many people have a hard time staying engaged in discussions of more than 10–15 minutes, so you need to carefully consider when to hold whole-group discussions.

16. In any one meeting, use a variety of conversation structures so that members are talking in pairs, trios, small groups, and the whole group. This allows different communication preferences to be met: Some people relish pair shares, whereas others need whole-group discussion time.

17. Use a variety of grouping structures so that members talk with a range of people in their team during the course of a meeting (so that they aren't just pair sharing with the person sitting next to them). This way ideas and perspectives cross-pollinate and people get to know each other more.

18. Use a timer and tell people how much time they'll have for a discussion or a pair share. For example, say, "You'll have 6 minutes to talk to your partner. I will let you know when we're half way through so in case you haven't switched you can do so."

19. Use a visible timer (projected or displayed on a screen) to help people self-regulate. As people take more responsibility for their airtime, you can do less management.

20. Be mindful of how much you speak in conversations and throughout the meeting. It's paramount that you model effective communication—that you listen to others, ask good questions, and ensure that your voice is not dominant.

> "Without mutually stimulating interactions, people and neurons wither and die. From birth until death, each of us needs others who seek us out, show interest in discovering who we are, and help us feel safe. Thus, understanding the brain requires knowledge of the healthy, living brain within a community of other brains: Relationships are our natural habitat."—Cozolino (2014)

GIVING FEEDBACK

We engage in many kinds of conversations with a team, and sometimes leaders need to give individual feedback. These conversations can be thought of as a directive coaching conversation—one in which you are not eliciting insight or reflection but rather raising an issue and asking for a change in behavior. Here are some guidelines for giving feedback.

Give timely feedback. Do this as soon after the situation or incident being described. In some situations, you or the person receiving the feedback may need some time between the incident and the feedback, but don't wait too long.

Ask for permission. There's no point in giving it if the other person isn't somewhat receptive. Ask: "Is now a good time for me to give you feedback?" If she says no, respect that and ask, "When do you anticipate would be good time?" or "Can we check in tomorrow about a good time for me to give you feedback?"

Look inward. Make sure that your feedback is coming from an honest and kind place in you. Feedback should help someone gain insight and grow. It's not an opportunity to shame someone.

Share your intention. Share why are you giving the feedback and the positive outcome you hope to achieve.

Begin with appreciation. In some cases, let the person know what she's doing well and what you appreciate about her. Don't prolong this step. Some people want you to get to the point and starting with appreciations can feel disingenuous if hard feedback is coming.

Be descriptive and specific. Tell the other person what you noticed or exactly what happened. Avoid evaluative comments or comments about her as a person.

Communicate impact. Share the impact that the other person's actions had on you. Avoid making assumptions about how the person's actions influenced others.

Check the feedback. Make sure your understanding feels fair and accurate to the other person.

Let the person know what you want. Make sure to be very clear about the changes, actions, or specific outcomes you would like to see. Make sure that your suggestions are ones that the person is capable of implementing.

Acknowledge the person. Thank the other person for the conversation, for listening, being open, and hearing your feedback.

Effective feedback is hard to give and can feel scary for many of us. It took me a while to feel comfortable and skilled at doing so. Usually, I waited too long to give it, spoke too abstractly about what had happened, and integrated too many evaluative comments into the discussion. Here's an example of what my ineffective feedback sounded like.

> A few weeks ago at our team meeting, you seemed really disengaged and checked out. I think it made everyone feel like you weren't part of the team.

In contrast, here's what more effective feedback sounds like.

> I want to give you some feedback on how I experienced you in our team meeting yesterday. I know you want to positively contribute to our team—and you usually do. My intention is to support your reflection and growth. During our meeting, I noticed that you checked your email several times while others were sharing the challenges they'd dealt with this week. I also noticed that you spoke up only once in our whole-group conversation. I find your insights very useful and missed hearing them. When I asked everyone to pair up and talk about their goals for this month, you sighed loudly and said you needed to step out for a few minutes. I'm open to hearing about what was going on with you, but I also need to ask that you follow the community agreements we've made about using technology and engage fully in our team meetings. Is this something you feel you can do?

Effective feedback yields openings—in conversations, in reflection, and in relationships. A conversation that begins as feedback has opportunities for growth for everyone involved.

EQUITY OF PARTICIPATION

Let's revisit the challenge posed in the opening of this chapter—that of the verbally dominating team member. A transactional approach to dealing with this person would be to have a hard conversation with him, tell him to stop talking so much, and maybe use a lot of rigid structures in team conversations to control his propensity.

Within a transformational model of team development, we take the time to cultivate awareness of our group's emotional intelligence. We examine the communication patterns that reflect our EI and consider their impact on our potential to accomplish the work we've come together to do. We engage in learning about communication together—in practicing our listening and questioning, in exploring the meaning behind the words we use, and in considering how our patterns of communication reflect societal values around who has voice, authority, and power. We seek to actively rupture those patterns that exist in our society at large and in our political structures—those that place greater value on the voices of some groups of people—because we know we need the insight, wisdom, perspectives, and opinions of everyone, especially those whose voices have not been heard as much as others. In a great team, members demonstrate self-awareness of how they are perceived in part because they ask their teammates for feedback and because they receive it. This awareness leads to self-regulation so that the facilitator doesn't need to play the role of airtime monitor.

Such explorations—of emotional intelligence and of communication patterns—take a great deal of time. But when we take the time necessary to develop the skills to lead our teams in such work, and when we take the time to do the work itself, equity of participation is possible. For the experience of children to be radically different than what it is today we'll have to make the time, acquire the skills, and engage in this critical component of the work.

Transformational Coaching Team, 2013

Early in our team's development, I noticed that member spoke way more than others and seemed not to be aware of it. He'd always be the first to respond to a question, and he'd talk far longer than anyone else. Rather than ignoring this behavior and hoping it would go away, I decided to confront it. As I prepared for what I imagined might be a difficult conversation, I thought about how much I liked this coach, how much I appreciated the perspective he brought to our team, how grateful I was that he was on our team.

During our regular weekly check-in, I raised the issue. I started with this question: "I'm curious what you notice about your participation in our team discussions?"

"Oh no, I'm talking too much, aren't I?" He dropped his head into his hands. "I just get so nervous, and I think if I keep talking no one will notice."

"Well, okay. That's a great start—that you're aware of how much you talk." I smiled. I hadn't anticipated that he was aware. "How do you think this behavior impacts the rest of the group?"

"You mean my talking so much? I guess it means less time for others. It just seems like some of the people on our team don't want to talk that much, and it feels uncomfortable when there's silence so I share my thoughts and hope that makes other want to share."

"I hear that your intentions are positive," I said. "I've noticed both how much you talk and also that you're often the first to talk. Are you aware of that?"

"Oh, that's another bad habit I have. I just want to say my ideas and then sit back."

"So when you do that, what effect do you notice it has on the group?"

"I don't know," he responded, looking confused. "I never thought about that."

"What I've noticed is that it sends our discussions in the direction you've introduced. Other team members validate your contribution and respond to the ideas of you've shared, and we often follow that train of thought. My concern is that we don't explore the trains of thought that others might hold. Does that make sense?"

"I guess so. I never even thought about that. But yeah, now that I think about it, I can see how I was setting the direction of the discussion by being the first to comment. Everyone is so nice, and I guess they don't want to take it in another direction."

"Could be that others need to be more assertive about shifting the discussion's gears," I said, "but you make interesting comments and I think they authentically engage those ideas. At the same time, I think our team would benefit from exploring the ideas that others make."

He nodded his head and sighed loudly. I held a few seconds of silence to let this suggestion sink in.

"What could I do," I said, "to help you bring awareness to your patterns of participation in discussions?"

"I don't know," he responded. "I'll really try to monitor my talking from now on."

"Ok, I appreciate your commitment. Would it be okay during meetings, if you are the first to respond to a prompt, if I say something like, 'Hold off for a minute. Let's see if someone else can get us started this time?'"

"Yeah, that's fine," he said. "I don't mind if you do that."

"Great. And if there are times when you're going on too long, could I do something similar? I'll try to be as respectful and tactful as possible."

"Definitely," he said.

Once I'd gotten his agreement to these proposals, I shifted the conversation to his underlying nervousness, which he said prompted some of the verbal dominance. He identified some strategies to manage those feelings, and in the subsequent months it was clear that he was making a great effort to do so. During discussions when he was the first to respond or went on too long, he frequently stopped himself, sometimes commenting, "Oh, I gotta stop. I'm trying to talk less," or he'd make a motion of zipping up his mouth. Sometimes just a glance from me would remind him of his commitment and I rarely had to cut him off verbally.

As I noticed our team discussions changing and becoming more equitable, I felt my relief that I'd been able to manage one of the biggest challenges I'd faced in facilitation. I recognized the groundwork I'd laid with this coach in the relationship I'd cultivated with him, I recognized the importance of having determined team norms and community agreements, and I recognized how I'd clearly laid out the work and purpose of our team. More than anything I acknowledged my own calm and confidence in managing this dynamic. I didn't see it as a battle to wage or the coach as someone to control; I noticed my genuine interest in understanding why he was acting as he did and my investment in helping him shift his behavior.

CHAPTER 8

Making Good Decisions

Humanities Team, 2008

The principal, Mr. Bain, shared the following year's master schedule with our team and told teachers that first period would be a reading intervention class.

"Each of you will teach a different level," I chimed in, "and we'll be on 6-week cycles. As kids master the material, they might move out of your class and into someone else's." There was an unusual silence. Teachers didn't lift their gaze from the documents they'd received.

Mr. Bain spoke up. "The new curriculum should arrive within a couple of weeks, so you'll have a few months to familiarize yourself with it."

"It's a really great program," I said, "backed by strong research. Kids get beautiful books, all nonfiction texts, and you won't have to make copies or dig out battered old sets of dusty novels."

Margaret lifted her head. "And who made this decision?" she said, removing her glasses and speaking slowly.

"We did," I said.

"Who is 'we'?" she responded.

I motioned to the principal and me. "Margaret," he said, "it's a district mandate that we have a reading intervention program. Over a third of our students read below grade level. We have to show that we're doing something about this."

"But why weren't we, the teachers, consulted about this? We know our kids best. We should have been involved." A couple other teachers nodded.

"I spent a lot of time this spring looking at different reading programs," I said. "I didn't think you'd want to be involved. You're always telling me how much you already work, so I figured it would be helpful if I did the research."

"So, let me just clarify," Margaret said. "You've decided what we'll teach, who will teach what, and how to group students."

"Well, yes," I said, "I used their latest reading assessment scores to determine the groupings."

Mr. Bain jumped in. "I asked her to do that."

"Ok, so it's all done." Margaret gathered up her papers. "Anything else we need to know? I have a stack of papers to grade. Correcting their egregious spelling alone takes hours. Will the new curriculum teach these kids to spell? I'd be thrilled if I didn't have to spend my weekends and evenings grading." She tucked her glasses onto her head and stood.

"Spelling is part of what the curriculum addresses," I said, "but it really targets reading comprehension."

"For years I've been saying that we need to address spelling and grammar, and no one listens to me. They don't need comprehension given where they're headed. But I'll teach whatever you tell me to teach, Mr. Bain." And Margaret walked out of the room.

Cassandra, who was usually very agreeable, leaned forward. "I would have liked to participate in this decision. It would have been interesting to look at different curricula and learn about them. I wish we'd been invited to participate if we wanted to. I could have made time."

"Me too," Bess added. "We used an intervention program at my old school that I was trained in and really liked."

I sighed and looked at Mr. Bain. "See," I thought, "I told you that they'd be resistant to this, too." But I also wondered if I'd made yet another mistake.

Effective decision making is a skill set that very few teachers or administrators systematically learn how to implement. It's one I struggled with the most—not knowing how to lead decision-making process with a team or even how to recognize *when* a decision was being made. I was nervous about group decision making, and I preferred to make decisions alone. Yet decision-making moments can be pivotal for teams as they are tightly connected to levels of trust in the group. A decision-making processes can strengthen or weaken trust between team members and the leader and between the teammates themselves. Given how essential trust is to developing an effective team, decision making merits thoughtful consideration.

If you are a department head or instructional coach, you most likely lead or facilitate some decision-making processes—and you're probably involved in others outside of your team. However, much of your team time might focus on learning and collaboration. Although many decisions are made within these contexts, you might not feel as if you are leading formal decision-making processes all that often. In contrast, certain groups, teams, and committees spend the majority of their time together making decisions. Site and central office leadership teams, administrative teams, and school boards are examples of groups whose primary role is to constantly assess the state of affairs, look for solutions, and formulate plans—and therefore these groups are often making decisions.

Reflect on Decision Making

1. What kinds of experiences have you had with either leading a team through a process or being part of a team and going through a decision-making experience?
2. What feelings come up for you when you need to make a decision as a leader?
3. What feelings come up for you when you're in a team and someone else makes a decision for the team?
4. What's hard about decision making for you?

INDICATORS OF EFFECTIVE DECISION MAKING

Let's get straight to the point—what makes for good decision making? What might we see, hear, and feel to indicate that the decision-making process we're leading or involved in has potential for being effective? Based on my experience and research, here are 10 indicators of an effective decision-making process:

- Everyone is clear about decision-making moments.
- Everyone knows his or her level of empowerment in the decision.

- The right people are present—the key stakeholders and decision makers.

- Everyone knows what kind of decision-making process will be used and is willing to use it.

- The conversation has a clear structure so that the discussion is objective, is focused on ideas and facts, and doesn't become personal and emotional.

- Ideas are freely exchanged and considered.

- No individual or subgroup dominates.

- If the decision-making process stalls, the group stops and reflects on its process and seeks ways to move forward.

- Discussions end with a sense of closure and clear next steps.

- The team engages in a reflection on the decision-making process.

This chapter offers some of the skills and tools necessary to engage a team in effective decision making. You'll also need to draw on your ability to structure group conversations (see Chapters 7 and 11) and to manage conflict (see Chapter 12). Keep in mind that the most effective decisions are made on solid foundations of trust and are guided by leaders with high self-awareness. The tools and technical support offered in this chapter will take root in teams where there's trust. Decision-making moments often boost levels of trust in a group or further erode them, which is why we need to pay close attention to decisions.

IDENTIFYING DECISION-MAKING MOMENTS

One sinkhole that many leaders fall into is making decisions without even knowing that we're making them. Sometimes I've been midsentence in a meeting when I realize I'm making a decision or inviting a decision to be made; sometimes a team member has called my awareness to a decision-making moment that's in process. At those times, I've felt a little sheepish as I realize that I was perhaps yet again moving toward making a decision without thoughtfully engaging others in a process.

One way I've honed my ability to anticipate decision making is by carefully planning meetings. Although Chapters 10 and 11 explore agenda planning in depth, here's a useful way of thinking about what happens during meetings. There are five big buckets that encompass the great majority of what happens in a meeting: information sharing, community building, learning, planning, and problem solving. Let's consider what happens in each of these components of a meeting and how much decision making happens in each.

1. *Information sharing*: This includes reviewing upcoming events and calendars, reading data reports, and sharing new procedures and protocols. This is typically what happens at many whole-staff meetings in schools but may also occur in team meetings when the facilitator or a team member needs to share information. There is rarely decision making in these components of an agenda.

2. *Community building*: These components of an agenda are intended to help people get to know each other and build community. This includes activities such as check-ins, team builders and energizers, icebreakers, norm reflections, and process observation. Decisions are sometimes made during these components of an agenda, but not always.

3. *Learning*: Many agenda components are professional development. A learning section does not include decision making; however, many learning sections can lead to planning or problem-solving discussions when decisions are made. It's important that a facilitator can distinguish when a learning section ends and when a decision-making conversation begins.

4. *Planning*: This includes discussions around upcoming school events, curriculum, assessments, work plans, strategic plans, vision and mission identification, and core values and norms. Many decisions are made during these conversations.

5. *Problem solving*: These conversations ask participants to identify and resolve issues. This includes analyzing student data, identifying challenges, and creating action plans. These discussions involve making many decisions.

When designing agendas for teams that make a lot of decisions, it can be useful to indicate the purpose of each section. Exhibit 8.1 is an example of an agenda that identifies the purpose for each part of a meeting and names the decision-making processes that will be used. I prepare agendas like this when I work with leadership teams, site administration teams, or strategic planning groups. It helps to clearly name *when* and *how* decisions will be made.

Exhibit 8.1. Example of Agenda for Decision Making

Rise Up Elementary School

Instructional Leadership Team Agenda

December 9, 2014 ★ 3:30-5:00

Intended Outcomes:

1. To analyze self-reflection data from PLC meetings
2. To identify priority areas for next month's whole staff PD session and determine plan for delivering PD

Roles

Process Checker: Sharon

Timekeeper: Francisca

Note taker: Martin

Facilitator: Elena

Time	Activity or Topic	Purpose	Decision-Making Process
3:30–3:45	**Opening** • Review agenda and outcomes • Team building activity	☐ Information Sharing X Community Building ☐ Learning ☐ Planning ☐ Problem Solving	None
3:45–4:15	**Data Analysis** • Share data on self-assessments from PLCs • Analyze data	☐ Information Sharing ☐ Community Building ☐ Learning X Planning ☐ Problem Solving	None
4:15–4:45	**PD Planning** • Review norms for decision making • Identify content areas • Determine who will design and facilitate which sections and when planning will be done	☐ Information Sharing ☐ Community Building ☐ Learning ☐ Planning X Problem Solving	1. Voting (with stickers) 2. Consensus
4:45–5:00	**Closing** • Review agreements and next steps • Reflection on norms and intentions • Process observer report • Feedback for facilitator • Appreciations	☐ Information Sharing X Community Building ☐ Learning ☐ Planning ☐ Problem Solving	None

WHO IS INVOLVED AND HOW MUCH
SAY DO THEY GET

Have you ever engaged in a discussion about a decision, only to find out at the end that actually you were only offering input and not able to make the decision yourself or with your colleagues? Or perhaps even more frustrating, have you ever sat through a discussion in which you've offered ideas and debated plans only to find out at the end that the decision had already been made? Unfortunately, many educators have had these kinds of experiences, which has led some to feel disempowered and distrusting. A key indicator of an effective decision-making process is that everyone involved knows exactly how much say he or she has in a decision.

Levels of Empowerment

Ingrid Bens (2012) offers some language to communicate how much say people have in a decision. She calls this *levels of empowerment* and suggests the following four levels:

Level 1: Administrators decide and then tell staff. People are told about a decision or directed to do something, and they are expected to comply. For example, the first day of school is usually a decision in which most of us have no say. The administrators who make this decision are entirely accountable for it.

Level 2: Administrators gain input before deciding. People are consulted and able to give input into a decision that is ultimately made by administrators or managers. For example, teachers might give input into a new initiative that their administration is considering, but the principal will make the final decision.

Level 3: Staff decide and recommend. People make a decision by themselves but must consult their supervisors before acting to get their approval. For example, perhaps a team of sixth-grade teachers decide where they'll take a weeklong field trip and when they want to take it, but they consult with the principal for final approval. On this level, accountability is shared.

Level 4: Staff decide and act. People make a decision and take action without getting anyone else's approval. They have the highest level of control and are most accountable for their decision. For example, a grade-level team might decide on the content of its advisory curriculum or its homework procedures.

Determining Levels of Empowerment

In advance of a meeting, a leader needs to identify the decisions that will be made and how much say the team will have—what the level of empowerment will be. If you are a site-based coach or a grade-level lead, this may mean that you need to consult with an administrator first. For example, perhaps a department team is considering a supplementary curriculum for the following school year. The team leader probably needs to talk to the principal and clarify the level of empowerment the group has to make this decision—perhaps the principal says, "Go ahead and just make it yourselves" (level 4), or perhaps she says, "Your team can make a proposal, and I'll weigh your input and make the decision" (level 2). To cultivate a team's trust, facilitators need to show up to a team meeting clear on the parameters of decision making.

More often than not, you'll probably determine the level of empowerment for a team that you lead. This can be a challenging decision-making moment for you as a leader—how do you decide what level of empowerment to offer your team? Here are a few considerations to guide this decision (and are you noticing how many decisions you have to make about decisions?)

Start with considering who is best qualified to make the decision in terms of expertise. Do team members have the *knowledge* necessary to make the decision? Perhaps a group of teachers will decide on a new high school advisory curriculum. Do team members have an understanding of the social and emotional learning skills that their students need to develop? What might they need to know to participate in a fully informed, level 3 decision-making process? Is there a way for them to gain this knowledge within the amount of time available to make the decision? Or perhaps because you have a background in counseling it would make more sense for you to *get input* and make the decision?

The next question to consider to suggest a level of empowerment is this: To what extent is it important that there are high levels of buy-in to the decision? If you're considering a decision that will greatly affect the daily lives of team members, then it might be worth involving them. For example, if all teachers will be expected to teach advisory every day, and if this program is to be the core of social and emotional learning in your school, then you'll probably want high buy-in to the curriculum that's selected.

Finally, ask yourself whether it's worth the time to deeply involve team members in every step of the decision-making process. We all know that time is limited and there's so much to do. If your team is newly forming, it might be important for them to participate in decisions—this can build trust in you as the leader and in the work you're doing together. If trust is fragile in the team, it can also be useful for them to participate extensively in decision making. Also consider what else is on everyone's plate—is investing the time in this decision making as or more important than attending to other responsibilities? Leaders need to guide some of the prioritizing around how time is spent.

Determining Levels of Empowerment

1. Do team members have the knowledge necessary to make the decision?

2. To what extent is it important that there are high levels of buy-in to the decision?

3. Is it worth the time to deeply involve team members in every step of the decision-making process?

When I apply these questions to reflect on my decision about the intervention classes in Wilson Middle School (as I described in the opening of this chapter), I'm stumped. The decision was very important. It directly impacted one-third of our students, who were reading below grade level. My level of expertise was far higher than that of other team members—I'd had extensive training in literacy instruction. But even then, I was aware that my choice to make the decision alone could potentially erode the trust that some of team members had in me. However, their trust in me was so low that I'm not sure it would have made a big difference had they been involved in the decision. Yet perhaps I could have led the team through a process of evaluating different intervention programs, which might have built their knowledge of reading intervention and offered them an opportunity for input. I think, if I could have done it over again, I would have taken Cassandra's suggestion and made participation in making the decision optional. I might have also said something like this:

> I'm not sure how to best lead this decision-making process. I'm aware of how much all of you already do and how many responsibilities you have as teachers. I also want you to know that, although I've had a lot of training in literacy instruction and I feel I could make this decision alone, this might be an area that we could explore together. Because we're all going to teach these courses next year, I hope there'll be a high level of buy-in to this decision, which makes me think that some, if not all, of you should be very involved in it. What are your thoughts about how to best go about making a decision that will affect our entire department?

An Opportunity for Self-Awareness

What feelings come up for you as you think about making decisions? Cultivating an awareness of our emotional experience gives us insights into ourselves as facilitators. Some leaders are anxious about making decisions because they fear the response of teammates or they want to *make sure* they're satisfying everyone. As leaders, we will rarely make everyone happy. This can feel uncomfortable, but we can learn to be okay with discomfort and with team members who don't like our decisions.

Some facilitators prioritize efficiency over full consideration and exploration of decisions. Again, notice the feelings that come up for you when you need to make a decision. Do you feel frustrated and impatient that a decision might need to involve discussion with your team? Would you prefer to just make decisions without getting their input? Does the thought of a consensus decision-making process fill you with anxiety and annoyance? Do you find that you usually make most of the decisions without getting team input or consensus?

For those of us who may identify with this later tendency, it helps to consider the origins of these inclinations. When I coached the humanities team at Wilson Middle School, I wanted to make 95% of the decisions quickly and by myself. I attributed this approach to my commitment to kids getting what they deserved and to the urgency I felt about acting on that commitment. I thought that the humanities team *needed* me to be directive or else we'd be stuck in endless dysfunctional inertia. The thing was, this didn't work. It led to many battles and exhausted me.

> *Patience does not mean to passively endure. It means to be farsighted enough to trust the end result of a process. It means to look at the thorn and see the rose, to look at the night and see the dawn.*
>
> RUMI

Even though this is how I understand my tendency toward directive leadership, I also recognize that some people take charge and do the work themselves because they were raised in households with that kind of leadership. Our society is predominantly hierarchical—from our homes to our schools to our economic system, hierarchical leadership abounds. It's hard to avoid replicating this kind of transactional leadership and takes intentionality. Transactional leaders might lead teams to produce impressive results—*temporarily*. However, transactional leadership does not lead to transformational changes and furthermore can result in the kinds of outcomes we don't want to see in schools—people becoming cynical, passively responding, disengaging, and quitting. Transaction leadership can't create a beloved community. Decision-making moments often surface these tensions around what kind of leader we want to be. Use these moments to reflect on the thoughts and feelings that emerge for you and to identify who you want to be as a leader.

DECISION-MAKING PROCESSES

Many groups commonly use five main decision-making processes: consensus, multivoting, compromise, majority voting, and unilateral decision. Each has advantages and disadvantages, and it's important to thoughtfully select a process and consider how it will affect levels of trust in a team. First, let's understand these five decision-making approaches.

Consensus

Building consensus with a group results in a decision that everyone can live with. Consensus doesn't mean everyone is enthusiastic, but it does mean that everyone clearly understands the situation or the problem to be decided, has analyzed all the facts together, and then has jointly developed solutions that represent the whole group's best thinking about the optimal decision. Consensus building takes time because there has to be a lot of listening, healthy debate, and option testing. There's generally the highest buy-in and most participation in decisions made by consensus.

Here are the steps involved in consensus building:

1. Name the problem, topic, or issue.

2. Share all of the known facts to create a shared understanding of the current situation.

3. Generate potential courses of action or solutions.

4. Generate criteria for sorting the courses of action or solutions.

5. Use the criteria to sort through the ideas. Use a decision grid (Exhibit 8.2), a vote, or a multivote.

6. Make a clear statement of the decision.

7. Ask for team members to either publically or privately share their vote. You can use a 0–5 scale like in Fist to Five (Exhibit 8.3).

8. If anyone votes lower than a three, ask them to speak about their reservations and follow up with a question such as, "What would it take to move you to a 3?"

9. The decision is not ratified until everyone has voted at a 4 or 5.

Exhibit 8.2. Decision-Making Grids

A decision-making grid is a matrix that uses criteria to assess a set of ideas to determine which are most likely to be effective. When a complex issue involves multiple elements, this process can help shift a conversation from a debate into a discussion in which solutions are weighed against an objective set of criteria.

The easiest decision-making grid is an impact/effort grid that looks like this:

Major improvement		Easy/Major	Difficult/Major
Minor Improvement	**Impact**	Easy/Minor	Difficult/Minor
		Effort	
		Easy to Do	Difficult to Do

As a group discusses the various choices on the table, they place each choice in one of the four boxes. For example, a leadership team considering how to better manage student behavior during passing periods might generate a dozen possible actions they could take. To create a strategic and doable action plan, they need to decide on just a few high-leverage actions. As they talk about the options, they determine that having a rotation of staff in the hallways would be easy to do and could have a major impact. They place the suggestion to institute detention for all students who are tardy into the difficult but minor category. Another idea to hold a monthly awards ceremony for students who have perfect attendance is determined to be easy but minor—the school has tried this approach for several years.

Before the team engaged in sorting the options into the different boxes, they had a discussion about what *easy* and *difficult* entailed and what *major* and *minor* meant to them. Being clear about the terminology from the start prevented debate and allowed the team to more quickly reach a decision about their next steps.

Exhibit 8.3. Fist to Five Decision Making

This is a strategy to use during consensus building either to determine where individuals are falling in their opinions or as a final voting method. After stating the decision, or proposed decision, ask the team to show their level of support using levels from fist to 5, where 3 indicates the point of consensus.

Fist = I object and block consensus.

1 finger = I am strongly opposed to this and will need to see some big changes to approve it.

2 fingers = I have serious reservations about this proposal but could accept it with some changes.

3 fingers = I have a couple reservations about this proposal, but I could let it pass without further discussion.

4 fingers = I think it's a good idea, and I can live with it.

5 fingers = I am in total agreement with the proposal.

A consensus process can feel intimidating to new facilitators because at times it can feel like a decision is far off and there's a lot of talk. But if the process passes the check test (Exhibit 8.4), then it's probably going to result in a team having the greatest possible buy-in and highest levels of group accountability. Everyone may not feel good or happy at the end of a consensus process, but the question to ask is, "Do we have a well-thought through outcome that we can all feel committed to implementing and that everyone can live with?" If the answer to that question is yes, then consensus building was a success.

Common challenges with consensus include some group members showing reluctance to support a particular decision. Although it might be tempting to pressure dissenters to give in, don't do it. Dissenters may have an important idea that's been overlooked by the group. First acknowledge and accept their dissent, allow them to express their concerns in concrete terms, and then ask them to propose solutions to issues that they've raised. This can sound like, "I acknowledge that you have some different views, and we want to hear those. Tell us the specific issue you have with the group's decision." Then ask, "What changes do you propose could be made to the group's solution that would make it acceptable to you? What are the solutions to the problems that you raise?"

Consensus building is time-consuming and requires strong facilitation skills. If it's done without proper data collection or if members have poor interpersonal skills, then it can produce low-quality decisions. But it's also a powerful method of making decisions that will affect everyone in a group, and it can be worth the time.

Exhibit 8.4. Consensus-Building Process Checking

A process checker can use this tool to assess its health of a consensus-building conversation. These are indicators of an effective consensus-building process.

1. Is the process that we're using explicit and clear? Is everyone onboard with using it?
2. Are lots of ideas being shared?
3. Are everyone's ideas being heard?
4. Are people paraphrasing each other's ideas?
5. Are people building on each other's ideas?
6. Is there an open and objective quest to find new options (rather than someone trying to push a predetermined solution)?
7. Is there healthy conflict (or does it seem like people are just being nice and trying to get along)?
8. If there's unproductive conflict, does the facilitator address it?
9. If we get stuck or the conversation starts spinning, does the facilitator stop us and guide us to reflect on our process?
10. Is the final decision based on sound information?
11. When the decision is reached, do people seem to feel satisfied that they were part of the decision?
12. Does it seem like everyone feels consulted and involved and can live with the final decision?
13. Are our next steps clear?

Multivoting

Multivoting is a priority ranking tool that's useful for making decisions when the group has a long set of options. Group members rank order the options, based on a set of criteria, and in doing so clarify the best course of action. This can be used after an idea-generating discussion. For example, this process would be a good choice for a sixth-grade team trying to decide on which of 14 locations is the best to take their students for an end-of-year camping trip. This is an important topic, and it's important that everyone can live with the decision. This process is also useful when a team is deciding on the norms or community agreements that all members agree to.

Steps to leading a multivoting process are as follows:

1. Clarify the items being prioritized. Make sure everyone understands the choices.

2. Identify the voting criteria to ensure that everyone votes with the same criteria in mind. Some situations benefit from voting several times and applying different criteria to each vote. Examples of criteria include the most cost-effective, the easiest to implement, the greatest potential impact on students, the most likely to meet our goals, or the most logistically feasible.

3. Vote.

    a. With sticker dots: Each person gets a set of sticker dots. Use slightly fewer dots than half the items to be sorted to force people to make choices. So if there are 10 items to choose from, give people four stickers each. Ask team members to place their stickers on their top four choices, and no one can put more than one sticker on any one item. After everyone has voted, tally the dots to arrive at the priorities.

    b. With points: Give each person points to distribute among the items to be sorted. The number of points is typically either 10 or 100. Members write their points next to the items they favor—but no one can place more than 50% of their points on any single item. After voting, add the scores to arrive at the priorities.

Multivoting is democratic, participatory, and objective. Usually everyone feels like he or she won something, and it's a fast way of sorting out a set of options. However, it doesn't always involve a lot of discussion (i.e., understanding of the options). Also, unless voting is done privately people can be influenced by each other. But it's a sound method to use especially when there are a lot of people involved and a lot of options.

Compromise

When a group is strongly polarized and there are two or more options, a compromise decision can be useful. In these situations, neither side is willing to accept the solution proposed by the other side, and a middle position is created incorporating ideas from both sides. The danger is that the outcome is one that no one really feels satisfied with—everyone feels that he or she lost something, although usually everyone also feels that he or she won something. The predominant response to a compromise decision is, "It's not what I really wanted, but I have to live with it."

Steps to leading a compromise decision are as follows:

1. Ask each side to describe the solution or action it favors.

2. Ask the other party to make notes and then summarize the other group's proposal.

3. Engage the whole group in identifying the strengths and weaknesses of each proposed approach. Surface the strengths of both sides.

4. Ask each group to willingly give up some aspect of its original approach to arrive at a decision that represents a middle ground.

5. Clarify, summarize, and vote on the middle-ground approach.

The risk with a compromise decision is that it can divide the group. However, when the group is strongly polarized compromise might be the only alternative. It also generates a lot of discussion and results in a decision.

Compromise decision making was useful with an elementary school staff with whom I worked when they needed to make a decision about how to spend a large amount of extra funding that was granted to the school. The site administrators felt it was important for the staff to have a level 3 empowerment—to make a recommendation—and they tried using a multivoting process. However, the staff was divided in two camps about how to spend the money. One group advocated for creating a new position and hiring someone for it, and another group advocated for technology supplies. A compromise was challenging because a part-time position couldn't be created, but ultimately it resulted in the money being spent in entirely new ways and resulted in the great majority of the staff accepting the final decision. Although the process was contentious at times, staff members also came to understand each other better through listening to the impassioned proposals of their colleagues. This process not only resulted in a decision that was acceptable but also increased trust amongst the staff and between staff and administrators.

Majority Voting

Most people are familiar with majority voting in which participants choose the option they favor and vote by a show of hands or secret ballot. An advantage with this method is that it's fast—although voting needs to be preceded by a good discussion and sharing of ideas. The challenge with majority voting is that can be used too fast and the decision can be a poor one if people have voted on their personal feelings without hearing each other's thoughts or the facts. The group can also feel divided since majority voting creates winner and losers. The voting process is usually best done in private so that members don't feel pressured to conform and aren't overtly influenced by each other. Majority voting can also be used if consensus has been attempted but couldn't be reached.

I used majority voting with a staff I worked with when we had a decision to make that was on a tight timeline and a compromise could not be found between two groups of teachers. The decision was about how to focus our professional learning time for the following year. It was very important that teachers were brought into this decision, and majority voting resulting in a satisfactory decision (that every one felt was "fair") within the time frame we were given to make it.

Steps in leading majority voting are as follows:

1. Ask members to describe the options in detail to build a shared understanding.

2. Identify criteria for deciding, such as cost-effectiveness, potential impact, and logistical ease.

3. Use a show of hands or paper vote to identify which option to implement.

Unilateral Decision

The final decision-making approach that can be used is to agree that one person will make a decision alone on behalf of the group. A one-person decision might be the fastest and most efficient way to reach an agreement. Of course, the designated person can seek input and advice from group members before deciding.

If team members have low trust in each other stage, this method may further divide the group. A one-person decision also doesn't result in the group's buy-in to the same extent as a shared decision-making process does. It's a useful approach to consider when the issue is small or unimportant, when there's a clear expert in the group, when only one person has the information needed to make the decision, or when one person is solely accountable for the outcome.

When I led the team of coaches in the Oakland schools, I had to make decisions about job assignments and responsibilities. There were many moments when I knew that I was the only one who had all of the information about both the coaches and their contexts and that I needed to make the decision. The issues weren't necessarily small, but they weren't ones my team was equipped to make a decision on.

There were other times, however, when I asked one member of the team to make a decision—for example, to select an online platform to use for one of our projects. In this moment, I knew I did not have the expertise to do so, and someone else on my team did. After inviting teammates to share their concerns and requests, we agreed to accept the decision of the person selected to make the decision. This was a moment in which my decision as a leader was that we shouldn't spend more than about 10 minutes as a whole group discussing this issue.

Steps to leading a one-person decision are as follows:

1. Identify the best person to make the decision. This might be someone who has some expertise in this area.

2. Engage the group in a conversation during which members can tell the decision maker about their needs and concerns regarding the item to be decided.

3. Gain agreement that everyone will accept the decision of the expert.

Deciding on a Decision-Making Process

There are many decision-making moments for leaders in a decision-making process, including how to decide which process to use. To determine the best process to employ in a decision-making meeting, I consider a couple of questions: How important is this topic or issue? How important is it that we are all onboard with the decision?

For example, if I'm planning an end-of-year celebration with a team and want to hold it at a restaurant, I think, "This is not really an important issue, and it's probably not a big deal if we decide to have it at a Mexican restaurant even though one person prefers Chinese." In this case, I choose a majority voting or compromise process.

However, if an instructional leadership team is going to decide on the electives that will be offered the following year, it's probably a very important topic and probably also very important that everyone is united and committed to the decision. A consensus process will probably be ideal, but if a decision can't be reached by consensus then a voting process will probably be second best.

Sometimes when I'm stuck, I ask the team I'm leading to help me decide which process might be most useful to use. I describe the five processes and ask for input. This can help them understand my decision, and it increases their awareness of the complicated nature of making decisions.

FACILITATING DISCUSSIONS

The skill sets for facilitating conversations that lead to effective decision making are described in many chapters in this book. Chapters 9, 10, and 11 offer suggestions for structures, processes, and protocols that you can incorporate into decision-making conversations. Chapters 5 and 12 offer guidance in managing group dynamics.

The strategies and approaches in those chapters are important to draw on when leading a discussion around a decision.

A team that makes a lot of decisions can benefit by having a set of norms specifically for decision-making moments (Exhibit 8.5). Specific behaviors are conducive to effective decision making, and a process observer can use this tool to pay attention to how a group interacts during decision-making meetings. I find that it's helpful to have these on an agenda as well as on the back of folded note cards, placed right in front of each team member, so that they're always visible in multiple places. Most people want to contribute productively in discussions—we just need reminders for how to do so.

Exhibit 8.5. Decision-Making Norms

When we make decisions in our team, we agree to:

- Listen to each others' ideas and seek to understand them, even if we don't agree with them.
- Paraphrase someone else's ideas before contradicting them.
- Acknowledge what's valuable about someone else's ideas (and not just criticize them).
- Build on the ideas of others (and not push our own).
- Ask for and accept feedback on our ideas (and not get defensive about our ideas).
- Be open to accepting alternate proposals (and not block suggestions).
- Focus on facts (and not engage in arguments based on feelings).
- Be aware of our emotions and manage them.
- Be kind and compassionate to each other.

WHEN CONVERSATIONS GET STUCK

Decision-making conversations can get stuck for many reasons. Some of these can be because of low levels of trust in the team or unproductive ways of dealing with conflict. Sometimes conversations can get stuck because our leadership skills are undeveloped and we're not sure how to facilitate a conversation. Sometimes conversations hit a wall because there's a lack of an agreed upon mission and vision for the team or organization. And sometimes conversations are challenging because team members are reluctant to share their true thoughts. Let's explore what that can be about.

Groupthink

Groupthink happens when people are afraid of the consequences of sharing their real thoughts and feelings. When this happens and people withhold their ideas, there is a danger that the decision won't be the best one or the most innovative or creative. It also indicates a low level of trust in the group and a fear of conflict. People start to feel that it's better to be quiet, go with the flow, and not challenge each other. Groupthink is one of the major causes of poor decision making.

How can you tell if groupthink is going on in a team? First, take a look at the context. Within hierarchical systems, it's natural for people to be concerned about speaking out. This is exacerbated if you're in a school or organization in which leadership is particularly authoritative or directive. In addition, if there's no regular practice of giving and receiving feedback, groupthink can flourish. If team members feel insecure about their jobs or positions, they can be reluctant to speak out. If there's a history of conflict in the group or unresolved conflict between two members, then you can also predict that there might be a reluctance to share thoughts and feelings. Finally, if the team doesn't have much experience with creative thinking or problem solving, they might lack the skills and knowledge for doing so.

Usually, as facilitators, we can tell when people aren't sharing their real thoughts. We can often see it in their body language—the absence of nodding heads, the distracted visual attention; we hear side conversations or mutterings of disagreements during breaks. We feel the lack of energy. If this is happening in a group you're working with, you may need to directly address this with the group by asking questions such as, "To what extent do people in this group feel free to speak their minds? Are opposing views seen as positive or negative by members of this team? Have there ever been repercussions for people who oppose a group opinion or idea presented by a leader?" Inviting members into awareness that groupthink has taken over their team and inviting them into a discussion of this is a first start. It can be empowering for a group when you are transparent about your leadership moves and when you invite them in to make decisions about how the group process will run.

If there's a positional leader in the team (e.g., an administrator), you might need to consider whether their leadership style is having a negative impact on the group. If there are some who feel threatened by this leader, then they may withhold their thoughts as long as that person is in the room. You may need to talk to the administrator about his or her presence. That might feel scary to do—and you may not actually be able to ask the leader to step out—but it might be what's causing the groupthink.

You'll also need to explicitly ask for, scaffold, and model the sharing of divergent ideas. And as soon as team members start to offer them, you'll need to acknowledge the risk they took and the positive impact it can have on the group's discussion. As a group gains confidence in its ability to engage in productive conflict and useful discussions, the groupthink will dissipate.

Our goal as team leaders is deceptively simple: We create the conditions in which healthy teams can make good decisions. However, the broad context in which we work is not necessarily conducive to this goal. In much of the national discourse, educators are blamed for far more than their share of problems in our country. Federal and state policies harshly penalize teachers and schools for not meeting absurd performance expectations. In many states and schools, teachers no longer even have union representation that might help ensure their right to a job. There's tremendous fear of speaking out against policies—and this breeds group think. It's important to acknowledge that we have a lot to contend with when we're trying to create a safe space for discussion.

REFLECTION AND FEEDBACK

When team members make big decisions, they need an opportunity to reflect on their process and offer the facilitator feedback. Exhibit 8.6 offers a tool that can do this. This tool is aligned to the indicators of an effective decision-making process that were presented at the beginning of this chapter. I share these indicators with teams to increase their awareness of what we're striving for when we make decisions.

There are a couple ways you can use the feedback. First, it's useful when planning for the next decision-making process, and it offers you feedback on your facilitation skills. It can also be used to engage the group in a reflective conversation about how they are working together. You can tally the responses and share them with the group and then invite the team to think about one or two areas in which they'd like to improve. Perhaps the ratings on active listening are amongst the lowest. At the next decision-making meeting, the team may agree to focus on using these strategies. Team members might start by practicing active listening before engaging in decision-making conversations so that they've warmed up those mental muscles. The more that individuals become aware of their patterns during discussions, the more choice they can make about how to engage. Reflection (and reflecting on reflections) often increases awareness.

Exhibit 8.6. Feedback on Decision-Making Process

Team: Date:

Please rate the following statements on a scale of 1–5, with one being lowest and 5 being highest. Use N/A if any don't apply. Below the statement, in italics, is the indicator of an effective decision-making process that we're aspiring to demonstrate.

Indicators of Effective Decision Making	Rating
The facilitator clearly identified when we were making decisions. *Everyone is clear about decision-making moments.*	
I was clear about the empowerment level we had in making today's decision. *Everyone knows his or her level of empowerment in the decision.*	
The people who needed to be involved in this decision were present. *The right people are present—the key stakeholders and decision makers.*	
The decision-making process we used (consensus, multivoting, majority voting, compromise, unilateral decision) felt appropriate. *Everyone knows what kind of decision-making process will be used and is willing to use it.*	
Team members used active listening and paraphrasing. *The conversation has a clear structure so that the discussion is objective, is focused on ideas and facts, and doesn't become personal and emotional.*	
People listened to each other's ideas. They weren't just arguing their own points. *The conversation has a clear structure so that the discussion is objective, focused on ideas and facts, and doesn't become personal and emotional.*	
There was objective debate about ideas and healthy conflict. *Ideas are freely exchanged and considered.*	
Everyone fully participated, and there was equal participation between members. *No individual or subgroup dominates.*	
The facilitator managed unproductive conflict well. *If the decision-making process stalls, the group stops and reflects on its process and seeks ways to move forward.*	
Our time was well managed and well used. *The conversation has a clear structure so that the discussion is objective, is focused on ideas and facts, and doesn't become personal and emotional.*	
We had true closure—the decision was clear. *Discussions end with a sense of closure and clear next steps.*	

Indicators of Effective Decision Making	Rating
We closed with action plans and next steps. *Discussions end with a sense of closure and clear next steps.*	
I think that the final decision is one that everyone can live with. *Discussions end with a sense of closure and clear next steps.*	
Overall, I feel that this was a healthy and positive decision-making process. *The team engages in a reflection on the decision-making process.*	
What suggestions do you have for improving our next decision-making process? *The team engages in a reflection on the decision-making process.*	

Transformational Coaching Team, 2012

I avoided making one big decision because I was afraid that I wouldn't be able to do it effectively. It was a very sensitive decision, one I can't tell you much about—and I couldn't tell the coaches much about the factors involved, either. In one-on-one meetings, I asked each one for their input by asking general, vague questions. I dragged this out over several months, keeping myself up at night, worrying about the possible implications of my decision, questioning my leadership capacities. My self-doubt surged, and I considered an escape plan in which I wouldn't need to make the decision. But then I did, and I felt confident enough that it was the right one.

One coach approached me privately after I shared my decision with the group. "I don't think you made a good decision," the coach said. To my own surprise, I didn't crumble. I had feared this—a response that wasn't in support of my decision. I feel so uncomfortable when people don't agree with me. I was afraid of damaging the trusting relationships I'd worked so hard to develop. But as the coach explained their thinking, I noticed that I was able to just listen and hear the coach's perspective and accept it.

"I'm really glad you shared this with me, and I appreciate hearing your opinion," I said. "It was a hard decision to make, and I'm not surprised by your response. I still feel that it was the best decision to make." The moment was a little tense—I can't deny that—and that tension lingered for some time.

A year later, as I reflected on that decision, I still felt that it was the best one to make. The uncomfortable feeling with the coach had dissipated, and it didn't seem like permanent damage had been done. What felt most apparent, in reflection, was my growth as a leader. I'd made a hard decision and survived a difficult and lonely moment. It wasn't a fun part of leadership, and I prefer for everyone to agree with each other, but it also wasn't devastating. It was part of the job, and somehow I'd acquired the skills to be able to do it.

CHAPTER 9

Supporting Adult Learners

Humanities Team, 2008

Our team included a teacher who had taught for 34 years and was in her final year before retirement, another who had taught for 15 years, two teachers with 3–5 years of experience, and two first-year teachers. As I began working with this diverse group, I recognized that one of my biggest challenges would be to design meetings and learning opportunities that met each teacher's levels of knowledge and experience. Unsure of how to differentiate for adults, I drew on what I'd done when I taught middle school.

Our focus for the first year was writing. We started by compiling a list of all the strategies that were being used to teach writing. The 34-year veteran used a brainstorming process in which students explored ideas through different modalities; the novice teachers were intrigued and wanted to observe her using the process. In her credentialing program, a new teacher had learned a creative strategy to help students organize their ideas; the veteran copied her materials and implemented the approach. Although there were challenging personalities in this group and many moments of troubled communication, there was also knowledge. I wanted to surface what these teachers knew, to validate what they brought to the table, and to help them see each other as resources.

There was agreement that students weren't writing at the levels we wanted—they had vast skill gaps. I asked teachers to fill in the blanks in this statement: "If our kids can't ___ (e.g., use correct grammar, write in complete sentences, organize their ideas), then that means we need to learn how to ____." The responses included comments such as, "Well, I taught that but they don't pay attention," and "They never do homework so of course they don't know how to do this." I tried to calmly acknowledge their frustration, and then I'd ask again, "So what do we need to learn to get kids' attention?" Over and over, I asked teachers to take responsibility for their students' learning and reflect on their own areas for growth.

Although I had many areas for growth as a leader, I knew something about designing learning experiences based on my years in the classroom, and we were learning together. In between the dysfunctional moments, there were moments of reflection and growth, such as one afternoon when the teacher who was about to retire said, "I've been teaching for 34 years, and I'm just realizing that I don't know how to teach kids to think. Can we focus on this?" As I saw teaching practices shift in tiny, almost microscopic ways, I became more intrigued by working with adult learners—the challenge was enticing, as was the potential for impact on children. These kinds of moments lured me deeper into the domain of coaching. Although I was wading through a mess not exclusively of my making, the desire to facilitate learning called me as it has for as long as I can remember.

While reading this book, have you wondered whether some of these strategies for team building could be applied in contexts outside of schools? Perhaps to strengthen a team of athletes or biochemists or even your family unit? If so, I'd affirm your inclination. I've used many of these approaches for managing emotions, developing good communication, and navigating conflict with groups outside of schools. This chapter, however, addresses one area in which team development in an educational setting differs from other contexts. This is because learning is one of the primary things that teams in schools do. Whether we are in a professional learning community or a department, we come together to refine our practices as teachers, coaches, or leaders—we come together to learn. While it's true that practitioners in other fields—from the sciences to sports to for-profit companies—also learn together (and their ability to learn often correlates to their success), in the education world learning is central. Anyone facilitating teams based in or related to education settings needs strategies for working with adults as learners.

But before thinking about how to help members of a team learn together, let's take a step back and consider some key organizational conditions that could best promote team learning. What conditions need to be in place in the schools where we work to promote our work together?

THE BIG PICTURE: THE LEARNING ORGANIZATION

I aspire to build educational organizations that are *places of learning* for *everyone* within them to meet the needs of all children. Our methods of understanding student learning change in response to new learning about learning, different beliefs and values about learning, and new tools available to measure learning. Our curricular and instructional approaches change due to shifts in demographics, to developing understandings of student needs, and to new resources for delivering curriculum and instruction. The rate of change in our world has never been faster; this holds true for the rate of change in schools. The only way to navigate this change is to learn how to understand it and adapt. Successful adaptation comes from learning.

Therefore, for example, the staff in a front office may need to learn new strategies for communicating across cultural differences when the population in a community changes. As new research emerges on supporting children with dyslexia, the resource specialist needs to learn new strategies based on this research. As administrators reflect on discipline practices that lead to an overrepresentation of suspension and expulsions for African American and Latino males, they need to learn new systems for creating school culture and managing behavior. If we are not all constantly engaged in learning, we run the risk of replicating the status quo and perpetuating systems that have not served all children. Leaders can cultivate the mind-set that school systems must be *learning organizations* to be effective and that everyone is expected to be a learner.

What Is a Learning Organization?

A learning organization is essentially what it sounds like: an organization in which everyone is learning. This not only ensures that the organization survives but also helps it thrive and generates new creations (Senge, 2006). Teams reach high functioning levels because they are extraordinary *learning organizations*—the learning that a group engages in propels it to greatness. Exhibit 9.1 can help you assess the extent to which you work in a learning organization. You might use this tool to reflect on your team, your school, and your district.

Exhibit 9.1. Indicators of a Learning Organization

Rate the following indicators of a learning organization on a scale of 1–5 (1 = low, 5 = high) as they apply to you and as you perceive they apply to your colleagues.

Element	Indicator	Rating (1–5)	Evidence, Comments, Reflections
Learning Environment			
Psychological safety	We can disagree with colleagues or supervisors; we can ask any kind of question; we can make mistakes; we can express divergent opinions.		
Appreciation of differences	Our discussions surface differences in ideas; we have healthy disagreements about ideas.		
Openness to new ideas	We are encouraged to take risks and try new things, and we do so.		
Time for reflection	We take time to pause, thoughtfully reflect on our processes, and learn from our experiences.		
Feedback	We get feedback on our work from multiple sources (including from colleagues and supervisors).		
Purpose	We feel that our work matters to us personally and is connected to something bigger than us.		
Learning Processes and Practices			
Orientation	Our learning is connected to and in support of organization's core purpose.		
Generation	We learn together.		
Interpretation	We make sense of our learning together.		
Dissemination	We share what we learn with each other and outside of our group and organization.		

Element	Indicator	Rating (1–5)	Evidence, Comments, Reflections
Leadership			
Listening and questioning	Leaders prompt dialogue and debate.		
Ensuring process	Leaders ensure time for reflection, generation, interpretation, and dissemination.		
Openness	Leaders are willing to entertain alternative points of view.		
Modeling	Leaders make their learning visible and model the practices of a learner.		

Source: Based on Garvin, Edmondson, and Gino (2008).

Reflect on the Learning Organization Self-Assessment

- Which of these indicators of a learning organization are present in my school? Which are absent?

- What are the present barriers to becoming a learning organization?

- Which practices or policies need to change so that we could become a learning organization?

- What could I do to help my school become a learning organization?

- How might our school be different if we were a learning organization?

FROM THEORY TO PRACTICE

If you are a coach who works with grade-level, departmental, or whole-school teams, it may be clear that you're facilitating learning. But in some teams, neither the leader nor the members may think of themselves as learners. To build learning organizations in schools, we can consider every team that we coach or lead as a developing learning organization. For example, if you lead a site leadership team that's responsible for analyzing student data, designing and delivering professional development, and monitoring progress toward goals, you could conceive of this as a team that simply does things. You may forget that members are also *learners*.

Let's take a department in a secondary school. Departments frequently meet to discuss curriculum, hiring, and programmatic issues. However, department heads may not think about the members of their team primarily as *learners* or of department meeting times as times for *learning*. For leaders, this shift in how we think about our teams could realign how we spend our time in meetings. It also suggests that we need to know something about guiding adult learners.

What the Research Says about Adult Learners

If you look into the research on adult learning, you'll undoubtedly come across the work of Malcolm Knowles(Knowles, 2015), a pioneer in the field who identified core characteristics of adult learners. Knowles's work is useful, but his ideas are really just basic good practices for teaching people of all ages. Furthermore, many of his assumptions are culturally bound: they may not be relevant among adults in other cultures, some are male-centric, and some do not take into account generational differences, which are becoming more accentuated. Furthermore, Knowles's assumptions exist in a vacuum of power. Without considering the power structures in which learning occurs, our understandings may be shortsighted and our actions may have limited impact. With these caveats, Knowles's work is helpful and greatly informs the principles of adult learning.

> *Humans are the learning organism par excellence. The drive to learn is as strong as the sexual drive—it begins earlier and it lasts longer.*
>
> HALL (2007)

I use the term *adult learning* intentionally, in spite of the fact that many of the approaches we take to guide the learning of children are the same as when we work with grown-ups. For educators who have worked with children for many years, the term conveys a useful reminder to shift our stance when working with adults from the way we approached working with children.

The Principles of Adult Learning

The following principles, informed by the work of Malcolm Knowles and other theorists, can serve as guideposts when working with adult learners. They encompass what is known about brain science, learning theory, behavioral and cognitive psychology, and to some extent sociology. These seven principles are foundational for working with adult learners and are essential for creating high-functioning teams. Following a brief explanation of the principle, you'll see a handful of implications for team leaders. These are intended to draw some quick connections between these principles and other strategies discussed in this book. Because every suggestion in this book is based in research about how adults learn and change, you will be able to make connections to additional strategies as you read these principles.

Adults must feel safe to learn.

Our emotional states are tied to our ability to receive new information. When we feel afraid, our brains shut down to learning, and new information can't be absorbed. There are volumes of research available on what happens in our bodies and minds when we feel afraid, when someone cuts us off in a discussion, when we perceive that our leaders don't have our best interests at heart, and when we are subtly threatened with negative consequences. This research says, essentially, that in such situations our physiological response helps us survive—we might fight, take flight, or freeze—and our ability to learn decreases.

In recent years, I've observed a number of professional development trainings in which an administrator opened the session with something like, "And after today's PD we'll expect to see these strategies in action in all classrooms starting next week." Anxious glances are exchanged between teachers. One representative might ask, "And what happens if we don't master these strategies after today's PD?" The response is never clear. Rather than focusing on learning, the minds of many educators in this kind of a situation drift into fears, frustration, anger, and perhaps planning for how to respond.

This first principle of adult learning compels us to consider power dynamics in a team to evaluate psychological safety levels. In a common scenario, when the team leader (or someone on the team) holds the power to make decisions about job security, roles, and responsibilities, team members may not feel safe. A leader needs to be conscious of power dynamics and take them into account when creating learning experiences. Furthermore, if a member regularly dominates discussions and decisions, adults won't feel safe to learn. This principle is an injunction to coaches and leaders to build trust in a team. We just can't get around it.

Implications for team leaders:

- When a team is forming, use structures to invite equity of participation in discussions.

- Do everything you can to address power dynamics between yourself and your team.
- Show up as a learner in this space—you are also a learner.
- Establish and use community agreements; have a process observer during meetings.
- Pay attention to feelings and cultivate your team's emotional intelligence.

Adults come to learning experiences with histories.

Adults come to the learning process with a wide range of previous experiences, knowledge, interests, and competencies. If these relationships between the new and the old are made explicit, the learning will be deeper and more permanent. This principle is particular to adults, who have a greater depth, breadth, and variation in the quality of previous life experiences than younger people. Children, of course, have rich experiences to draw from and explore, but as we age we have a greater quantity of experiences.

This principle reminds team leaders that most educators have had experience working in teams. These previous experiences accompany adult learners wherever we go—sometimes we may be conscious of them, but often we're not. As leaders, we'd be missing an opportunity if we didn't see members' prior experiences as learners and team members as a rich resource. Discussions, for example, about previous experiences in teams (the good and bad) help members understand each other, differentiate between past and present, and create visions and goals for their work together.

In addition, acknowledging that team members hold a treasure of experience and knowledge can increase trust in our efforts. Instead of implying through our actions that our team members are empty vessels to be filled with the latest educational whatever, we can find ways to validate who they are and what they bring to the table. This principle suggests that our job is to create structures for members to share their experiences and knowledge with each other. Acting on this principle helps communicate a value each member holds useful knowledge and experiences set and can contribute to the team.

Implications for team leaders:

- Find out what team members know and can do.
- Create opportunities for people to tell stories and share past experiences.
- Invite team members to take on roles and responsibilities within the team that match their skill set.
- When a team is forming, facilitate discussions about previous experiences working in teams.

- Begin activities, discussions, and readings by asking people to activate their background knowledge and make connections between what they're learning about what they already know.

Adults need to know why we have to learn something.

Anyone who has taught middle school can anticipate a student's first question in response to most of our lessons: "Why do we have to learn this?" As children age and internalize social norms, some stop asking, but the great majority of us *think* about this every time we're asked to learn something new. For many the answer (or lack of an answer) may be the moment when we either embrace the learning or check out and start grading papers, browsing email, or daydreaming.

Many adult learners commit to learning when we believe that the objectives are realistic and important for our personal and professional needs. We need to see that what we learn through professional development is applicable to our day-to-day activities and problems. Adults can seem reluctant when we don't know why we're being asked to learn something. Whether the reason we're learning is connected to a personal interest and need or to a school's purpose, it has to be clear.

Implications for team leaders:

- Include a section on agendas that articulates the reason for each activity.
- At the start of each meeting or PD session, share your reason for the learning, and give learners an opportunity to make meaning of what they'll do and how it might help them.
- Draw a connection between that day's learning and the school's goals, mission, or vision.
- At the start of PD sessions, ask participants to identify a challenge they're facing that the day's PD might address. Ask them to reflect on their connections at the end of the session.
- Connect the learning to previous questions and challenges that members of the group have raised.

Adults want agency in our learning.

Adults want some control over the what, who, how, why, when, and where of our learning. Whenever possible, facilitators can invite input into what we do as a team, what we learn, why we do what we do, and even when and where we meet. Although a leader might make the final decisions, team members can give input. This helps members feel heard, which is often enough for them to engage and commit to learning. For team members to participate in directing their learning, they'll need to give the leader regular, honest feedback, and lines of communication will need to be open and strong.

Implications for team leaders:

- Ask team members to reflect on and share how they learn best. Be responsive to these needs.
- Guide participants to identify their areas for growth and professional learning goals.
- Ask for input and feedback in person and anonymously.
- Use all kinds of data to help adults make decisions about their learning.
- Invite people to name their colleagues with whom they want to collaborate or learn.
- Give participants surveys to assess their learning needs.

Adults need practice to internalize learning.

To internalize learning, we need direct, concrete experiences to apply what we have learned to our work—we don't automatically transfer learning into daily practice. Adult learners need feedback on our practice from someone we trust, which is precisely where coaches play a critical role. This principle is essential to remember to avoid the sinkhole of one-shot PD. Many teachers have sat through a 2-day summer training on some new curriculum or instructional approach and return to their classrooms with the expectation that they'll now implement it. Professor Linda Darling-Hammond (2009) says that, for a teacher to learn a new skill to the extent that it will positively impact student learning, he or she needs approximately 50 hours of professional development (which can include hours spent with a coach). Professional learning for educators would be transformed if we heeded this 50-hour rule.

One undervalued component of practice is reflection time. When we have opportunities for reflection (thinking, writing, and talking time), we make connections between our previous experiences and our present; we identify the why for which we're engaging in learning; we connect learning components and uncover solutions to our problems (Garvin, 1993).

Implications for team leaders:

- On any agenda, include time to practice new skills and time to reflect.
- Reduce the number of objectives on an agenda.

- Contain the new information to less than a third of the meeting time, and use the rest of the time to practice, make meaning of the information, and draw connections.

- Close learning sessions with quiet writing time, and ask participants to name their takeaways and ideas about how they'll apply their learning.

- Use structures such as role-plays where participants give each other feedback.

Adults have a problem-centered orientation to learning.

Because of our life and work experience, many adults have a task-centered or problem-centered orientation to learning. When trainings are developed around problem solving, then we grapple with content with the intention of using it. We can be highly motivated to acquire new skills if we think they'll help us solve an issue we're struggling with.

Because we're problem centered and have limited time, when many of us attend a PD session or meeting we want to feel like we are getting something useful out of it. Facilitators have to balance this with the need to engage in deep learning. Sometimes PD or meetings that are action oriented and provide quick fixes and tools are superficial. We need time for learning and reflection that allow us to explore the root causes to our challenges and to make transformational change.

This is one area of adult learning, however, where the theorists disagree. Tennant (1988) suggests that adults are able to tolerate the postponed application of knowledge because of an innate fascination with learning. He challenges Knowles's assumption that our approach to learning is so strictly utilitarian and suggests that our motivation to learn is far more expansive and comprehensive. This is a useful reminder that in most groups there's a range of people. There are some who urgently need (demand!) activities, tools, and strategies they can use the next day, and there are some who thrive in contemplative, imaginative activities that may not have immediate application but that satisfy a part of their learning self.

Implications for team leaders:

- Facilitate processes for educators to identify the problems in their schools, teams, or departments.

- Engage team members in naming their individual challenges and areas for growth.

- Balance meeting time that builds skill that can be applied immediately with opportunities for reflection.

- Use structures such as the consultancy protocol (in Appendix E.1), which blend depth of thinking with application.
- Use role-play practices or other experiential activities that simulate real challenges.

Adults want to learn.

As human beings, we are intrinsically inquisitive: we want to learn from the time we are born, and we love to learn. It is our role as facilitators to spark this desire in others. Sometimes recognizing a will for learning in others can be hard—some adults show up to team meetings and PD sessions reluctant to learn—but we need to remember that it is there and will emerge when the conditions are right.

Remembering that adults come to learning experiences with history can be helpful. If some of those prior learning experiences were negative, then there's a chance the learner may not be open to new learning. Regardless, it's our responsibility to do all we can to create a safe environment, to articulate purpose, to invite past experience and already existing knowledge, to offer choices, to make the learning relevant, and to provide opportunities so that the learning can be internalized. All human beings at some level really do want to learn.

Implications for team leaders:

> *People who don't take risks generally make about two big mistakes a year. People who do take risks generally make about two big mistakes a year.*
>
> PETER DRUCKER

- If someone seems uninterested in learning, keep reminding yourself that all adults want to learn.
- If there's low interest in learning, consider the conditions for learning—is the learning relevant? Have participants had a say in their learning? Do they feel safe?
- Find out what team members want to learn about—keep asking and asking.
- Ask about previous learning experiences—as an adult and a child.
- Whenever possible, make learning fun.

COMMON CHALLENGES

Coaches face a number of common challenges in designing and facilitating learning spaces. Let's consider how to respond to a handful of those.

Designing PDs That Meet a Learner's Developmental Stage

The Russian psychologist Lev Vygotsky introduced the concept of the zone of proximal development (ZPD): the area that falls between what a learner can't do and what a learner can do independently. This concept is often used when teaching children, but it is equally useful when thinking about adult learning. Whenever I'm coaching someone and I make a suggestion for something he or she might practice, I make that suggestion based on what I know about his or her skill set—I aim for the ZPD. I plan on guiding him or her through that practice and providing the necessary scaffolding, but I want to make sure I'm not asking the person to do something he or she cannot accomplish, even with my support. As we start practicing, I can quickly tell whether my aim was correct—I can see whether the person is able to practice the skill with my support or whether the task is too easy or too hard. If so, I adjust my approach.

A team also has a ZPD. As the facilitator, you provide the structure for participants to collaboratively engage in learning. You'll want to pay close attention to how and when they struggle to ensure that you're in their ZPD as much as possible. For example, you might ask yourself, "Can this team do this (e.g., engage in a discussion protocol) with my facilitation and support? Can the members together make meaning of the student work they've brought to share with the short protocol I've provided, or does it need to be more spelled out and more heavily facilitated?"

The concept of the ZPD also invites us to reflect on the scaffolding we provide a team. For example, teams that are high functioning may work fine with lighter facilitation, looser discussion protocols, and more fluid, emergent agendas. Teams in the forming stage probably need more structure and scaffolding as they come together and norm. In this case, the ZPD corresponds to a developmental stage.

Perhaps for facilitators one of the key ideas to hold is this: Whenever something isn't working in a team of adults, it probably reflects a learning area of our own. Maybe we've been overestimating a team's ability to work together (e.g., the team's ZPD is narrower than we thought), or perhaps individuals in a team haven't bought into the work they're doing together (e.g., they haven't been able to give input or have choice in their learning). If we can make this shift from looking for external factors to blame (It's those resistant teachers! It's the principal's mandates!) to our own sphere of control and influence, we'll likely be much more effective.

Using an Assets-Based Approach

We can think about change in two basic ways: We can focus on what we're doing wrong and try to do less of it, or we can focus on what we're doing right and try to do more of it. Researchers in many fields have found that by focusing on strengths, talents, competencies, and things we're doing right we are far more likely to make long-lasting change. And a good way to start thinking about designing adult learning is with an assets-based or strengths perspective.

It's useful to understand why an assets-based approach works—and it comes back to the way our brains are wired. When we're focusing on what we're not good at, at our deficiencies and areas of struggle, negative neural pathways—the ones that produce self-defeating statements like, "I'm such a failure; this won't work; I know I'm not good at X, and I've been trying to get better for many years; What's wrong with me? Why am I so bad at this?"—are reinforced. Take just a moment to think about something you've tried improving in (perhaps eating healthier or getting more exercise) and notice how that internal dialogue amplifies. The majority of us are well aware of our areas of weakness, and casting more light on them creates distress. This decreases our ability to take action, to learn, and to see possibilities. It's not that we can't learn when we focus on areas for growth, but there's more struggle. We're at odds with our brain.

When we focus on our strengths, we can access the positive emotions that inspire action and open us to learning. Assets-based coaching strives to magnify strengths assuming that what we focus on grows. In partnership with our client, we seek out what's working, effective practices, and hidden skills. We want to be careful that we're not doing too much pointing. Although sometimes we might shed light on a strength, our clients need to see and embrace their strengths to really benefit from them.

When I became a coach, I focused almost exclusively on closing the big gaps in a teacher's instructional practices. I thought we needed to start with the areas of greatest need—and deficits command a lot of attention. In addition, many of our organizational cultures are focused exclusively on what's not working, what we need to improve on, and the big goals we have to reach. We're constantly reminded that we're never meeting our goals, always underperforming, and still facing a Grand Canyon–sized gap. These messages trigger individual and group emotional experiences of shame, failure, and hopelessness, emotions that are rarely inspirational and certainly not transformational. Using shame as a means to produce positive results has never worked, and shame as a management tool has contributed to a whole slew of messes in schools.

I now primarily coach strengths and look for the places where we can use those strengths as a foundation to explore an area of growth. For example, if a teacher is struggling to build productive relationships with parents, I will first coach him to strengthen relationships with his colleagues—which might already be solid and positive. I'll work with him to identify the moves he makes to develop relationships with peers, and then slowly we'll transfer those skills to working with parents. I'll use the positive emotions about the relationships he's developed with colleagues to build confidence in his areas for growth and to develop concrete skills and actions.

When we focus on strengths, clients naturally enlarge their vision to include the areas in the periphery of strengths, their own areas for growth. They move toward them as they come into focus—we don't have to push. Assets-based coaching isn't about ignoring the areas of greatest need; rather, it's about first solidifying strengths, helping someone cultivate a growth mind-set and developing the momentum needed to successfully tackle areas for growth.

See what happens if you start with yourself—focus on building your strengths and doing more of what you're doing well. And then see what happens if you use this approach with individuals or a team. I promise it will feel a whole lot better, and you will see positive changes.

Holding Others Accountable

Leaders struggle to hold others accountable—especially if we're in a role such as a coach or department head where we may not feel we have the positional authority. Sometimes our supervisors ask us to hold team members accountable, and other times we feel it's part of our role. If you've experienced this tension, then I hope what I'm about to share will come as a relief: *You can't hold anyone accountable to anything.* People always have a choice about what they do and what they think. If you give up the question—*How can I hold others accountable?*—you'll have a lot more energy to direct in productive places.

The opposite of accountability is commitment. People respond to demands by choosing commitment, compliance, or the appearance of compliance (Showkeir and Showkeir, 2008). When we choose commitment, we are held accountable because we choose to be, not because of someone else's perceived authority. We make progress toward our goals because of our passion, energy, and enthusiasm.

When we choose compliance, we do what we are told because we like our boss or are afraid of his authority. We're motivated by fear (of losing our job, a relationship, or a position), or we might do what's asked of us because we're afraid of being seen as uncooperative. Our motivation is extrinsic as we do acceptable work, focus on getting along with others, and do what we're told.

We may also choose the appearance of compliance so that we appear to be accountable. We are driven by fear, frustration, or anger. What we are asked to do often makes no sense, so we find workarounds or undermine initiatives. We spend time trying to recruit others to our views and use our energy to highlight everything that's wrong or not working.

Since the Industrial Revolution, organizations (including most school systems) have been built based on a prevailing philosophy that adults won't choose accountability on their own and therefore must be bribed, coerced, or threatened. This reflects a cynical view of human beings' will, and most of us who have worked in schools or large organizations have seen that this view doesn't get us where we need to go.

Compliance won't transform schools. We can't hold others accountable for anything, and we waste a lot of energy trying to devise measures of accountability. Leaders can facilitate conversations about individual commitment and can ask new questions starting with, "What am I willing to be held accountable for?" As team leaders build cultures of learning, many people choose accountability. They choose to learn, and there's a greater likelihood that they'll make commitments that will benefit all children.

DEALING WITH RESISTANCE

The question I'm most often asked about coaching and team development is, "How do you deal with resistance?"

First, let's name the behaviors that we often perceive as resistance. To me, it looks and sounds like claiming confusion, questioning rationale, questioning competence, giving superficial compliance, and never being satisfied with information. If a conversation can't focus on the content or the issue, I sense resistance. Agreeing to do something but never taking action is a form of passive-aggressive resistance. In some, resistance takes the form of attacking the messenger, getting angry, and blaming others. Resistance also sounds like changing the subject, denying a difficult reality, rambling, and jumping to conclusions. When I'm given one-word answers or someone else goes silent, I experience this as resistance.

The strategies I've offered in this book can go a long way to create the kinds of teams where communication is direct and effective and resistance is rare. However, sometimes we'll need time to create those healthy communities. Here are some ways of understanding and dealing with resistance.

Look Inward

When you find yourself thinking, "Why are they so resistant?" first look at your own leadership. How are you showing up with this group? What kinds of judgments have you made about them? When facing resistance, notice your feelings. Do you want to avoid it? Are you inclined to charge forward and tackle it? How are you managing these feelings, and how might your team experience your feelings? In any situation we have the most control over how we think, feel, and respond. Start there.

Resistance Masks Fear

Resistance is a camouflaged expression of underlying emotional distress, particularly fear. When emotional concerns are expressed directly or there's open disagreement, this isn't resistance—it's just disagreement. Resistance is an *indirect expression* of fear, concern, or anger.

When you sense resistance in others, activate your compassion for them. Compassion might be the most underused resource in school transformation. It allows us to make connections, have empathy, seek understanding, and listen. Resistance in others is strengthened by anger, lecturing, counterarguments, and placating—compassion can prevent us from wandering into these ineffective places. When I experience resistance in others, I've learned to say to myself, "This person is afraid of something. I wonder what's going on," and then I'm no longer dealing with resistance—I'm dealing with powerful emotions.

What Looks Like Resistance Is Often a Need for Help

Before making the assumption that someone's behavior is a reflection of their *will* (i.e., before designating them as a resister), consider whether he or she has the *abilities* to do what is being asked of them. To effectively implement something, we need the knowledge and skills to do so, the emotional intelligence to manage the feelings that come up, and the capacity to do what we're being asked to do. Sometimes if someone has a skill gap—for example, a teacher just doesn't know how to teach English learners—it can show up as a *will gap*.

Changes and new initiatives often incur an implementation dip, as Michael Fullan (2014) calls it. This is a small setback during a change process. During this time, learners can appear resistant if they aren't getting the right kind of help. I've found that this happens when I haven't provided enough scaffolding for learning or enough practice. The pushback I get from a team or an individual really means, "I want to do this well and I'm trying, but I can't yet. I need more help."

Be Clear

It's true that some people block collaboration by asking endless questions and being perpetually confused—no amount of information is ever enough. And it's also true that sometimes leaders don't provide enough information or aren't clear. It can be hard to tell whether questions are an attempt to block a process or truly a request for more needed information.

If you find yourself in this situation, reflect on the questions you receive: Are they logistical and technical or substantive? How are you communicating your answers? Ask for feedback from team members and talk individually with those who have many questions and really listen to understand their questions. Also consider your personality type (see Chapter 2) and that of the person asking a lot of questions. Because of my personality type, I often need less information for me to buy in to a project, whereas other personality types need more. I've learned that questions can come from a genuine need for more information to secure true commitment.

Trust Reduces Resistance

I've found that it really helps my own will and resolve to remember some lessons from social science and neuroscience: Human beings want to be with others, and we crave trusting relationships the same way we want nourishing food. Then the question about resistance becomes how do I create spaces for trusting relationships to flourish? How do I increase my team's trust in me as its leader?

Perhaps a plan for building trust is the most important kind of strategic plan we could create. Perhaps if we spend time strategically planning for building resilient, trusting communities we'll deal with less resistance.

Confront Cynicism

Some teachers have become disenchanted. They may have once been enthusiastic about change and might have supported three or four initiatives until the efforts ended or were thwarted. Perhaps a beloved principal left or their team was disbanded or funding ran out. Although they became disenchanted, teachers in this group can reengage in a healthy way.

If you are working with cynical team members, start with committed, deep listening. When I first coached disenchanted teachers, I tried to hurry this stage, which didn't work. We need to take the time to help people process their disenchantment and find other ways to think about those unsatisfying experiences. We can help teachers think about change in a way that's empowering so that they don't show up as cynical and resistant.

Reflect on Team Structures

If you're feeling resistance from more than one team member, reflect on how the team operates: Is there space, time, and structure for healthy conflict about ideas? Is there clarity around decision-making processes? Do you regularly ask for feedback on your facilitation and leadership? Are you responsive to the feedback you get? Do team members have input into what happens in the team? Are team members clear about the team's purpose and have they bought into it? Most likely, there are actions you can take with your team to reduce the resistance.

Don't Focus on the Resisters—Focus on Those around Them

Often resistant teachers build a following. They rally others to whatever cause they're championing and create friction and factions among staff. However, I've seen staff cultures shift over a period of years when leaders focus on those who are receptive to change. Create the teams and spaces for those who are onboard to come together away from the resisters; provide time for them to learn together and develop healthy ways of being together. Focus on the willing and some of the others might follow.

Know That Some People Are Not Coachable

For some teachers and leaders, the conditions that allow them to be open, vulnerable learners are not present in that particular time and place. Perhaps they were once receptive learners and they could be again. But perhaps in the moment you're in with them, for whatever reasons that may or may not have to do with you and your school, they aren't open to learning. You can't make people learn.

Sometimes leaders and coaches have to accept someone's resistance to learning and change. It may or may not be within the parameters of your role to give them an ultimatum. If you are the principal of a school, you might be able to say, "It's an expectation that everyone at our school engages in a process of learning," and take whatever appropriate actions you can. If you're a department head or coach, this decision lies outside of your purview. You may need to skillfully consider how to bring an administrator into the conversation, or you may need to just accept the resistance, let it go, and focus on where you have control and influence.

Battling Resistance Is a Futile Endeavor

If someone's resistance has a negative impact on a group or obstructs change that can benefit children, then your responsibility is to explore it, reflect on your own leadership, address cynicism, and create the conditions for learning. Use all your communication and emotional intelligence skills to address the resistance. However, engaging in a battle with a resistor is useless.

Once you feel yourself in a battle with a trainee or a team, you've already lost. Battles mean that psychological barriers have been erected: those behind the barricades are looking for ways to defend and protect themselves. If you get to this point, surrender. You can't win, and it'll exhaust you. It takes two to battle. Don't walk onto that field.

Distinguish between Individual Resistance and a Toxic Organization

High numbers of resistant staff are commonly found in highly dysfunctional, toxic organizations where communication has been ineffective for a long time. When I'm told that there are a lot of resistors in a school or district, I ask questions about systems, structures, and leaders. It is also in these places where I've seen coaches asked to play a fix-it role—they are often directed to work with the most struggling and sometimes difficult teachers.

The responsibility to remedy a dysfunctional system cannot be heaped upon one person. If you are dealing with a lot of resistors and a dysfunctional system, you need to find others who can support you and with whom you can partner. You also need to draw boundaries around what kind of behavior you will and will not tolerate. It always helps to be compassionate, but being compassionate doesn't mean that others can be abusive. If resisters become mean and nasty, we don't have to stay in their presence. If you say to a teacher, "I'd really like to hear more about your feelings around this decision because I want to support you," and the teacher says, "There's nothing I want to share with you, and I don't want your support. I never asked for it. I don't think you should be a coach anyway," you can say, "I hear your anger. It's probably better that we don't have this conversation right now." I'm not suggesting that you avoid conflict or dismiss anger, but you can draw boundaries around how you are treated.

Without one another, we risk bitterness. With one another, we have the opportunity to stay vulnerable, stay determined, stay the course.

MARTIN (2010)

What we often experience as resistance is a big challenge in schools and teams. It can prevent us from navigating change, making important decisions, addressing problems, and facing big dilemmas. When resistance prevents us from learning together, it blocks our efforts at transformation. Resistance is a symptom of something going on for an individual and sometimes for an organization—it's like the tip of an iceberg. If we feel like we're facing a lot of resistance, it's also an opportunity for us to turn inward and look at ourselves as leaders, to look out at the system, and to look deeper into the resistor. When we take such a holistic and systemic approach to responding to resistance, we're much more likely to make meaningful changes.

Transformational Coaching Team, 2013

Coaches took turns bringing dilemmas for consultancy, and that week Noelle, who was a leadership coach, shared a challenge she was grappling with. The new site leader she coached seemed overly concerned about her physical safety in her school. She'd refused an office on the street side of the building because she feared a stray bullet might hit her, she asked the security guard to walk her to her car every evening, and she wouldn't close her door when meeting with parents out of concern that they would lose control. Noelle worried that the leader's fears were impeding her ability to connect with students and families.

Furthermore, Noelle wondered about the race dynamics: the student population was 100% Latino and African American, and the leader was white. How might the leader's fears (which seemed exaggerated to Noelle) impact how she viewed and worked with our middle school students? If she perceived the adults in the community as criminals, would she project those assumptions onto the children who lived there? Given that the leader played a role in discipline, would she lean more heavily toward punitive responses to behavior because of the beliefs she held? Finally, was she aware of the implicit bias she carried and how this affected the way she felt? And if not, how could Noelle help raise her awareness?

Consultancies always yielded rich discussion and surfaced the complexities of the dilemmas facing us. Following the discussion, I grouped coaches into trios and sent them off to different corners of the office to role-play Noelle's scenario. When Angela played the role of the coach, her approach led the leader to get defensive and shut down. When Dave played the coach, his kindness and compassion didn't shift the leader's thinking. When Michele was the coach, the conversation went around in circles.

As I observed these three role-playing, I wondered how to identify the skills and knowledge that they were missing. When we regrouped as a team and debriefed the experience, I asked, "I guess I'm wondering if you feel like you have the skills to address the reflections of racism when they appear?" Without pause, Dave responded,

---

"I don't. I know I don't." Michele chimed in, "Me either." Heads shook around the table. I shared that this was also an area I wanted to grow in. "OK," I said. "So what do we already know, and what do we need to know?" I opened my notebook and picked up a pen. With input from the coaches, I designed a plan for learning to increase our capacity to take up perhaps the most challenging of coaching conversations. There was knowledge and experience in the room already—I knew I could draw from that, and there were learning gaps that we could close.

Several months later, after much reading, discussion, and practice, we returned to Noelle's scenario and role-played it again. By repeating the activity that had launched us onto this learning path, coaches recognized their growth. "These are still conversations that make me nervous," Michele said in reflection, "And I need a lot more practice, but I feel a little more confident."

"It's been so helpful in these role-plays to hear all the different ways these conversations can go," Han said. "I feel like I have all of you in my head now, and I can remember what you said and try using your strategies when I need."

In reflection, I also recognized my own growth as a facilitator of adult learning. I could identify the elements that allowed this to be an effective learning experience: the need for learning had emerged from an authentic situation, they had input into the goals for the learning, the content could have a meaningful impact on students, and coaches were given time to practice the skills they were striving to acquire. Although I could still improve in many aspects of designing a learning experience, I acknowledged the growth I'd made.

CHAPTER 10

Orchestrating Meaningful Meetings

Humanities Team, 2009

Partway through that first year, in an attempt to differentiate professional development, I divided the members of this team into two groups during our meeting times. Those who wanted support on instructional planning and design worked with an administrator—Bess and Margaret joined this group—and those who wanted to engage in an inquiry project worked with me.

For several months, we dug into the kinds of activities I'd envisioned offering this team. Participating alongside teachers (I was also teaching a class), we each identified a handful of students who were not succeeding and set out to understand the obstacles in their way. We learned to use new tools for assessing reading comprehension and uncovered learning gaps that had been obscured for years—such as an eighth grader's inability to decode. We had conversations that revealed our misconceptions about students, and we challenged each other to try new approaches. We designed lessons together and then analyzed the student work that was produced. We observed each other teaching and provided encouraging feedback and observations about the specific student the teacher was focused on. We constructed questions for interviews with our students and their parents and then shared the results and our insights into our students. And as our inquiry proceeded, we saw our students learn.

What a difference it made, I reflected, to share a purpose.

Recall some meetings or professional development sessions you've attended as a participant, from which you left thinking, "That was a good meeting." What made the meeting a good one? Some years ago, I asked a group of teachers this question. Their responses were as follows:

- I knew why I had to go and I knew what we were going to do.
- The facilitator was organized and prepared.
- The furniture was arranged to foster collaboration.
- The room was clean and there were snacks.
- We had a realistic agenda and stuck to it.
- We started and ended on time.
- The meeting opened with a transition activity, but we didn't spend too long settling in and getting to work.
- We did something—not just talk or listen to someone else talk.
- There were structures that invited equitable participation.
- I learned something new.
- I could see how our meeting might impact kids in a positive way.
- We had a meaningful closing, and I gave the facilitator feedback.
- I left feeling energized, hopeful, and connected to other people.

What would you add to this list?

A first step in holding meaningful meetings is to know what you're trying to create. This chapter explores how to design and facilitate meetings to which team members arrive early and from which they leave smiling. Appendix D can be used when you are creating an agenda and when you lead meetings.

TO MEET OR NOT TO MEET?

We all dread meetings that feel like a waste of time. If you're going to convene a group of people, make sure you are clear about why they all need to meet at the same time, and then make that reason clear for those who attend. What will they do that can happen only if they're physically gathered together?

Sometimes a group is summoned to receive information. Perhaps next year's calendar needs to be presented or information about a specific student needs to be shared. In some cases, a meeting may not be necessary. If the information is sensitive and important to discuss, come together. If the content is something you want team members to talk about, come together. Otherwise, send an email. Don't convene a group just to talk at them: being a passive recipient of information only makes us dislike meetings.

One reason that leaders call a meeting to share information is because they are concerned that unless everyone is in the same room the information may not be received by all staff. Many times I've heard leaders say, "People don't read it if I send an email." I'm sure that some of us are guilty of not reading such emails. Here's what I say to staff and team members on this issue: "To attend fewer meetings that feel like a waste of time, we need to take responsibility for reading whatever we're asked to read. We'll need to agree to check school email on a daily basis. Is this something we can all agree to?"

Leaders also need to check that recipients read and understand what is shared. When I send an email to a team with information, I ask recipients to respond to me with one question and one comment, and I give them a date and time by which this must happen. This shifts accountability onto others—they play a role in having meaningful meetings. My part is to write up the information I need them to have and to be succinct and clear, and their part is to read it and respond.

Given how many tools we have for communication in the digital world, we should see fewer meetings in which we're not learning or actively engaged in problem solving. Leaders can be creative to ensure that information is received; team members can take responsibility for receiving information. The purpose for a meeting should not be to sit and listen to someone talking; there's way too much meaningful work we can do together.

WHY MEET?

The reasons for meeting fall into six big buckets: to share information, to learn something, to solve problems, to make decisions, to plan, and to build community. Some teams, like Professional Learning Communities (PLCs), meet primarily to learn together, whereas others, like leadership teams, engage in a variety of purposes in one meeting. The first step in planning a meeting is to decide on the big-bucket purpose for the meeting, which should be determined by the work plan (see Chapter 4). Exhibit 10.1 illustrates how a semester of meetings connects to a team's work plan.

Exhibit 10.1. Example of a Team's Meeting Schedule

The fifth-grade team at Rise Up Elementary School planned its meetings for the first semester of the year based on its work plan (see Exhibit 4.7). Team members met for 2 hours every week on their school's early release day. They spent 15 minutes of each meeting building community with each other or practicing strategies to cultivate emotional resilience. They also spent 10–15 minutes when necessary taking care of business such as testing schedules and field trips. In the remaining time, they engaged in the following activities.

Date	Work Plan Goal Number and Outcomes (See Exhibit 4.7)	What (Activities)
OCTOBER		
First Tuesday	Goal 1: To figure out how we're going to learn more about our focal students. Goal 2: To observe each other's focal students during the Month of Compassion unit.	• Design interviews we're going to do with focal students. • Design protocol for observations during Month of Compassion unit.
Second Tuesday	Goal 1: To gain a deeper understanding of our focal students. To co-plan a reading comprehension lesson and access each other's knowledge and skills.	• Share interviews with focal students. • Plan science text reading comprehension lesson.
Third Tuesday	Goal 1: To gain insight into our focal students by hearing what others observed. Goal 2: To observe each other's focal students during a lesson on the Month of Compassion. Goal 2: To divide up tasks around planning for November's service learning activities.	• Share observations of each other's focal students during reading lesson and lesson on Month of Compassion. • Plan for November service learning activities.

Date	Work Plan Goal Number and Outcomes (See Exhibit 4.7)	What (Activities)
OCTOBER		
Fourth Tuesday	Goal 1: To get feedback on our teaching (and encouragement) from sharing our videos with the team. Goal 2: To get to know our and each other's focal students better.	• Share video recordings of the lesson we taught. • Debrief the overnight trip, and share observations of each other's focal students.

Next, determine the outcomes or objectives for the meeting. When articulating the wording of an objective or outcome, I look for verbs that are clear and precise and that give participants an indication of the level of thinking that they'll be engaging in. I also use verbs that indicate particular activities. We identify, review, report, and discuss. Whenever possible, I avoid the verb *understand,* because as a facilitator it's hard for me to know at the end of a meeting whether I achieved my intended outcome. Exhibit 10.2 offers examples of outcomes for different team meetings.

I use a variety of possible agenda formats, choosing the format for a given meeting depending on the team and its needs. Sometimes purpose and outcomes are listed at the top of the agenda, and sometimes I embed purpose within the document (see, e.g., Exhibit 5.2 and Exhibit 8.1).

Exhibit 10.2. Outcomes for Team Meetings

Team	Outcomes for Meeting
School leadership team	• To analyze teacher retention data to inform our plan for next year's new teacher support systems. • To assess the impact of our PD on reading comprehension in Semester 1 so that we can revise our plan for Semester 2. • To understand the work plans for each department so that we can support each other and hold each other accountable. • To analyze student attendance data so we can modify our advisory curriculum. • To make decisions about next year's master schedule.

(continued)

Team	Outcomes for Meeting
School administrative team	• To understand the new protocol for receiving new students and agree on a schedule. • To decide on the teacher evaluation calendar and align our practices for evaluations. • To review office referral data and identify the key moments in the day when we need to be in the halls. • To discuss the conflict we had last week in the staff meeting and identify next steps. • To understand each other's leadership history and styles so that we can align on our roles and empathize with each other.
District math leadership team	• To report on the implementation of the new math curriculum and share challenges and successes. • To plan for district-wide professional development on new curriculum. • To decide on a focus area for the second semester's PD for teachers. • To review the new assessment tools, clarify confusion about the process, and plan for how to introduce these to teachers.

When meetings fail, vague or missing outcomes can be the culprit: sometimes it's because these aren't clear in the leader's mind; other times they just aren't effectively communicated. An agenda can also have too many outcomes; when in doubt, cut and prune your objectives. As you open a meeting and review why the team has gathered, you can get feedback on your effort to communicate purpose by asking, "Does anyone have questions about why we're meeting today or what we hope to accomplish?"

When I plan a meeting, I strive to connect what we'll do at that meeting with the children we work with. Sometimes this end goal becomes obscured. Regardless of the team, I ask myself, "How does what we'll do here today connect with student learning? How can our meeting serve the needs of children?" Even when our discussion feels distant from the student experience, I keep this in my mind. It helps me stay focused and invested in the work.

Finally, when I'm thinking about outcomes, I also imagine what I want team members to say about the meeting as they walk into the parking lot together. I call these my unstated outcomes, which are often about the emotional experience I want to create. I think about how I want participants to leave feeling inspired, connected to each other, aware of their learning and growth, and excited about their work.

Scribbling these kinds of outcomes on the side of my notes ensures that they don't get lost in my planning.

As I plan I think about what might be evidence that these intentions were met. I imagine teachers lingering in the room after the training has ended, still sharing ideas with each other, laughing, and making plans to visit each other's classrooms. This imagining helps reinforce my planning process—what do I need to do during the meeting to see this happen at the end? How will I make it safe for teachers to invite each other to their classrooms? How will I create an atmosphere that invites laughter? This leads me to plan and review my agenda with these intentions in mind. I might select an opening activity that will evoke laughter and silliness, or I might invite a discussion around what we need to feel safe visiting each other's classrooms. I plan backward from the emotional experience I want people to have—as well as from that meeting's objectives.

WHICH ACTIVITIES SHOULD WE DO?

After naming the meeting's purpose and identifying its outcomes, you need to make choices about which activities will lead team members to these outcomes. Other chapters in this book include descriptions of activities you can use in meetings. For activities on decision making, see Chapter 8. For activities that support learning, also see Chapter 9. For activities that support community building, also see Chapter 3. Here I'll share some activities that are applicable to many different kinds of teams—from a department, to a leadership team, to a central office curriculum team. I'll describe the activity, discuss why you might select it, and offer some tips on how to lead those activities. Then I'll explore how to make decisions about selecting activities for a meeting.

Some of these activities align primarily with one purpose—for example, using a protocol for a discussion about a text is an activity that helps people learn. Many can be used for multiple purposes: they can both help a team learn and make a decision; they can both help build community and problem solve. Appendix F provides a list of books containing additional activities.

Making Meaning

Purpose: Learning, information sharing, planning, decision making, problem solving

We make meaning primarily in two ways—through talking and writing. These are both forms of reflection and mental processing that allow us to sort through thoughts, make connections to prior knowledge, surface questions, and arrive at new understandings. Meaning making can be brief or extended.

Most people benefit from engaging in a combination of talking and writing, sometimes in that order and sometimes in the reverse order. I often incorporate poetry in meetings. Sometimes I ask people to read the poem, then talk to a partner, and then capture a written reflection. Other times I invite people to write first and then talk. It's useful to know that in general extroverts prefer to talk first (and sometimes only to talk and not write) and that introverts often need quiet time to write or think before they talk to others. I often do a quick poll at the outset of a meeting with a new group, asking those who know they are extroverts to raise their hands. When I work with groups composed entirely of extroverts, I adjust my processes to accommodate their preferences.

Exhibit 10.3 presents a structure you can use with a variety of inputs—student work, a rubric, an article, a data spreadsheet, a master schedule, a testing calendar.

Exhibit 10.3. Meaning-Making Protocol

I. Read and Think:

1. Connections: Read the text and note connections. Connections are anything you've heard about before. If you'd like, code the text with a "C" at those points.
2. Questions: Read the text and note your questions on the side or on a sticky note.
   a. Determine which questions are clarifying questions—you need information or the definition of a term (indicate these with a "C?") and which questions are Big Questions—probing or reflective and probably in need of discussion (you can note these with a "B?").
3. Feelings: Read the text and notice any feelings that come up. Note those on the side or on a sticky note.

II. Talk and Share:

4. Turn to a partner and share your connections.
5. Share connections with the whole group.
6. Turn to a partner and share your clarifying questions. If your partner can answer your clarifying question, cross it off.

7. With the whole group, share your clarifying questions and see if others can answer them.

8. With your partner, share your big questions. Identify the biggest of your big questions you think the team should discuss. Write this one down on a sticky note and give it to the facilitator. The facilitator can decide when to address them.

9. Turn to a partner and acknowledge the feelings that surfaced. Just listen to each other and hold space for the feelings without trying to fix them or make them go away. If either of you feels that it would benefit the team to share some of your emotional responses, offer these in a whole-group discussion.

Look back at Exhibit 10.2. Which outcomes listed in this table will likely require a process for making meaning? It's likely, I think, that to reach just about all of these outcomes you'd need to provide team members with an opportunity to make meaning from the content at hand. Too often this meaning-making stage is skipped because a facilitator perceives that there are too many decisions to make and just too much to get done. Even though there might be a lot to do, we have to consider that if we don't understand what we're doing there may not be much point. Whether we are receiving information, planning, problem solving, making decisions, or learning something together, we need time to make meaning.

Identifying Implications

Purpose: Learning, information sharing, planning, decision making, problem solving

After using a process such as the meaning-making protocol to understand a document or text, leaders need to guide a team in drawing conclusions and identifying implications. Even if we've simply offered a poem, we might want to ask, "What might this poem suggest for your work?" or "Based on the meaning you made of this poem, are there any actions you might want to take?" We offer texts, rubrics, and data so that people will get new ideas that will manifest in their practice. This process also requires guidance.

When looking at data such as student work or assessment results, there are additional questions to consider before drawing conclusions. The National School Reform Faculty (http://www.nsrfharomony.org) offers a simple data analysis tool called Data Driven Dialogue. This protocol guides teachers through making predictions, observations, and inferences. It is easy to use, fosters real dialogue, and can result in meaningful decisions.

Then we consider implications and next steps for our work. These questions can prompt a team to explore implications. You may need to modify the language so that it is appropriate to the task—some of these questions are useful when analyzing data, whereas others apply to items such as a rubric or calendar.

Determining Implications

- What are some of the conclusions we can draw from the meaning we've made?

- What does this imply for our work? Brainstorm as many implications as possible.

- Of these implications, which might most serve children and particularly our most vulnerable children?

- Of these implications, which are closest to our sphere of influence and control?

- Of these implications, for which do we already have the skills and knowledge to execute the ideas?

Implications often lead us on a path to decision making. If you're facilitating this process, be very clear about how the decision will be made (see Chapter 8). Engaging in meaning making and determining implications before making decisions can result in sound decisions.

Consultancy Protocol

Purpose: Problem solving, decision making

The consultancy protocol (Appendix E) offers a highly structured way for a team to think through and discuss a dilemma. This is a powerful way to prepare to make decisions, as it surfaces root causes behind problems. I have used it in many contexts: with teams of coaches, administrators, and teachers and with leadership and grade-level teams.

I love this structure for many reasons: it engages a group of people in rigorous thinking and deep conversation; it helps people see their situation in entirely new ways; it often results in solutions to problems that no one had ever considered; and it builds community. There's a good kind of accountability built into this structure. Teammates tend to want to support each other, so they participate actively; however, parameters also create equitable participation.

This protocol takes some time to master. Be sure to closely follow the suggestions for facilitation—they've been thoroughly tried and tested, and there are often multiple reasons for each suggestion. For example, the request for the presenter to move her chair away from the group or turns her back to it allows her to have private thinking space and not be put on the spot to respond in a discussion. It also allows the group more freedom in talking. Although some groups initially grumble about sending the presenter out, I encourage you to try it a dozen times before you abandon the practice.

Ensuring that clarifying questions are truly clarifying questions also takes some practice. At first it can feel awkward to cut off a questioner and tell him that his question is a probing question, but to protect the presenter this is necessary. I always say, "That's a good question—but it's a probing question, so save it for the discussion." Of course, clarifying and probing questions can overlap. As a facilitator, I pay attention to how the presenter seems to receive the question. If she can blurt out the answer quickly, it is probably a clarifying question. And if she pauses, gazes up, or responds with a long answer, it's probably not.

The first few times you use this protocol, make sure to debrief the experience with your team. Ask how they think the process could be improved next time. As team members rotate through the roles—as they get a turn to present and perhaps to facilitate—they'll buy in to the structure.

My website has a video of me leading a team of coaches in a consultancy protocol.

The Feedback Protocol

Purpose: Learning, problem solving, planning

Many of the structural elements of a feedback protocol (Appendix E) are the same as those in a consultancy protocol. A feedback protocol can be used for just what it sounds—to give feedback to a teacher on a lesson plan or a video of a lesson, or a coach on a video or transcript of a coaching session, or team leader on a draft of an agenda.

Discussion Protocols

Purpose: Learning, problem solving, planning, relationship building

Whenever you hold space for any kind of verbal commentary or discussion during a meeting, it's important to think about how you'll structure the conversation. Protocols can invite equitable participation, keep the conversation focused, and direct it to deeper levels. The National School Reform Faculty (http://www.nsrfharomony.org) has dozens of protocols on its website. For discussing articles, I particularly like the "Text Rendering" and "Three Levels of Text." In addition to using these tools, I often create my own protocols with simple prompts for discussion and clear structures for engaging in reflection. I aim to make sure everyone has time to talk—sometimes in a pair share and other times with the whole group.

Routines to Build Positive Culture

Purpose: Relationship building

The following rituals and routines can be incorporated into any meeting to build relationships among team members and to create a positive team culture. The community-building activities discussed in Chapter 3 also support a group toward these ends. A team might select several of the routines described below to include in every meeting. For example, the team may decide to start each meeting with a group check-in and to close each meeting with a poem. In contrast, the community building activities described in Chapter 3 are not routines that are repeated in each meeting. A facilitator might select a different community building activity to use at each meeting.

Group Check-In

To transition into a meeting and come together as a group. Offer the group a simple question such as, "How are you right now?" or "Share a moment from your day or week." Each person shares with the whole group. The purpose is for everyone to hear from each other. On my website you can view a video clip of me facilitating this process with my team of coaches. Time: 30–60 seconds for each person (which means this doesn't work well with groups larger than 10 people).

Community Agreements or Norms

Although ideally all of the norms are held during all meetings, sometimes it helps to focus in on one or two at a particular meeting. The group can select a norm to focus on, the leader might suggest a norm to pay attention to, or each participant can select the norm that he or she feels would be most helpful for his or her own work that day (see Chapter 5).

Five Deep Breaths

To transition into a meeting. Invite participants to close their eyes or find a place to gaze that allows them to focus inward. Say, "Take five deep breaths, allowing each breath to help you transition from what you were doing into this space together." This can be expanded on to include relaxation or mindfulness meditation. Time: 1 minute.

Poetry or Quotes

To generate inspiration, curiosity, and empathy; also as way to lead into the content of the meeting. The facilitator or a team member can read the poem aloud, or individuals can read silently. Participants can then discuss it with a partner or with the whole group. Quotes can be drawn from inspirational material, scholarly articles on education, or many other places. Time: 5–10 minutes.

Intention Setting

To provide each person with an opportunity to reflect on how he or she wants to show up at the meeting. See Chapter 5 for a description. Time: 3–5 minutes. On my website you can view a video clip of me facilitating this process with my team of coaches.

Student Profile

To anchor the work of the team in the experience of one child. One school that I work with begins leadership team meetings and whole-staff PD with this ritual: a student's photo is printed on the agenda, and staff are invited to share positive stories about themselves. Everyone learns more about students, and participants are emotionally energized. The principal closes the activity by saying, "Let's keep _____ in our heart and thoughts today during our meeting." Time: 5 minutes.

Dyads

To provide time for emotional release, to process their thoughts, and to provide a way for individuals to connect with each other and develop empathy for each other. See description in Appendix E. Time: 5–15 minutes.

Walk and Talk

To help a group get physically energized and process something related to the meeting content. Offer the group a prompt such as, "What connections can you make between our work today and your teaching?" or "What thoughts and feelings has this work brought up for you?" Sometimes I even give people a document to read and talk about while they walk. Then pair team members and send them out for a defined period of time to walk. You can suggest that they take a timer and keep track of time so that both people have time to talk. If a group is meeting and sitting for more than 90 minutes, this is a great way to keep moving forward with the content while honoring our body's need to move. Time: 10–20 minutes.

> Learn, discuss, then take a walk.... The brain is not built for continuous focused input. Instead, leaders need to make sure that stimuli are shut down and the brain can pause to link new information. Terry Sejnowski

Appreciations

To allow people to express gratitude.

Silent appreciations

Say, "Close your eyes and take a moment first to appreciate yourself for all you do, for showing up here today, for giving so much. [Pause] Now if there's anyone else in the room to whom you feel grateful, perhaps who contributed to your learning today or helped you in any way, send them a telepathic thank you."

Written appreciations

Provide cards or sticky notes on which appreciations can be written and then handed to the recipient.

Verbal appreciations

It's common for people to feel initially uncomfortable. Encourage the speaker to directly address the person, saying, for example, "Sandra, thanks for helping me understand that data set today. You explained it clearly and simply." And you can suggest that the recipient acknowledges the appreciation with a nod and a thank you. Verbal appreciations are important culture builders, but pay attention to ensure that they are widely distributed and there isn't one person who is rarely appreciated.

On my website you can view a video clip of me facilitating this process with my team of coaches.

In addition to creating routines or rituals a team uses every time participants meet, you might also want rituals for special events. For example, birthdays might be opportunity to shower appreciations and recognition on someone and eat cake.

Think about what your team needs—do members need rituals to help them transition into the meeting? To recognize each other's contributions? To show up as their best selves? You can also engage the team in thinking about what kinds of rituals will help them create meetings that they love attending.

A Word on Shared Facilitation

If you're sharing facilitation of a meeting, it's essential that you either plan the meeting together or your individual sections and then prepare together. It doesn't work to hand a co-facilitator an agenda at the start of a meeting and ask them to facilitate.

That said, in teams that regularly meet and use recurring structures, it is not only appropriate but also wise to share facilitation of some sections of an agenda. For example, if a team meeting regularly starts with a grounding activity, members can take turns leading this section. This builds greater buy-in to the activity and allows for others to bring knowledge and expertise you may not know about. They'll need to know basic parameters, such as how long they'll have or what the themes for the meeting are, but it's great to have others take up components of an agenda. Doing so also allows you to build leadership capacity in others and to delegate pieces that you don't need to do.

Make sure that before someone else takes on a piece of facilitation he or she is ready to do so—make sure that you're setting the person up for success. For example, the consultancy protocol (Appendix E) is a powerful learning structure for teams. Once you've modeled it a few times you can invite someone else to facilitate. Make sure to offer him or her real-time feedback so that you're developing a culture where everyone is seen as a learner and so you truly are building the capacity of another team member.

You may also find that there are members of your team with experience or skills in a particular area you'd like the rest of the team to learn from: perhaps one person might share his experience with building strong relationships with students' families, whereas another explains how to use a particular instructional strategy. As you get to know your team, be sure to listen for opportunities for other members to demonstrate their skills, share their knowledge, or contribute in some other leadership capacity.

HOW DO I CHOOSE WHAT TO DO?

Once you have a bank of activities from which to draw on when you're designing a team meeting, you need to have some ways to decide among the activities. You'll want to anticipate how much energy participants will have during the meeting—physical, emotional, and cognitive energy. You'll also need to think about how to group people. Finally, you'll need to consider where the team is in its development.

Working with Energy

Start by anticipating what kind of physical energy participants will have. If the meeting is held at 3:30 p.m. after a day of teaching, consider a grounding activity that will get people moving—even just a 10-minute walk and talk makes a big difference during the subsequent hour and a half of sitting and thinking. Structures such as chalk talk (Appendix E) also get people up, sharing ideas, and responding.

Most educators work in emotionally challenging contexts. Providing time to process some of these feelings can help participants be ready for a meeting. For example, the dyad structure (Appendix E) helps to release emotions. Other emotional needs include feeling connected to each other, feeling inspired and hopeful, and feeling valued and validated. Activities that can help meet these emotional needs include reading poetry, check-ins, and appreciations. When you start thinking about team members as complex, whole human beings, you can think about designing agendas that really work for all participants.

When I learned to teach, I was told not to introduce new content and new structures at the same time because it was too much for the brain to process. The same rule of thumb applies to adult learners, and when we consider how we need to anticipate how much cognitive energy participants will have. We don't want to introduce a complicated new protocol that will take time to discuss, understand, and apply, at the same time as we're introducing complex content. Our minds have a limited amount of cognitive energy. Leaders make decisions about how to direct that energy in meetings.

Pairing and Grouping

When planning meetings, you need to make decisions about how to group people. Will they come in and sit anywhere? Will you ask them to turn to a partner and talk? Will you say, "Break into two groups," or will you direct individuals into specific groupings?

When I plan agendas, every time I anticipate having a turn and talk or a small-group discussion, I think about how to group participants. I've moved away from saying, "Find a partner" because this is anxiety producing and energy draining for some people. I'll often use random grouping methods to make pairs, trios, or groups (Appendix C). This allows people to mix with each other and collaborate with others with whom they don't usually work. Or sometimes I say, "Today you'll be in trios, and how about if Anna, Han, and Manny work together." When team members trust you, they won't mind if you configure groups. Sometimes it makes sense to group people by their role or content area ("Math teachers at this table,

English at that table") or to mix groups up ("Configure yourselves into groups with a teacher from each grade level"). If a group meets over an extended period, I often put them in pairs or trios for the whole time. This allows them to build a closer relationship, understand each other better, and form a little community within the larger one.

Heeding the Stages of Team Development

One way of deciding what to do in a meeting is to consider in what stage a team is in its development. Bruce Tuckman's (1965) stages of development have been invaluable in helping me make decisions about what to do in team meetings. Tuckman suggests that teams go through five stages of development—forming, storming, norming, performing, and adjourning or transforming. Although this description suggests a linear process, the processes can be cyclical—for example, a team can be at the norming stage but return to the forming stage when its composition changes. What follows is an overview of each stage and suggestions for facilitation moves to shift a team into the next stage.

Stage 1: Forming

In the forming stage, a group is coming together, learning about each other, and learning about what the team is meant to do. Members may be excited to be on the team and eager to engage in their work, although it's also common for members to feel anxious about fitting in or wonder whether their work will measure up to other members'. At this stage meetings may feel more tiring than those at later stages. Members absorb a tremendous amount of information and learn a great deal about each other, the leader, the purpose, and how the group will work together. Sometimes this stage can also be characterized by politeness as team members get to know each other. Trust has not yet been developed, and team members closely observe each other to assess levels of safety.

At this stage, it's essential to focus on building trust, to establish community agreements, and to clarify decision-making structures. The team also needs to understand its purpose for existing and what it will do together. At the forming stage, teams need to have opportunities to make meaning together, learn, and engage in discussions.

Stage 2: Storming

Just as it sounds, storming is about conflict. During this stage, members express differences of opinion, ideas, and feelings between each other and with the leader.

They may question their purpose for being a team and there can be frustration or anger at the group's process. Splinter groups may form, anxiety levels increase, and individuals may push for power. There can also be competition between team members, personal attacks, and little team spirit. Levels of participation can vary greatly—some members may participate significantly while others disengage. When problems come up, it can be a struggle to address them. Most of us know when we're in a team that's storming: it doesn't feel very good, not much gets done, and we may dread meetings.

A leader needs a robust tool set to move a team through the storming stage. You'll need to be attuned to recognizing feelings and the ways they manifest: you may notice people resisting suggestions by other members, arguing and bickering, individuals setting unrealistic goals, or individuals who are retreating to avoid conflict. Although some issues may need to be addressed privately between two individuals, conflict may need to be named and addressed with the whole group (see Chapter 12). It's also possible that the team's projects may need to be modified—goals might need to be broken into manageable steps or roles, and responsibilities might need clearer articulation. This is a challenging phase when a leader needs to balance the implementation of a team's work plan while also attending to communication and conflict.

At this stage, establishing a number of feedback loops is essential. Ask for feedback on your leadership and facilitation and offer feedback to individuals. Team members also benefit from giving each other feedback as this builds trust in the group and buy in to the team's work. Exhibit 10.4 is one way to do this. Furthermore, team members need opportunities to reflect on how they work together and what they get done. Appendix B and Exhibit 3.1 facilitate this process.

While you directly address unproductive conflict and communication, you also need to continually cultivate trust. As trust grows, unhealthy conflict can decrease. Members need time to listen to each other, learn about each other, and do work together—which is why we can't just relegate team building to the beginning of the year. In addition, during the storming phase, sharing Tuckman's (1965) framework of team development can normalize the rough moments. Congratulate the team for passing through the polite forming stage, and ask members what it might take for them to move to the norming stage. This model is a reminder that we won't storm forever and that this phase paves the way for performing.

Tuckman (1965) argues that storming is an essential stage and that teams that skip this stage never really become effective teams. Although I acknowledge this, I've also seen teams go through the storming stage very quickly. Unproductive conflict might surface only between a couple members and can be addressed quickly when a facilitator recognizes it and the individuals have the skills, will, and emotional intelligence to resolve it.

Storming has a great deal to do with the organizational conditions in which the team exists. When conditions are optimal, a team might storm quickly. In contrast, if you're leading a team that seems to be doomed to eternal storming, it may be that the organizational conditions for team development are poor. For example, if site leadership is ineffective, the team may be receiving confusing or contradictory messages about their purpose and role. Changes at the federal and local level in curriculum and assessment will also shape how a team of teachers works, especially during the initial period of implementation of a new initiative. Chapter 13 explores organizational conditions for team development.

Exhibit 10.4. Team Feedback Process

This activity (which I've modified from one designed by Lencioni, 2012) is useful to do at any time of year and at any stage of team development and can help a team move through storming. A baseline level of trust does need to exist among the group—if a team is too stormy or there is very little trust, this activity is useless or even damaging. I encourage you to take risks as a leader and not be afraid of conflict, but you'll need to use your best judgment about whether a team can manage this.

The process starts with everyone writing down one thing that each of the other team members does to contribute to the team—for example, "Jessica: asks inquiry-based questions when we're making decisions." This should be the person's single biggest area of strength as it impacts the group—not an extensive list of appreciations. It should also be about the way the person behaves when he or she is with the group—not about his or her technical skills. It's a behavior that makes the team stronger. Next, everyone writes down one behavior that each team member does to negatively impact the team—for example, "Jessica: makes excuses for not following through on commitments." Most teams need about 10–15 minutes to write.

In the second part of this activity, the feedback is verbally delivered. The leader is the first to receive feedback, and one at a time members share what they identified as the leader's positive contribution. After everyone has shared, the leader says thank you or offers a brief (one-sentence) reaction. Next, everyone shares the one behavior that the leader needs to work on. In response, the leader says thank you or offers a brief (one-sentence) reaction—but not a rebuttal. This process continues for each member of the team.

This can be a powerful experience as everyone gets direct, honest, and helpful feedback. It can also build trust among team members as they begin to learn that because they'll engage in this process on a regular basis (perhaps annually) they'll be both appreciated and held accountable for their behavior by their peers.

It can be hard to know whether enough trust exists in a team for this process to go well. Often, we might feel confident that most team members will respond well and will appreciate the feedback, but we might doubt the capacity of one or two individuals. We want to be mindful not to make those one or two people unbearably uncomfortable, but we also want to make sure we're not treading too carefully. If you have reasonable trust that people will be able to share hard feedback that won't sound personal and mean, then give this a try. It's a risk worth taking because it has tremendous potential for increasing accountability in each other and for creating a culture where feedback is the norm.

Stage 3: Norming

You know when a team hits the norming stage because members feel clearer about their purpose and have developed more trust in each other and in you. You can hear these changes in peoples' words, and you can sense them in the energy and flow of your time together. Ideas and feelings are expressed with more ease, and members elicit each other's opinions and experiences. At this point, many of the structures that were established to develop a team, such as community agreements and appreciations, fade slightly into the background of the group's work. Norms are self-reinforced. Appreciations are offered regularly at various points of a meeting. Members offer each other feedback outside of formal structures to do so, and the feedback is well received.

When conflict surfaces, members feel less anxiety and either make conscious efforts to resolve it or transform it into a learning opportunity. Members also engage in productive conflict with each other, discussing ideas and pushing each other's thinking. Meetings are punctuated by laughter, references to previous positive experiences, and appreciation for each other.

In the norming stage, leaders balance taking a directive and facilitative approach and push the team toward higher performance. At times, you'll need to give the team some leeway in how they work together—letting them try new ways of engaging with each other, allowing them to experience some disagreements, giving members opportunities to take leadership roles. At other times, you'll need to be more direct and call team members' attention to their ways of working, making suggestions for improvement and refinement. Communication continues to be essential and must flow smoothly in all directions: between members as well as between yourself and members.

Stage 4: Performing

At the performing stage, the group has established a unique identity and takes great pride in their team. Members care about each other deeply, put team needs above their own, and work interdependently and collaboratively. Because of the high levels of openness, support, empathy, and trust, members challenge each other and take risks. Roles on the team may become more fluid, with members taking on various responsibilities as needed. Differences among members are viewed as assets and enhance the team's performance. Commitment to the mission is strong, the competence of team members is high, and progress toward meeting goals is clear. A team at the performing stage also confidently embraces new projects and tasks.

Performing teams seldom fall back into a storming phase. When they do, they resolve conflict effectively and quickly. Individual team members may join or leave the team without affecting its performance levels. Being part of the team feels easy at this stage compared with earlier stages.

In the performing stage, a leader focuses on developing other leaders in the team. Most of the time, you seem like a participant and leadership is distributed. There are still times when you might play a facilitative leadership role, but the sense of hierarchy has greatly diminished or disappeared. At times, the team will need to focus on its process. Significant changes in membership or in organizational conditions can cause a team to cycle back to an earlier stage. A leader needs to stay attuned to recognizing these changes and the ways they might affect the team and address them directly. A team at the performing stage is a great team, as I defined in Chapter 1.

Stage 5: Adjourning or Transforming

Some teams end when their work is completed or organizational conditions change. At this stage, team members need to celebrate and process their growth and learning. It is an opportune moment for members to reflect on their growth individually and to recognize the role they played in the team's success. Team members will likely feel sad at parting and will need time and opportunities to say good-bye to each other. It's very common for people who worked together in a high-performing team to stay in touch for years—participating in a joyful, resilient community creates bonds that endure.

Using the Stages of Team Development

This framework can help a leader make decisions about what to do during meetings and to respond in the moment to group dynamics. Because teams don't progress into the next stage in one definitive moment—there will always be overlap and gray areas as teams move—it's important for you to notice the behaviors that indicate a team's stage and take action to help it move to the next one. As this process unfolds, name the indicators that suggest that the team is moving. This might sound like, "That lively discussion you two just had is a great sign that we're moving into a norming stage. I noticed that no one got defensive and you were both so open to shifting your perspectives." Naming the behavior that you want to see helps members know what to strive for and gives them hope. You can also invite team members to share their observations of how the team is moving and to be on the lookout for indicators of growth. Exhibit 10.5 is a tool that can guide you in this reflection.

Fall down 53 times. Get up 54.

ZEN SAYING

Transformational Coaching Team, 2013

The storming happened during the first year in brief bursts. Sometimes it happened during a meeting, and I'd observe a tense exchange between two coaches. Sometimes it happened outside of meetings, but a team member would let me know that a challenging moment had transpired. Whenever I got wind of conflict, I addressed it immediately with the individuals. It wasn't easy or comfortable for me to do, and my feedback wasn't always polished. However, I knew I couldn't ignore even the littlest moments of distress. Sometimes during a meeting, if an exchange seemed tense, I simply said, "Hey, let me check in. Was that okay for both of you, or was it heading in an unproductive direction? Anything need to be addressed?" Other times I spoke to an individual after a meeting, saying something like, "Your response to ___ today seemed off. Can you check in with her and see if there's anything to clear up?" There were times when I needed to coach the coach on how to resolve the conflict, and there were other times when the coach knew exactly what needed to be done. What I insisted on, gently and with care, was that unproductive conflict be addressed.

Some of the storming was with me—there was some pushback on what I asked of coaches. I held tight to my expectations: our team's work needed to be exceptionally high quality. For example, coaches designed and delivered professional development for teachers and administrators. Some of the PD agendas were exceptional: they were designed based on adult learning principles, they were detailed and precise, and activities flowed well. In contrast, coaches with less experience created weaker plans. Recognizing their need for more learning around designing agendas, I allocated significant chunks of time during meetings to planning and sharing PD agendas. Using a feedback protocol (see Appendix E.2), coaches reviewed each other's PD plans and offered feedback. Sometimes these were difficult moments as a coach's work was picked apart. Most of the time coaches felt that their learning increased, the quality of their PD improved, and their trust in each other expanded.

Conflict makes me nervous, but in tough moments I consciously managed my feelings. That year, I often reminded myself that the conflict would resolve and that others had the ability to manage their own discomfort. I asked, and asked, and asked for feedback—and I gave it, too. I asked coaches to own how they showed up in meetings: "Are you here as your best self? Are you showing up the way you want to be here?" And I reflected on these questions myself. I stayed grounded in my vision for our team and in the conviction that we could move to a high level of performance—and I asked members, "What needs to happen so that we can improve how we work together?"

As coaches began taking responsibility for sections of our agendas—leading the grounding activity, facilitating protocols, designing plans—I suspected we'd moved into norming. We were no longer forming or storming was evident by the feeling in the room during meetings—the genuine care expressed for each other, the spontaneous appreciations, the laughter, the openness. I'd never felt anything like this with a group of colleagues, and sometimes I worried that I was misreading the situation, that things weren't as good as I thought they were. After meetings ended, I'd sit at my desk and read feedback that was full of appreciation for each other, our team, and our time together. "This is what feels like to be in a healthy professional community," I'd think, "and just let the experience sink it."

Exhibit 10.5. Stages of Team Development

Stage	Indicators	Key Leadership Moves
	Some of these might be present. If so, try the leadership moves in the next column.	*Focus on these activities in meetings.*
Forming	If: ☐ Varied levels of participation in discussion—some might talk a lot whereas others sit back and listen. ☐ Discussions feel awkward. ☐ It feels like people are holding back. ☐ There are lots of questions for the leader. ☐ There's excessive politeness between members. ☐ Members (and leaders) leave meetings feeling tired—not good tired.	Then try: • Building trust. • Establishing community agreements and decision-making processes. • Articulating the team's purpose and ensure understanding and buy-in. • Structuring learning experiences, meaning making and discussions. • Modeling vulnerability, risk taking, engagement, and transparency.
Storming	If: ☐ Members question how the leader runs the team and may advocate for changes to the goals or process. ☐ Not a lot gets done at meetings. Agendas are hijacked or diverted to discuss process and purpose. ☐ Productive and unhealthy conflict erupts during meetings and outside of them between members. ☐ Outside of meetings, members communicate with each other about their frustration or disagreement with the leader with other members. ☐ Some members are more actively engaged in discussions while others step farther back. ☐ No one feels excited about attending meetings and the leader also questions whether he or she wants to lead the team.	Then try: • Normalizing this stage and ensuring the team that members can move through it. • Continuing to build trust. • Paying close attention to your own emotions. • Incorporating strategies to build the team's emotional intelligence. • Addressing conflict between members as soon as possible—sometimes publically in the moment, sometimes privately. • Engaging the team in reflecting on how they work together. Use the Effectiveness Survey and Team Temperature Check. • Pushing forward on the team's work, but consider modifying projects or goals.

Stage	Indicators	Key Leadership Moves
	Some of these might be present. If so, try the leadership moves in the next column.	*Focus on these activities in meetings.*
		• Asking for feedback on your leadership—anonymously and publically. • Offering members feedback on their behavior privately. • Structuring opportunities for members to give each other feedback. Use the team feedback process. • Highlighting moments of success, especially those indicating that the team is moving out of storming. • Acknowledging organizational conditions that might contribute to storming.
Norming	If: ☐ There is more laughter in meetings. ☐ Members seem to like each other, they appreciate each other, and communication feels easier. ☐ Members push back on each other's ideas, and this leads to deeper understanding. ☐ Feedback is offered in the moment and is received with appreciation. ☐ Norms and structures to support norms (e.g., a process observer) are less often used. ☐ Members know what they're doing together as a team and why they're doing it. ☐ The leader participates in some of the activities as a colleague and during others plays a directive leadership role.	Then try: • Starting to build the capacity of leaders within the team: Identify team members who have the skills to take on leadership roles. Give them leadership tasks. • Structuring opportunities for productive conflict—encourage the exchange of ideas. • Participating in some of the team's discussions and activities as a colleague. • Giving the team more challenging tasks. • Modeling your vulnerability and transparency and inviting others to do so.

(continued)

Stage	Indicators	Key Leadership Moves
	Some of these might be present. If so, try the leadership moves in the next column.	*Focus on these activities in meetings.*
Performing	If: ☐ A lot gets done and members feel proud of their work and learning together. ☐ The work done independently and collaboratively is high quality. ☐ There's obvious warmth between members, laughter, and appreciations. ☐ Members take risks and make mistakes and clearly see their areas for growth (both individually and as team). ☐ Discussions can be lively and heated, but members don't take it personally. ☐ Facilitation of meetings is shared. ☐ Members don't feel like the leader has authority over them. ☐ Members leave meetings feeling good tired. ☐ As the leader, it feels easy, enjoyable, and rewarding to work with this team.	Then try: • Continuing to distribute leadership and hand over elements of team facilitation to members. • Acknowledging all the indicators that the team is at a performing level. • Paying attention to changes in organizational conditions that might affect your team. • Continuing to encourage healthy conflict and promoting even deeper levels of engagement and learning. • Outside of meetings: Sharing the story of your team with other leaders and other teams so that they can learn. • Relaxing and enjoying your team.
Adjourning or transforming	If: ☐ A significant number of members are leaving. ☐ The team is disbanding.	Then try: • Creating opportunities for team members to tell their stories about their experience in the team. • Engaging members in reflecting on their individual growth and learning. • Celebrating successes. • Offering structures for closure, including holding space for sadness. • Sharing your own feelings about the team ending.

CHAPTER 11

Setting the Stage for Artful Meetings

Humanities Team, 2008

In my second year at Wilson Middle School, I developed a strategy for working in toxic environments. Staff meetings and whole-school professional development meetings were often just as difficult and contentious as our humanities team meetings. Inspired by an afternoon with my young son that we spent blowing human-size soap bubbles with a huge bubble wand, I began using a visualization strategy before entering meetings. I'd see myself stepping into a strong, translucent bubble. I'd tell myself that the toxicity in the staff meeting couldn't penetrate my bubble and that inside the air was clean and pure. While I was at the meeting, I stayed in my bubble and reminded myself, "I'm not inhaling any of this yuckiness—it's not in my space." I'd notice that I felt calmer when in my bubble, less triggered by unprofessional behavior, more able to react thoughtfully to the questions and comments I received when I was leading the meeting. And when the meeting was over and I'd left the grounds I'd pop the bubble.

This chapter pulls the curtain all the way back on meeting design and facilitation. Smoothly flowing, productive, and focused meetings that leave participants feeling accomplished, connected, and satisfied are carefully planned and prepared for.

The preparation routine for an artful meeting includes much more than writing an agenda: It begins by reviewing feedback and thinking about the team's needs. It involves thinking through what you'll say during key moments in the meeting and capturing those thoughts in your facilitator's agenda. Preparation also includes reflecting on yourself as a leader, determining who you want to be during the meeting, and imagining how you want to show up. Finally, preparation involves setting up a space and creating a tone for a meeting.

START WITH FEEDBACK

If you could have seen me planning for a Friday meeting with my team of coaches, you would have seen a yellow highlighter in my hand, a stack of feedback forms from our last meeting spread across my desk, and our team work plan and goals pinned to the wall in the periphery of my vision (below photos of former students, inspirational quotes, and my core values). Whenever I plan for a meeting or Professional Development session, I always start by reviewing feedback. I would be lost without it.

Why and How to Ask for Feedback

There are several reasons to gather feedback: to plan for subsequent meetings, to refine your facilitation skills, and to gain insight into group dynamics. Individual written reflections allow people to privately communicate about their experience and to leave facilitators with a record to reference. I've observed some leaders engage a group in collectively generation reflections about what worked and what could be improved at the end of a meeting. Even though such a process can serve the purpose of reflecting on a team's effectiveness, it does not reveal the same kind of information as a written reflection from each person.

Feedback can be solicited anonymously, or individuals can identify themselves. If you hold evaluative or supervisorial power over team members, then occasionally invite anonymous feedback perhaps through an online survey. Most of the time when I lead small teams or deliver professional development sessions, I ask participants to identify themselves on their feedback. I explain that this allows me to more effectively differentiate learning and that I may want to follow up about something they wrote. I also believe that identifying yourself can make you more accountable for what you say and how you say it. Inviting feedback is a step toward shifting culture and creating learning organizations.

I always let a group know at the beginning of our time together that I will ask them for feedback at the end of the meeting. I provide them with the feedback form from the start and suggest they jot down questions or comments as we proceed. When the time comes for feedback, I say, "I really value your feedback. It's incredibly helpful to me for planning our time and developing my facilitation skills. Please write as much or as little as you want."

One technical challenge in gathering feedback is timing: Because getting feedback happens at the end of an agenda, it's often cut short or cut entirely if a meeting is running behind. It's imperative to budget time so that this doesn't happen. If during a meeting you anticipate that feedback time is dwindling, cut anything and everything else to preserve time for it. Eliminating the brief opportunity for team members to offer feedback can chip away at their trust in you.

What to Ask

If the meeting is one in which learning is the primary purpose, then I ask these questions:

1. What are a couple of big lessons you're taking away from today?
2. Which activities worked best for you?
3. What didn't work?
4. What questions or concerns do you have?
5. Is there anything else you want me to know about your experience today?

My first question is intentionally about learning. I measure my own success based on whether participants learn, so although it might be possible that they didn't like an aspect of the meeting or even didn't want to attend, if they learned something I feel somewhat satisfied. This question also provides insight into participants as learners and what they value. I also need to know how they experienced the different activities I engaged them in. I look for patterns in these responses. If every team member says that a particular exercise didn't work, I won't do that one with them again. Of course, when there's overwhelming appreciation for an activity, it's one we'll repeat.

The fourth and fifth questions often provide insights into the group and my facilitation. Someone might write, "I like doing role plays but today my partner kept interrupting with random questions," or "I'm sorry I was kind of disengaged today— I have some personal issues that are distracting me," or "I really appreciated your comments at the start of the day about taking risks in our team, but later when I asked a difficult question I felt like you dismissed it." Open-ended questions can yield information that you otherwise might not receive.

If the purpose for the meeting was primarily to share information, solve problems, or make decisions, I modify my questions. In those cases, I want to know whether participants felt that the meeting outcomes were reached as well as how they experienced the process, and any other responses they had. Chapter 8 has an example of a feedback form that I use for decision-making meetings.

When to Read Feedback

Feedback can be encouraging or hard to receive—and usually a mixture of both. Sometimes I hunker down at my desk or rush out to my car and scan it immediately after the meeting while the experience is fresh on my mind. When feedback is good, it affirms my hard work, and I go home feeling content. However, after most meetings or PD sessions that I lead, I'm usually pretty drained, and I often need to replenish my energy before I can clearly process the meeting. When I'm tired, I'm also more emotionally sensitive. It's in those moments when I can read 47 positive feedback forms and one with a negative comment, which I'll then obsess over while the other 47 comments are deleted from my working memory. Giving myself a day or two before reading the feedback allows it to be more useful.

What to Do with Feedback

I read feedback with a highlighter pen in hand so that I can circle comments that are useful for future planning or that I need to respond to. The feedback informs subsequent planning, and I also reference it when I meet with the group. I start by reviewing feedback from our previous meeting. Sometimes I might say, "Last time several of you asked for more time to write before moving into a pair share, so I've made that adjustment." Or, "We'll be doing role plays again today. Last time one member struggled in a role-play because their partner was not following the protocol and interrupted. I want to ask that you make explicit agreements in your trios about how you'll follow the protocol. If things aren't working during role playing, please speak up in your trio or let me know that you need support."

Sharing feedback also cultivates understanding and empathy between teammates. Sometimes I tally up responses or select specific comments to share with the team. For example, when there is a range of feedback on a particular activity, I share this with the group. I might say, or include on a PowerPoint slide, that 6 of the 12 team members appreciated the discussion protocol. I may also project a quote from a participant (without identifying the author) such as, "I love using a protocol to discuss an article. As an introvert this helps me feel comfortable in a group discussion." And then I project another slide with someone else's response: "I really don't like using protocols for discussion. I feel like they stifle conversation." I do this because I want the group to gain insight into how others engage in our learning and how I make decisions about what we do. Whenever possible, I look to be transparent about my decisions as a facilitator. I might also say, "Given this feedback, we'll have one discussion today using a protocol and one that's unstructured."

Sharing feedback with a team subtly shifts culture. When I facilitate meetings where a significant number of people are on phones or computers at inappropriate times or for reasons unrelated to learning, I can feel conflicted about how to respond. I suspect that this behavior might bother some learners, but sometimes I'm not sure how to address it, and don't want to engage in a power struggle with those who are using their technological devices for things other than learning. When I receive feedback saying something like, "I was distracted by the number of people texting during our group conversations," I share this with the whole group and suggest that phones to be put away. Most team members receive this feedback well and want to be respectful of their colleagues, which allows me to step away from policing behavior. This again is another opportunity to make transparent my requests as a facilitator: When I can share the impact of behavior on others, as reported by them, it helps people understand a request.

I'm also intentional about reporting positive feedback about how people experience the group. For example, especially when a team is forming, I share comments such as, "I love this team. I feel so safe and like I can trust everyone and I love coming to our meetings." Or, "I'm really grateful that my trio challenged my thinking yesterday. It was hard for a moment, but I know it's helping me grow." When I see evidence in feedback that a team is developing the culture that we're striving for, I share it. This encourages others, helps them see how we're making progress, and gently nudges them onward.

Making Sense of Critical Feedback

Sometimes feedback feels hurtful or confusing. I always listen for the kernels of truth in difficult feedback, but I also consider the conditions in which the feedback is offered. I think about whether there's evidence that the organization is a learning organization. I remind myself that in learning organizations the giving and receiving of feedback is a regular practice that allows people to develop skills at effectively communicating feedback. When there isn't a culture of giving constructive feedback in a school, when trust levels are low across the organization, and when people are really frustrated about many things, their anonymous feedback can be more critical. Sometimes I feel like educators are so desperate to have their experiences heard that they unload complaints on me that aren't about my facilitation.

At the same time, I always listen carefully for feedback that is about my facilitation. Even when conditions in a district or school are not optimal, I need to consider critical feedback about how I communicate. For example, feedback such as, "You seemed frustrated with us," stings for a moment, but when I reflect on the meeting, I can usually see how someone might have experienced something I said as frustration. I am grateful for this kind of feedback. It has helped me become a more mindful facilitator.

Feedback that's just mean—that feels personal—has become easier for me to dismiss. I've learned to differentiate between my delivery of a professional development session and someone's anger and frustration that has nothing to do with me. Once my knee-jerk irritation subsides after reading the feedback, I wish the individual well and do what I can to mentally delete the comments from my memory.

The feedback I struggle with most comes from groups where just about everyone says, "Everything was great" and says little more. When I get vague and minimal feedback like this, I attribute it to the organizational culture. I suspect that a practice of sharing authentic feedback doesn't yet exist or that levels of trust are low. If I continue to work with the group, I'll reiterate my desire for honest feedback and work on building trust, and I assume that one day I'll get meaningful feedback.

Regardless of how functional or toxic an organization is and how much trust exists, I believe it's critical that you always ask for feedback. Always. Dysfunctional organizations are full of people whose voices haven't been heard. Yes, they may be cynical, disengaged, and outright nasty. And although it will take many years to shift such a culture, I believe all people deserve to give feedback. This doesn't mean you have to accept it or take it personally, but as a coach, facilitator, or leader, it's your responsibility to begin creating the space for voices to be heard.

DON'T FORGET THE FACILITATOR'S AGENDA

I've coached many leaders who tell me that they don't need to create a facilitator's agenda because it's all in their heads. Even though it might be in there, often during a meeting, what's in their head gets muddied and forgotten. After the meeting they reflect that they didn't say everything they wanted to say or hadn't thought through a specific step of the agenda. "Next time, put it down on paper," I insist, being very directive in my coaching.

A facilitator's agenda differs from a participant's agenda because it includes the precise time allotment for each activity and section and your detailed notes about procedures: for example, how you'll create pairs, the order for sharing ideas. Your agenda also includes your talking points and framing comments. You'll especially want to think about transitions between sections of the agenda and how you'll help your team make connections between the meeting components. Sometimes, especially if I'm preparing for a potentially contentious meeting, I anticipate questions that might be asked, and I come up with possible responses. When I recall disastrous meetings I facilitated, it was because I hadn't anticipated and planned for participant questions and comments. You can find an example of a facilitator's agenda at the end of Chapter 5.

Planning a meeting takes time—on average between 1 and 2 hours of planning for every hour of facilitation. Therefore, planning and preparing for a daylong team retreat means you'll need 8–16 hours. You might think, "How can I do that? I have so many things I'm expected to do!" And even though I believe you, it's essential to figure out how to advocate for the time you need to plan and how to prioritize tasks so that you can have the hours to prepare.

Designing agendas gets easier and faster with practice, especially when preparing for meetings with the same group. But when you're in the forming, storming, and norming stage of team development, or when new members join, or when a new project is taken up by the group, planning takes a lot of time. I use two tools to guide my planning process (see Appendix D and Exhibit 11.1). Sometimes I use both of these and at other times just one.

The facilitator agenda is your best friend. The process of creating it allows you to anticipate what might happen in a meeting. Even if nothing goes as you planned, your preparation often equips you to navigate digressions and challenges, and you'll feel more comfortable with making deci-

If words come out of the heart, they will enter the heart.

RUMI

sions in the moment. You'll walk into the meeting feeling confident and prepared, knowing that you did everything possible to ensure success. I can just about guarantee that you'll *always* be glad you made one.

Exhibit 11.1. Checklist for Facilitating Meetings and Professional Development

Opening

- [ ] How will I know who is in the room and what they're bringing in with them—as far as their backgrounds, experiences, and feelings about the session? How do I get that information?
- [ ] How do I communicate the session's objectives and activities?
- [ ] How do I share where these objectives and activities come from?
- [ ] How do they see how these objectives are relevant to their work and where the learning will be applicable?
- [ ] How do I communicate expectations for behavior, norms, and engagement?
- [ ] Are there any norms that need to be requested (confidentiality?) and agreed on?
- [ ] Are there any other decision-making moments in the day? If so, how will they be decided?
- [ ] How do I make this an emotionally safe space?
- [ ] How do I show up as a compassionate listener?
- [ ] How do I communicate what to do with questions, concerns, and requests? What structures capture these?
- [ ] How do I help participants get grounded and present for the session's learning?

Pacing and Tone

- [ ] How are participants seated? Random groups or predetermined? Can these change during the session?
- [ ] Do participants move physically throughout the day? Do people get up at least every 60 minutes?
- [ ] Does any segment go for more than 20 minutes without a shift?
- [ ] If participants don't know each other, what do they need to know in the beginning? (Names?)

Collaboration

- [ ] Are there structures for participants to learn from each other?
- [ ] How often do they talk to each other? How much of that talk is structured and how much is open?
- [ ] What is the purpose for each talk time (e.g., meaning making, story telling, reflection, planning)?

- [ ] Are meaning-making talk times varied in the numbers of participants who are engaged? Are there opportunities for dyads, pair shares, trios, small groups, whole group?
- [ ] Are there opportunities to hear from each other in a nonverbal way (e.g., a chalk talk)?
- [ ] Are there opportunities to role-play?
- [ ] Can participants coach each other? How do I set this up to be safe?
- [ ] Is there a "problem" that participants can solve together?
- [ ] Do participants have a chance to tell their stories? Does some of the talk invite personal stories?

Learning

- [ ] When do participants have choice during the day? Where do they get to direct their learning?
- [ ] How will participants remember what they learn?
- [ ] How can they have some experiences during the same day when they can apply their learning?
- [ ] Are there different ways for participants to experience input (e.g., reading, listening, watching a video or role-play)?
- [ ] How many visuals am I using? Are there a few memorable visuals?
- [ ] How many stories will I tell? When will I tell stories? For what purpose?
- [ ] Is there an opportunity to visualize some piece of the new learning?
- [ ] Can metaphor, simile, analogy be incorporated as a way to make meaning or remember learning?
- [ ] When can a graphic organizer be used?
- [ ] Are there opportunities for participants to write?
- [ ] Is there an opportunity to incorporate drawing?
- [ ] Are participants given an opportunity after every input piece to make meaning and capture learning?

Shifting Energies

- [ ] Are there moments when we might laugh? How can I plan for laughter?
- [ ] Is there an opportunity to include a video?
- [ ] When could I play music?
- [ ] Can I use quotes, a short story, or poetry to engage participants in reflection and discussion?
- [ ] What can I do after lunch to avoid the sleepy slumber?
- [ ] Is there an opportunity for a walk and talk?

- [ ] How do I solicit the support that participants need to continue their learning?
- [ ] How will participants recognize and reflect on their learning during the day?
- [ ] How will they be able to assess how much they've learned?
- [ ] How will participants offer me feedback?
- [ ] How will I close the day and appreciate their participation?
- [ ] How can participants appreciate each other?

PREPARE YOUR INTERNAL SELF

The final element to consider when preparing for a meeting is who you want to be and how you want participants to experience you. Ultimately, this is what you have the most control over as a leader. It's an opportunity to cultivate your emotional intelligence and communication skills.

My process begins when I'm creating my facilitator's agenda. As I read feedback and think back to my previous time with the group for which I'm planning, I pay attention to the feelings that come up for me. If I remember being frustrated with one individual, I explore those feelings and investigate the possible triggers for my frustration. Perhaps he'd asked a random, off-topic question in a key moment of the discussion, or perhaps he pushed back on my idea before I'd fully expressed it. I wonder if the participant sensed that I was annoyed with him and what impact my behavior had on his ability to engage and learn. I ask myself, "What might happen in this meeting if I were to listen and try to understand him?" I anticipate what might trigger me in the next meeting, which primes me to be aware in that moment if I do get triggered. When I am aware of my frustration, then I can make choices about how to respond, choices that might be aligned to my intention for how I want to be in that meeting.

As I'm planning, I ask myself, "What does this group need from me? How do I want them to feel when they leave our meeting? How might I best meet their needs?" For example, if I work with a group that's going through a lot of transition, then I anticipate it needs a space that feels calm, safe, and grounded. If participants are about to deliver a big project, I will need to recognize their readiness and my confidence in them. Whether I'm leading a meeting or facilitating a day of PD, I want people to leave feeling emotionally energized, inspired, and connected to others.

Once I've named this outcome, I ask myself: "Who do I want to be in this meeting?" Even if there are people in the group who trigger me, even if I anticipate grumpy feedback, I still push myself to identify how I want to show up, how I want others to experience me, and what I want people to think about my leadership. Sometimes my responses differ depending on the group I'm working with, but often they are a reflection of my core values: compassion, justice, and community. So I think, "I want people to know that I care about them. I want to be confident and humble. I want to be a presence for healing and transformation." I visualize myself walking into a meeting room and being these things.

Then I ask myself, "How will I communicate my intention? What will it look and sound like if I'm being this way?" I recognize that I can't entirely control someone else's response, but I can do my best. I suspect that expressing frustration at an off-topic question won't make someone feel cared for, and I think about different ways I might respond if someone asks random questions at inappropriate times. This process helps me mentally prepare to manage challenges when they arise.

I think through these prompts—"What does this group need from me? Who do I want to be? How will I communicate my intention?"—when I'm planning for a meeting and then right before it starts. Sometime I write my intention down on the top of my facilitator's agenda. When I leave the meeting, this is what I reflect on before reading feedback. I think about how I held my intention and the moments when I felt like I was really being who I want to be. I think about moments when my intention might have faltered. I commit to learning about those moments, and I also don't use them as an opportunity to ruthlessly critique myself. And when I do read feedback, I look for indicators that participants experienced me and our learning space as I wanted them to. When I read a comment such as, "I feel inspired to use these strategies," or "Thank you for being transparent about the process we used," I take this as evidence that I fulfilled my intention.

PUT ON THE FINISHING TOUCHES

When I'm planning for meetings, I think about setting a stage for a mood. I consider how I can help people feel inspired, cared for, and excited to be meeting.

Physical space affects our moods. When I'm planning a meeting, I visualize the space and how I'll organize chairs and tables. I strive to counter the hierarchies in our society, so I usually favor a circle or U-shape set-up. Especially for meetings of smaller teams and groups that will collaborate with each other, members need to be able to see each other.

When you arrive at the meeting space, consider your options for lighting. Natural light is best, but light of any kind will elevate mood. If the meeting is held at the end of the day, don't keep the lights off or dimmed, even if there are windows—people get sleepy. Make sure there's air in the room but that it's not too cold. Pay attention to all the elements in the space, including how noisy it is. If it's loud outside, close the door or windows or ask if there are other places where the meeting can be held. Every little thing contributes to a good meeting, and we are easily distracted by feeling physically uncomfortable.

Many school meeting spaces are not very inspiring places. Whenever possible, I take plants, flowers, tablecloths, and other such decorative items into meeting rooms. Sometimes it's necessary to simply straighten up the room a little, throw out trash, and stack the random piles of paper covering the counters. When I prepare for meetings, I think about the physical and cognitive energy that participants will have and how to direct it toward our learning goals or the work we'll do together. I don't want participants to be distracted by the room.

Snacks always make meetings better. Many educators skip meals and are chronically low on energy. Beyond that, breaking bread together is an ancient and universal way of connecting and acknowledging our shared humanity. Even on a low teacher salary, I found that it was worth spending $8.00 of my own money on a bag of chocolate-covered almonds to take to a meeting. Team members can rotate bringing food, or you could ask for a small budget for snacks. Sharing food makes a difference in how we feel about each other—and if the snacks are healthy, they make a difference in our physical and cognitive energy.

Finally, think of your meeting as a party you're hosting for treasured friends. Is there anything else you'd do to create a space that's welcoming and energizing? I love playing lively music while people arrive and instrumental music during quiet reflection. I leave boxes of supplies on the tables so that people have pens, sticky notes, paper clips, markers, and other office supplies. I also often leave snacks in these boxes (like mints or chocolate) and Aaron's Thinking Putty (search for it online), which is like Silly Putty but much better.

FIND THE JOY IN PLANNING

Although planning takes a lot of time and thinking, I often find it fun. Sometimes it's like figuring out a puzzle and other times like organizing a dinner party. I love thinking about how to help a group of people feel energized and hopeful, how to cultivate their curiosity and wonder, and how to guide them to new awareness about themselves, their colleagues, and the students we serve. I love searching out the perfect poem that will symbolically reflect the work we'll do together. Thinking through groups and pairs of participants makes me feel like a professional yenta—I always hope that people will form new connections with each other. I get energized thinking about the treats I'll provide or the materials I'll include in the supply box. I hope that the meeting might be a moment in which we can experience a different way of being together—a way of learning that invites vulnerability and an opportunity for building community. When these conditions are present, then I think we'll be able to more effectively get to the hard work of transforming schools. When I engage in planning toward this vision, the planning is joyful.

Transformational Coaching Team, 2014.

It's around 8:00 a.m. on a Friday morning, and I'm the first to arrive in our office, an old portable on a former elementary school campus. I turn on the lights and heat, start the coffee, and set the pastries I've brought onto the center of the large wooden oval table where we'll all gather. I select some lively music and turn the volume up high. I print out the agendas for participants and my facilitator's agenda. I copy a couple pages from a book and a protocol we'll need. By 8:30, when Dave arrives, I've tidied up the room, have gathered our materials for the day, and am getting myself into the necessary frame of mind for me to facilitate a day of learning for my team.

I know that this internal preparation is far more important than the organization of materials and the hot coffee. I wake up before dawn, and my mornings are a blur of activities before I walk out my front door. Sometimes, by the time I've dropped my son off at his school, I feel frenzied and tired, yet I know that to lead my team I need to shift this energy. I've learned some effective ways to do so: I listen to music as I drive, I practice mindful breathing for a few minutes before getting out of my car,

---

and I remember who my team needs me to be—a calm, focused facilitator who can guide our journey.

Emotions are contagious, I remind myself, and emotions are like weather—they come and go. I find the parts of me that are grounded and hopeful, I notice my fatigue dissipating, I imagine how I want the day to go and what I want my team to get from our experience together. I've designed our learning time based on our team's goals and feedback from previous meetings. I've thought through how I'll introduce our day, reference prior requests, and make connections to other learning we've engaged in. I've thought through how to engage each individual person—what each coach needs to leave with the feeling that this was time well spent. I've thought about what I need today and what I can learn.

By 9:00 a.m., when our meeting starts, I'm truly feeling calm, happy to see everyone gathered around the table, and excited for our time together.

CHAPTER 12

Navigating Conflict

Humanities Team, 2008

Cassandra showed me an email that Margaret had sent to many staff members at Wilson Middle. It included a litany of complaints about my coaching and team leadership, a long description of how the school was out of control, and a proposal to have me removed from my position. "Reply all if you agree that she should be fired," was the closing line.

"I just thought you should know what's going on," Cassandra said. "I think her behavior is totally unprofessional, but I don't know what to do." I thanked Cassandra and left the building to walk around the neighborhood so I could clear my head. Perhaps because it was a Monday and I'd had a rejuvenating weekend, or perhaps because I'd recently been inspired by a workshop I'd attended, I calmly decided that it was time for a hard conversation with Margaret. I'd tried dodging her behavior, but that hadn't worked. I didn't like confrontations—who does?—but I needed to respond.

The next day, I went to her classroom during her prep period. "Margaret," I said, "I need to talk with you. It's somewhat urgent, so I hope you can make time now." She had a red pen in hand and was grading papers.

"What's up?" she said, putting down the pen.

"I understand that you have some concerns about my leadership," I said calmly and confidently. "I know that you sent an email out to staff expressing these. I want to hear directly from you about your concerns, and I also want to talk about how you can communicate with me and others in a way that might be more professional. Are you willing to have this conversation now?"

"Okay," she responded.

"The issue is that when you send out emails to segments of the staff, it creates division, distrust, and rumors. We need to be on the same page and united if we're going to make a difference for our students." I stopped and waited for her response. She looked down at her hands folded in her lap.

I continued. "What needs to happen so that you can come directly to me, or even to our principal, with your concerns?"

"You don't listen to me," she said.

"Why don't you take these concerns to our principal then? He wasn't on the email. Have you tried talking to him?" I asked.

"He doesn't listen to me, either," she said. "The only way I can get him to listen is when I remind him that I'm the union representative and I tell him it's official business."

"I'm listening, right now," I said. "Can we talk about some of these complaints you have about me?"

And we talked. And I listened. There were some kernels of truth that resonated with me in what she said. I acknowledged that I hadn't joined the staff in a very effective way, that I had indeed thought their teaching practices were weak. Margaret defended her right to email her colleagues and vent when she needed, but she also agreed to come to me first with her concerns. I admitted that I was tempted to share her email with our principal—I felt hurt and embarrassed by the fact that she was trying to instigate an uprising against me—and she said she understood.

Things didn't get dramatically better after this. Margaret continued venting in emails and in the hallways and meetings, but she also made attempts to share her concerns with me in private. What improved was my confidence in initiating hard conversations and my ability to have them. I engaged my principal—who also avoided conflict—in a hard conversation about staff professionalism. I asked for his support to draw clear boundaries around what teachers could and couldn't do. I asked him to attend some of our department meetings so that he could observe how challenging it was to get through an agenda and make progress on our department goals. And I also had a hard conversation with myself: "How much more can you put up with?"

Although many facilitators name dealing with conflict as the hardest part of coaching a team, this chapter intentionally comes toward the end of this book. We can't effectively respond to conflict until we've done the thinking in the preceding chapters of this book: until we've explored our own emotional intelligence (EI) and that of our team, considered the power structures that frame our teams, and thought about teams as entities in development.

Conflict can be *healthy* and *unhealthy*. Healthy conflict brings group members closer to each other and contributes to strengthening the work or product they're focused on. Unhealthy conflict does the opposite. It erodes trust among teammates and distracts the group from their goals and objectives.

Conversation around conflict sometimes focuses on how to manage—to control, change, or deal with—a difficult teacher. We need strategies for responding to individual behavior, but we also need to make sure we're identifying and examining the threads of conflict. Rarely is the problem due to one person's behavior. Usually there's a culture and system that fosters and supports this behavior, and usually the behaviors of a number of others in the organization allow for and feed an individual's dysfunctional behavior.

Furthermore, focusing on dealing with unhealthy behavior can draw attention from another challenge that teams have with conflict: the inability to have healthy conflict. Fear of conflict can prevent us from having honest conversations about our practice as teachers, coaches, and leaders, conversations that could have significant impact on our students and the communities that we serve. These are two sides of one coin: To have healthy conflict, we'll have to know we can manage unhealthy conflict; and unhealthy conflict is bound to happen, but teams can learn to recuperate from it and emerge stronger and more cohesive than before.

To get started on thinking about these ideas, you might take some time to reflect on the questions in Exhibit 12.1. It may also be helpful to engage your team in reflecting on these questions and sharing their responses with each other.

WHAT IS CONFLICT AND WHY IS IT SO SCARY?

Exhibit 12.1. Reflecting on Conflict

1. How was conflict expressed in your family of origin?
2. How could you tell if people were sharing their opinions and ideas? What did this look and sound like?
3. How did it feel to you when adults expressed their opinions and ideas?
4. What were you told about how and when to express your opinions and ideas?
5. What does healthy conflict look and sound like to you?

Many people feel uncomfortable with conflict, which may have to do with the evolution of our species. For hundreds of thousands of years, humans relied on each other to survive; any threat to the bonds between social groups could be dangerous to the little bands of hominids that roamed the African savannah. Add to this social evolutionary history that cultural groups communicate disagreement, deal with conflict, and even think about conflict differently. Conflict in a Caucasian British family often looks very different from conflict in a Russian Jewish family. Furthermore, men and women express conflict differently. Then there is the way our brains respond to perceived threats—they often overreact and flood our bodies with stress hormones that shut down our ability to think clearly; our brains send us into fight, flight, or freeze mode. Finally, many of us have never acquired the communication skills to deal with conflict—it's just not something we've learned. Let me assure you that if conflict makes you nervous, or if you avoid it at all costs, you're very normal.

However, the path to transforming our schools inevitably passes through a vast terrain of conflict. We'll need to explore our disagreements, values, beliefs, and opinions to build the kinds of strong and effective teams that will make a difference to our students. We need to learn how to manage unhealthy conflict, and we also need to learn how to cultivate the kind of conflict that will be productive and that will help us learn. We need to transform our relationship to conflict.

What might be possible if we could experience conflict in a way that was healthy? What could such an exploration teach us about ourselves, each other, our students, and our practice of teaching and learning? What if we could experience conflict as *opportunity*, and what if we embraced exploring our conflicts together? Before we explore dealing with unhealthy conflict—which is necessary—let's start with the kind of conflict we might aspire to see in teams.

> *When an old culture is dying, the new culture is born from a few people who are not afraid to be insecure.*
>
> RUDOLF BAHRO

WHAT IS HEALTHY CONFLICT IN A TEAM?

Kelly: I'm surprised to hear you say that, Joe. I see the situation with that student very differently, and I was going to suggest a completely different course of action. I want to understand your perspective, so could you tell me more?

Joe: Really? Huh, I imagined you'd agree with me. The reason I thought that we should … is because … what I noticed when I worked with that student was … and … That's how I came to my conclusion. Does that make sense?

Kelly: It does, and I didn't realize … but I still have some questions about … because your suggestion makes me feel really uncomfortable. I still disagree about that plan, and I'd like to suggest … What are your thoughts on that?

Joe: Well, I can see how you'd have those questions … I wasn't sure about that either. I hadn't really thought about … and I probably need to explain that other idea more clearly … I'd also like to hear your perspective on … I think you might have more information about that.

These are fragments of a real conversation between two deans at a school about a very serious issue with a student. What you can't read in this text is what I observed in their nonverbal communication—the way their bodies leaned in toward each other, the openness conveyed by their relaxed postures, their truly inquisitive tones of voice, the nodding and affirmative gestures indicating their listening, the long pauses and silence between what each person said. So much meaning is communicated through our nonverbal message, and if we intend to participate in healthy conflict we need to be mindful of those as well as of the words we use.

Healthy conflict includes an exchange of ideas, a sincere asking of questions, a genuine willingness on everyone's part to listen, learn, and even to experience moments of discomfort. Healthy conflict can make me feel nervous and excited at the same time—my heart might beat a little faster than usual—but healthy conflict also feels hopeful. When healthy conflict surfaces with a colleague, I sometimes worry that I'll uncover some deep, serious disagreement in how we see reality, but I also know there's a good chance we'll make a deeper connection. The conversation feels like a risk worth taking because usually healthy conflict is about discussing something we've previously tried to ignore. Even if we find out we're in disagreement, it's often a relief to have the conversation.

Why Do We Need Healthy Conflict?

Patrick Lencioni, an expert in organizational development, is the author of the well-known *Five Dysfunctions of a Team* (2005). He offers a simple framework that explains what teams need to accomplish their objectives—and which dysfunctions prevent them from doing so. The first dysfunction is the absence of trust. Without the ability to be vulnerable and completely open with each other, members of a great team can't engage in conflict. The fear of conflict is the second dysfunction of a team. Lencioni argues that teams must passionately debate issues, decisions, and ideas to make progress on their work together. The third dysfunction is the lack of commitment. If a team hasn't engaged in healthy conflict, then its members can't be sure they have genuine buy-in around important decisions. And lack of commitment leads to the next dysfunction: avoiding accountability. If teammates have committed to doing something, members hold each other accountable. The final dysfunction of teams is the inattention to results—nothing gets done.

We can also think about this framework as the functions necessary for a team to be effective. With the team of transformational coaches, I focused intensely on building trust. This foundation allowed for there to be healthy conflict—coaches challenged each other's thinking, offered each other hard feedback on professional development sessions, and questioned each other's coaching strategies. This resulted in team members making agreements about how to facilitate PD and committing to these decisions. Coaches held each other accountable for what they said they'd do and to the high expectations we determined for our work. And this meant that things got done—we saw results.

Even among the strongest teams, conflict is always a little uncomfortable. Although we might focus on issues, it's inevitable that some might feel like they're under personal attack. This is why it's essential to cultivate emotional intelligence: Our EI boosts our awareness of how we're feeling and helps us manage our responses. We can cultivate emotional intelligence and also commit to conflict.

Lencioni (2005) also offers a conflict continuum that is invaluable. Artificial harmony is on one end of the continuum, and mean-spirited, personal attacks are on the other end. Both of these extremes are equally damaging to a team. In the middle is a dividing line where conflict moves from constructive to destructive. The ideal conflict zone, says Lencioni, is the area just before conflict gets destructive. In this space, a team is engaged in every opportunity for constructive conflict. Of course, it isn't always possible for a team to stay in that productive conflict ground: even in the strongest teams, sometimes people cross into the destructive conflict zone. But when teammates do cross the line, it can be an opportunity for trust building. As a team recovers from an incident of destructive conflict, members build confidence that their team can survive such an event—which boosts their confidence in exploring conflict.

HOW CAN I FACILITATE HEALTHY CONFLICT?

Whether your team has been mired in artificial harmony or destructive conflict, you can cultivate healthy conflict by recalling your role as a facilitator of learning. Assume that your team craves healthy exchanges of ideas but that they don't have the skills or knowledge to do so. The following activities can help a team move toward healthy conflict.

Raise Individual and Group Awareness

We start by individually understanding who we are in relationship to conflict. Our viewpoints and comfort with conflict are determined by many factors including our personalities, cultural backgrounds, and family norms. Our Myers-Briggs type (see Chapter 2) can give insight on this, as can the reflection questions in Exhibit 12.1. Team members need time to engage in these reflections and share their insights about themselves with each other. Sharing builds empathy and understanding and will help in creating norms for conflict.

Get Buy-In on the Need for Conflict

Engage team members in reflecting on how they work together and on the need for healthy conflict. Whether you need to shift them away from destructive conflict or out of artificial harmony, you'll need to have buy-in if you are asking for a different kind of conflict. This can come from reflecting on how they work together and what might be possible if they were to commit to not holding back on opinions and to expressing them in a constructive way.

Articulate a Shared Vision for Conflict

A team needs to agree on what healthy conflict will look and sound like to ensure the exchange of good ideas. Team members can write down and then share their individual preferences relating to acceptable and unacceptable behavior around discussion and debate. During the sharing, a note taker can capture key areas of similarity and difference. The team then discusses collective preferences and agrees on some acceptable and unacceptable behaviors that everyone can commit to. Exhibit 12.2 is one team's statement that reflects its shared vision for conflict.

Exhibit 12.2. Five Indicators That Conflict Is Healthy

- We wrestle with ideas.
- We ask questions to probe for deeper understanding.
- We change our minds.
- We demonstrate curiosity.
- We hold student needs at the center of our work.

Identify Sentence Stems That Promote Healthy Conflict

Some of us don't know what words to use to express our ideas in a way that feels authentic but that also keeps our team from moving into the zone of destructive conflict. We need to engage our teams in discussing how we can skillfully say what we want to say and create tools to do so. Sentence starts and sample statements are a great beginning. In the heat of an emotional moment, we may want to contribute effectively to a discussion, but we may not know how to say it. There's nothing wrong with equipping ourselves with every tool possible to reach our end goal of healthy conflict. Exhibit 12.3 offers some useful suggestions.

Exhibit 12.3. Sentence Stems for Healthy Conflict

- Can you elaborate on your thinking because I'm not sure I understand?
- I have some concerns about that suggestion. Could you explain it more?
- I want to push back on that idea. I've noticed … and I would suggest …
- I hear what you're saying, but have you considered … ?
- What do you think the unintended consequences of doing that might be?
- I'm curious about … I have some reservations about doing that.
- That's an innovative idea. I'm having a hard time imaging how that could work. Could you explain?
- Can you help me understand why you believe that? My experience has led me to a different conclusion, but I want to understand your perspective.
- I disagree with you about that, but I want to hear your thoughts.
- I disagree with you about that. Can I share my reasoning?
- I disagree with you about that, but I'm willing to change my mind.
- It would help me get behind that idea if I could hear more about …
- I agree with several points you made, but I want to challenge you on this idea …
- I have a request to make. Are you open to hearing it?
- I think we've jumped into decision making too fast and haven't gotten to the root of the problem. Could we spend some more time exploring what it might be?
- Let me see if I understand what you're saying. I hear that you think … Did I get that right? Ok, I still disagree with that idea, assessment, and suggestion.
- I hear that we have a difference in beliefs, and I understand that it comes from our different experiences.
- I hear that our beliefs are very different. To make a decision about what to do, it seems like we need to get additional perspectives.

Facilitators: Cultivate Your Own Emotional Intelligence around Conflict

We need to hone our awareness of the feelings that come up for us when there's conflict and be mindful of how we respond, especially if conflict is particularly hard for us. As leaders of a group, our emotions are contagious—so if we're calm and grounded when conflict surfaces, our team will take a cue from us. We will also need to be especially attuned to how others are experiencing conflict as we foment healthy conflict and also as we hold everyone accountable to the norms they've agreed on. We won't have the mental energy pay attention to all of this if our own emotions override our thinking capacities.

Instigate and Validate Conflict

Many of us will do anything we can to avoid disagreement and conflict, even if we know its necessary and could be useful. Lencioni (2005) warns, "The leader is going to have to be ready to not only light the fuse of good conflict but to gently fan the flames for a while too" (p. 45). This means that we have to excavate buried conflict and invite team members to address those issues. Leaders can also request shared responsibility by asking the entire team to listen for and unearth conflict that may need to be addressed.

As team members get used to challenging each other's opinions and ideas, you can alleviate the discomfort by validating and normalizing it. Don't hesitate to interrupt two debating team members and say, "I want to point out that you two are engaging in healthy conflict. Even though it might feel uncomfortable, this is good for our team and our work. Keep going." Finally, during a meeting debrief, it's also useful for the facilitator to invite reflection by asking, "We had some healthy conflict today. How do you think this might affect our team and our work together?" It's important that team members recognize the way conflict can lead to more commitment and better work together.

Facilitate Conflict Resolution

To have healthy conflict, our team needs to know we'll deal with unhealthy conflict. We can't just avoid it when we see it, and focusing on the other suggestions in this section will go only so far if we don't directly address unhealthy conflict.

A NOTE ON TALKING ABOUT RACE AND OTHER REALLY HARD THINGS

For many people, talking about race might be the most difficult topic to talk about. For me, these are the discussions in which my heart beats faster, my palms perspire, and my mind can feel muddled. Yet we must have them. We cannot transform our schools without talking about race. (If you or some members of your team are not convinced of this need, see recommendations in Appendix E for more reading.)

In this book, I hope I'm providing you with many strategies to create the conditions in which these essential conversations can be had, including how to build a foundation of trust and boost effective communication. I also want to emphasize the urgency for you, as a leader, to have the time and space to do some of your own reflection and learning *before* you engage a team in these conversations. You need to be aware of the emotions that will likely surface when you facilitate conversations about race and other really hard things. You need to have done some sorting through those feelings so that you can effectively hold and facilitate space for others to do so. For most of us, this sorting through is a lifelong process, so don't expect to resolve all your thoughts and feelings. But you need to do some of it.

I'd like to offer the way I think about these issues when I'm working on them with a team or individual. My assumptions are as follows:

1. *This isn't going to be easy.* Whether we're talking to people who share our particular cultural group or skin tones, or we're in mixed company, speaking about race—and classism, patriarchy, homophobia, and the other things that have divided us—is going to be uncomfortable.

2. *But it will get easier.* One reason that it's hard to have these conversations is because we don't have them. We can learn how to have them—our inability reflects a *skill gap* that we can close and we can learn to acknowledge and manage the feelings that come up. With practice, these conversations get easier.

3. *There is no "right way" to have these conversations.* We're going to struggle to find the right words and get them out.

4. *But we have to do it anyway.* We need to acquire skills, manage our own discomfort, and engage in conversations about race, class, privilege, and power because children need us to.

5. *Racism is learned and can be unlearned.* No one is born with distorted perceptions of others. Conversation, community, education, and reflection can dismantle bias and the structures of oppression that riddle our society.

Conversations about race can feel like healthy conflict or unhealthy conflict. They can be constructive or destructive. They can also be healing and transformational—but usually not unless the journey has been a little bumpy. There are more resources for engaging in conversations about race in Appendix E.

HOW CAN I RESPOND TO UNHEALTHY CONFLICT?

To foster healthy conflict in a team, we'll have to know what unhealthy conflict is and how to deal with it. Like healthy conflict, unhealthy conflict will look different depending on, for example, the configuration of the team, the cultural backgrounds of teammates, their ages, and genders. In some teams, unhealthy conflict appears in the parking lot in the form of nasty back-talking and complaining. And in some teams, the conflict will be displayed openly during meetings. In teams where I've witnessed these dysfunctional dynamics, I've heard people blaming and attacking each other, refusing to take responsibility for their words or behavior, and using language that's provocative and seems intended to set others off.

Unhealthy conflict can emerge from or, if it goes on unchecked, can create a toxic culture—you can almost smell the sulfuric fumes and see the bubbles of anger. In its extreme, when this is the culture of a team or staff, the consequences are serious. Meetings are often derailed—usually by a handful of people who act like bullies. There's usually an absence of effective leadership and no meeting norms. And the majority of members disengage. Not much gets done, and ultimately children suffer.

Reflect on Conditions

As a facilitator, if you are in a team on which there's unhealthy conflict, start by reflecting on the broader conditions in which the team exists. Look at Exhibit 13.1 and

Exhibit 13.4 to determine whether your team is a reflection of a larger culture that's challenged in your school or organization. If you are in a team that's dysfunctional and also in a school where there's widespread dysfunction, then your work will be much more challenging. You'll need to find allies with whom you can partner to shift the whole school's culture. If this is the case, it might help to know that it will probably take some 5–7 years of concentrated effort by a strong group of people to shift the school's culture. I offer this as a reminder of the limits of your power as a facilitator. Even the most skilled and effective facilitator can't turn around a team (or staff) by herself if the whole school is riddled with unhealthy conflict.

Hone Your Own Emotional Intelligence

A facilitator needs to be aware of her triggers, which are often rooted in decades-old experiences. Our own emotions will be activated when there's conflict—the more we understand them, the better we can respond to them. We can't help a group manage their unhealthy dynamics if we're consumed or distracted by our own emotions. This is hard to do, and we need practice.

You can start by honing your awareness of the feelings you experience. For example, if I'm leading a conversation that gets tense, I say to myself, "I'm feeling a little anxious because Charles just interrupted Veronica and told her that her idea will never work. I feel protective of her and am worried that if I don't say anything the team won't respect me, but I'm also afraid that Charles will shut me down. Being interrupted is one of my triggers and now I'm feeling insecure." When I find distance between what's going on and how I'm responding and I recognize my feelings, I can think clearly. I can say, without charged emotion in my voice, "Charles, we've agreed not to interrupt each other in our team meetings. Veronica, would you please continue what you were saying?" My clarity when I say that can often be enough to set the discussion back on course; others pick up on my confidence that everything is really okay, and we can move on. As leaders, our emotions are the most contagious in a group, so if we start feeling anxious and scared the conversation might deteriorate. If we find a way to genuinely feel confident and calm, the conversation might shift. We have tremendous influence, and when we're aware of our feelings we can effectively use our power of influence.

Return to Norms

If conflict between team members becomes unproductive, the second step is to return to the norms or community agreements. Simply saying, "We've agreed not to interrupt each other," or "I want to remind us that one of our norms is to assume positive intent" can often be enough to subtly shift how a group is engaging. Sometimes it's useful to state how the unproductive behavior is affecting the group by saying, for example, "When we interrupt, we don't get to hear someone's full idea. We need everyone to contribute and share their thoughts so that we can be sure we're making the best decision. If we don't make good decisions, we're less likely to get full commitment from each other. Let's be mindful of giving everyone the full time they need to express their thoughts." It's helpful to assume that the team *wants* to engage with each other productively and is just having a moment of forgetting or falling into old behaviors. If a team has spent the necessary time developing norms and reflecting on them, and if there are agreed on processes for using them, then this approach often works.

If unhealthy conflict continuously bubbles up in your team, you need to go back to norms (see Chapter 6), and team members need to recommit to how they want to work together. Sometimes the norms that were developed, perhaps at the beginning of the school year, become irrelevant as a team develops. Maybe they worked for the team's launching phase but need to be revised or expanded. Maybe individuals on the team understand the norms to mean different things, and there needs to be some shared meaning-making. Or perhaps a group of people can't see how they're interacting with each other. In this case, team members need to see or hear how they're working together and recognize the negative impact. Unless they acknowledge and own their behavior, they won't be invested in changing it. As a facilitator, you can ask for permission to video record the team and then facilitate an observation of it, or you can record a meeting and offer a transcript. Of course, in a transcript you can't see body language or hear tone of voice, and those are often powerful indicators of dysfunctional behaviors.

Identify the Conflict

Sometimes, if conflict surfaces in a group, it can be immediately addressed by identifying what the conflict is about. Often just being able to name it—"We're experiencing some conflict because our personal core values are different"—can relieve what feels like interpersonal conflict. Participants can then move on to discussing personal and school values and mission. Other times, conflicts escalate because of the emotions that arise. As a facilitator, if you have a hunch about the source of the conflict, try saying something like, "I think we're disagreeing on our goals," or "I hear that people hold different values." This can deescalate a situation and help teammates get perspective on their disagreements.

Conflict can become unhealthy when team members trip over extraneous obstacles that prevent them from focusing on the real issues. These obstacles can be informational—perhaps team members need more time to share opinions, perspectives, and facts related to the topic they're discussing. As a facilitator, sometimes I've overestimated how much time people need to understand a shift in instructional strategies, for example. Conflict has surfaced because people just didn't have the information they needed.

Conflict can also surface because of environmental factors that have to do with the atmosphere and context in which the discussion is happening. This can include a shortage of time, organizational politics, and organizational dysfunction on a larger scale. For example, if a school is facing consolidation of staff, this will have a profound impact on a team's conversations even if the people engaged in the discussion are not directly affected. Sometimes when conflict bubbles up, prompt yourself to ask: What else might be going on in this school or organization that's contributing to the conflict? The conflict might also be stemming from one member who is simply in a bad mood.

Problems or issues between members of a team can lead to conflict, as I'm sure many of us have experienced. For example, something might have happened between two teammates some years ago that is contributing to conflict that we notice, or other teammates may have stark differences in their styles. A person's position in an organization can also affect the levels of conflict in a team—for example, teachers on a leadership team may be reluctant to challenge the principal's plans because of the power he holds.

Finally, unhealthy conflict can be due to one person who may lack the experience, knowledge, self-esteem, or emotional intelligence to positively contribute to a team. An individual may hold a set of values or beliefs that differ substantially from those of the rest of the group.

Identifying some possible sources of the conflict you observe in a team can help a group make a decision about how to move forward. Most often, we experience conflict as interpersonal. When I led the humanities team at Wilson Middle School, I usually interpreted one teacher's questions as resistance to my leadership. It took me a long time to acknowledge that she simply needed more information. If we feel that conflict is interpersonal, it seems much more challenging to address. If we recognize that it might have something to do with an organizational challenge, or a difference in values, we can sometimes see pathways that open for our work together.

Consider Addressing the Conflict Now or Later

When you notice unhealthy conflict in your team, you'll need to make an assessment about whether it needs to be addressed in the moment, with the team, or whether it's a conflict between two team members that needs to be addressed later. Most likely, you'll know if the situation is the latter—you'll have seen these team members engage in unhealthy conflict with each other before or you'll be able to see the clearly interpersonal conflict between two people.

Let It Go

If the conflict doesn't need to be addressed later, and if you attempt, either successfully or unsuccessfully, to address it in the moment, sometimes the best move you can make is to let it go. You recognize that someone else's behavior is not personal (i.e., not toward you or to others in the team), and you shift your attention away from his or her behavior. You might need to address the behavior one-on-one with the individual or it might resolve itself—but for that moment, for the sake of the team's greater needs and objectives that day, you don't respond. Here's an example of a meeting where I observed a facilitator not engaging with a teammate's potentially provocative behavior:

Cassie: Let's ask admin if we can _____ next year. That would be so cool for us and for our kids!

Rhonda: That'll never happen. We tried that already. Who has another brilliant idea? *(With a markedly sarcastic tone of voice)*

Facilitator: Rhonda, what's going on with you right now? Your response to Cassie's suggestion was strong.

Rhonda: Nothing! Her idea won't work, that's all!

Facilitator: We've made agreements here about how we respond to the suggestions of others, and telling them that their idea could never work is a breach of that agreement. It makes it hard for us to share ideas if we respond like that so I need to ask you to be mindful of how you respond to the ideas that others put out. If you have doubts, consider how you might ask a question that is grounded in inquiry such as, "I'm curious about what you think the challenges might be to taking that action? How do you anticipate our administration might respond?" Perhaps you can rethink what you'd like to ask and try again because we value your perspective.

Rhonda: I feel like you're silencing me and don't let me talk. I was just expressing my thoughts.

Facilitator: My intention isn't to silence you. My intention is to hold a safe space for our team where everyone can contribute in conversations and feel heard—at our August retreat, we all identified that we need to feel heard if we're going to have conversations that will help us meet our goals.

Rhonda: I still felt silenced.

Facilitator: Can you suggest a way that I could help you bring awareness to the way to communicate and not make you feel silenced? What could I have said?

Rhonda: I don't know.

This was a tense moment, although the facilitator seemed calm throughout. For the rest of the meeting, Rhonda sat in silence. The rest of the group, however, engaged in a lively discussion and seemed unaffected by the tense moment. Later the facilitator explained that she had attributed the conflict to Rhonda's mood, which was regularly off, and recognized that she needed to follow up with a private conversation with Rhonda. But in the moment, I observed that the team didn't get stuck—the facilitator seemed to let it go, and the team followed her lead.

Managing Unhealthy Conflict in the Moment

1. Ground yourself: Acknowledge what you're feeling and take a deep breath.
2. Return to the team's norms and share the impact on the team when a norm isn't adhered to.
3. Identify the conflict or impasse.
4. Decide to address the conflict now or later.
5. If necessary, address it in the moment.
6. Let it go.

WHAT IF NONE OF THESE SUGGESTIONS WORK?

If I had read this chapter when I worked with the humanities team at Wilson Middle School, I probably still would have said, "None of this will work!" Some of that was because I just didn't have the skills or they were too rudimentary to manage the team I was coaching, but other factors would have made even these strategies hard to implement. If you're in a situation like I was where it all seems hopeless, let me offer a few more ideas.

Get Help from Others

If conflict has been brewing between two individuals, then you'll need additional tools for conflict resolution or support from someone outside of the team. Many of us don't have the refined skills or knowledge for mediating interpersonal conflict between two adults—we've never learned it. If this is the case, I encourage you to search out someone else to help you: another colleague, a conflict mediator, a school counselor, a restorative justice practitioner, or a trusted and skilled administrator. You can ask the two people in conflict to meet with you, and you can say, "You two clearly have some unresolved conflict with each other. It is affecting our team negatively and preventing us from reaching our goals. I need to find someone else to help you two mediate your conflict. Do you have any suggestions for who that could be?" Ideally, both people would agree on that outside individual, but if that isn't the case then you can say, "It's unfortunate that you can't agree on someone to help because our team needs you two to resolve your issues. I will ask around and will try to give you two options to choose from. If you can't agree on one of these, I'll make the decision."

Have a Hard Conversation

We must strive to do everything possible to create a team culture in which we can take care of unhealthy conflict. However, as we do this, there are sure to be times when we have to deal with someone individually, when we have to have a hard conversation. I encourage you to do additional reading and learning in the area of hard conversations, and I've found a couple of resources incredibly useful in learning to navigate difficult moments.

The first recommendation is for the work of Jennifer Abrams. Her book *Having Hard Conversations* (2009) offers invaluable tools. She suggests that we begin hard conversations by setting the tone and purpose for the conversation. Then she suggests we get to the point and name it professionally. When we name the issue with someone else's behavior, she reminds us to give a couple of specific examples. Abrams explains that we need to describe the effect of this behavior on colleagues, students, and the school, describing the consequences and impact of the behavior without dramatizing it. Finally, Abrams encourages us to share our willingness to resolve the issue and have a dialogue and discussion about it.

The other resource I've found useful is *Crucial Conversations* by Patterson et al. (2002). They suggest that when preparing for a crucial conversation you ask yourself four questions:

1. What do I really want for myself?
2. What do I really want for others?
3. What do I really want for the relationship?
4. How would I behave if I really wanted these results? (pp. 34–35)

In Appendix F, you can find other suggestions for developing your knowledge and skill set for having difficult conversations.

Set Boundaries

We all have a responsibility to learn and be reflective and work on our leadership skills. But even if you're a novice leader and you're working hard on building your own skill set, you also don't need to be a punching bag. You can invite people to behave differently, you can give them tools, can involve them in creating a vision and community agreements, and can ask them to follow certain agreements—but you can't *make* people change. You have a responsibility to create a safe space for your team (and don't forget that you are a part of this team), and that trumps all. Sometimes you have to accept that someone doesn't have capacity to be reflective, and although you can empathize with that person you still need to establish boundaries around how they act. You can't let one person silence his or her colleagues or stifle the work of a group or dump his or her anger on you. This is a hard conversation. Setting boundaries is really about you saying to yourself, "This isn't okay. I've done my very best," and then considering the next suggestion.

Enlist Administrators or Supervisors

Sometimes when unhealthy conflict is unmanageable between two people or in a team, you need to ask someone else for help—ideally, the person who supervises the individuals. This is a last resort, and there can be consequences when doing this. For example, some team members might feel that you breached confidentiality agreements or that you're going over their heads and telling on them. Sometimes when you've tried everything else and drawn a clear boundary, you need to enlist help.

When you approach an administrator, explain what you've tried with this team, describe how the unhealthy conflict is affecting the group and your work together, and ask for the administrator's support with very specific requests. Most likely, the administrator won't be surprised and will have seen this kind of behavior before. You might ask the administrator to have a direct, hard conversation with the teacher or team or to attend a couple of team meetings. You will probably need to make some suggestions for what the support might look like and recognize that you're asking him or her to do something difficult, something for which he or she may not even have the skills. You still need to ask. In this case, it's useful to remember that you might be coaching up: use your tools as a coach to engage this administrator in this conversation.

Here's what I said to a team I once coached when I took this step:

> *Never doubt that a small group of thoughtful, committed citizens can change the world; indeed, it's the only thing that ever has.*
>
> MARGARET MEAD

I really want to help you all with the project you're working on. In the last 6 months, I've tried all of the tools in my facilitator box, but I'm stuck. There's a lot of unhealthy conflict getting in the way of reaching our goals. Unless someone can offer a suggestion for what we can do, I need to ask that Mr. X [their supervisor] attend our meetings. I am hoping he might be able to offer support, but I also need to let him know that we've reached an impasse. I wanted to let you know that I'm going to do this.

Build Culture

Unhealthy team dynamics and difficult individuals can consume a lot of energy. The problem is rarely one person—a difficult or resistant teacher—or even a group of them. The problem is a culture that has allowed unhealthy conflict to mushroom out of control, a culture that has tolerated and permitted this behavior, and a culture that hasn't attended to building a team's emotional intelligence. Culture is made by people. The culture of a school or organization can be shifted—it can take years, but it can be done.

Make sure that you're putting 90% of your effort into shaping a healthy culture and limited time and energy into responding to the individuals who are not willing to shift. In most schools, the truly challenging members are very few in number but occupy a great deal of our thoughts, feelings, time, and energy. It is much more effective to focus on those who are willing to change or even those who seem disengaged or neutral. Build pockets of healthy culture. These can grow and spread just as the toxic ones did.

Have Hope

The organizational development expert Danah Zohar tells us, "It is a well-known sociological law that a ten percent minority in any culture begins to unsettle and change that culture" (Zohar and Marshall, 2004, p. 145). I find great encouragement in this. If you're in a leadership position, the research is even better. Zohar and Marshall found that if 2–5% of the top leadership in an organization undergoes profound personal transformation, another 10% of their direct reports will follow their lead. This is precisely why transformational leadership coaching is such high-leverage work and why I advocate for it across the country.

Keep Learning

As a team lead and as someone who is striving to grow, you are responsible for your own learning. If possible, get the support of a leadership coach. Read. Use the reflections offered in this book to understand yourself better and to create your own learning plan. Seek out effective leaders and watch them. Videotape yourself facilitating a meeting and reflect on it. Ask for feedback from your team and listen to it—remember, you can't see your own blind spots, and it's possible you are enabling the unhealthy conflict.

Know When to Go

Sometimes you just need to get out of a dysfunctional culture or team. When you've tried everything possible and when you see the toxicity affecting your physical and emotional well-being, it's time to go. Being a martyr won't help your school, team, or students—it will only undermine your ability to put your skills into play somewhere else. Don't let fear hold you back from moving into a position in which your leadership will be respected and appreciated and in which you'll be able to more effectively serve students. If you're not sure when the time has come for you to leave, listen to the people around you who care about you. Sometimes when we're in the thick of dysfunction, we can't see as clearly as others. If your loved ones are telling you it's time to quit, it might just be.

The question we need to ask ourselves is whether there is any place we can stand in ourselves where we can look at all that's happening around us without freaking out, where we can be quiet enough to hear our predicament, and where we can begin to find ways of acting that are at least not contributing to further destabilization. Ram Dass

Transformational Coaching Team, 2012

It happened toward the end of the first year, on a Friday afternoon when I knew everyone was tired. One team member made a disparaging comment about the teachers in our schools, and another echoed it. "That doesn't align with the values of our team," I thought, reflecting on our value of holding a compassionate growth mind-set. My inclination was to say something, to remind the team of our values, but I held back. I wondered if the comment reflected more than the coach's emotional fatigue. I wondered whether the comment resonated with others or bothered them. I wondered whether anyone else would say something if I didn't.

The two team members continued complaining about the teachers. One said, "If it wasn't for them, you all would see that I'm a good coach." This person had fallen behind on some commitments expected from coaches: reports were unfinished, meetings had been canceled, professional development sessions were haphazardly prepared for.

A stillness seemed to encompass the room. One coach glanced at me, and then another leaned forward. "I'm feeling uncomfortable by your comments," she said. There was a long, awkward moment when I had to restrain myself from jumping in to try to resolve the tension. "Wait," I told myself. She continued, "I hear what you're saying and know how challenging some of those teachers can be. You've got a hard load, but ... " Her voice trailed off. Another coach spoke up. "I've worked with some of those teacher in our department," he said. "I've seen potential in a few."

The team member who had made the initial comment looked flustered. Again, I restrained myself from jumping in to stop the discomfort. I sensed that others wanted me to do or say something, but I wanted to see what would happen if I didn't.

Someone else spoke up, directing a question at the coach who seemed to be in distress. "What do you think you can influence and control when it comes to coaching your teachers?" The distressed coach responded defensively.

I spoke then. "I've been unsure of whether to say anything about what's come up. I know this feels uncomfortable—it does to me, too—and I want to acknowledge that we're experiencing conflict. I want to ask that we all stay in this, keep listening to each other, and see where this takes us. Can I suggest we all take a deep breath?" I did so, loudly. "I want to make sure we hear from everyone who wants to speak. What's coming up for you in response to the comments that others have shared?"

With the team's agreement, I modified the agenda so that we could continue the conversation. Over the next hour, many moments were tense, and others felt hopeful and insightful. Several coaches challenged the suggestion that our efficacy was contingent upon the perceived quality of the teachers we worked with. One made a suggestion: "I feel like we need to return to our team's values and commitments and make sure we're all onboard with those." There was unanimous agreement.

As the following weeks unfolded and we reflected on our values and commitments, I observed how coaches took increasing ownership over the products our team was responsible for—the coaching of teachers, the leadership of department meetings, the delivery of professional development. Far in advance, they solicited feedback on agendas for upcoming PD sessions; they called each other for support when preparing for coaching conversations; they reflected on the stress they were under and their desire to demonstrate their competence.

During the meeting when the initial conflict had bubbled up, I wasn't sure if it would be healthy or unhealthy—I didn't know what the long-term effects would be on our levels of trust or on the quality of our work. But it didn't take too long, and I didn't need too much evidence to see that this had been worthy conflict that would strengthen our team and the work that we did.

CHAPTER 13

Assessing Organizational Conditions

Humanities Team, 2009

It was a warm, February afternoon, and I was in my office preparing for a department meeting when I was inundated by a barrage of physical symptoms: my heart raced, my breathing was shallow, and I felt lightheaded and dizzy. A colleague happened to call at that moment. "That sounds like a panic attack," he said. The feelings subsided, although I felt rattled. I'd never had panic attacks and felt competent at managing anxiety. But I also acknowledged that I was heading into what I suspected might be yet another difficult department meeting. I'd been struggling with this team for a year and a half and was getting tired.

Year 2 at Wilson Middle was better than Year 1. The humanities team had a focus. We attempted to use norms. There was more clarity around my role as a team leader. There were some changes in team composition, and the new blood was good. I found support outside the school in a coach of my own and a community of like-minded leaders. My skills increased, as did my self-awareness. I began to distinguish between

---

my own areas for growth and the pervasive toxicity in the school that impacted my ability to coach and lead.

I also began coaching a team of educators in another school, in another city—a team that was excited about collaborating, that welcomed me and appreciated my support, and that enthusiastically dove into the work of equity. This team energized me and gave me perspective on the conditions for leadership at Wilson Middle. I felt affirmed that I could meaningfully contribute to schools and recognizing that I probably needed to find another place to work.

I have a stubborn streak in me, and I like to see projects to their end. There were some promising shifts under way at Wilson Middle, and I was tempted to see if they would make a difference. But then there was the fact that the principal—with whom I had a solid partnership—had decided to leave. The district leadership was changing also, and I doubted that with the incoming leaders the school would receive the guidance it needed. There was also my husband admonishing me for putting up with so much dysfunction. "I don't understand why you'd want to stay there," he'd say when I'd come home and relay another meeting fiasco. And after that department meeting on that warm, February afternoon, a meeting that had been another contentious waste of time, I knew I needed to leave.

Look around you at the landscape in which you are building a team. What's the weather like? What's happening in other areas of the field? How crowded are the watering holes? Now that we've looked closely at team development, let's step back and survey the landscape in which you are building a team. An accurate picture of organizational conditions will help you identify the boundaries of your sphere of influence, take strategic action, and manage your emotions.

Many factors affect whether teams—and their leaders—can fulfill their potential. These include the culture of the organization in which the team lives and allocation of resources, including how time is used, levels of trust among stakeholders, and approaches to problem solving. This chapter describes 12 organizational categories that affect team development and suggests steps to establish optimal conditions. Exhibit 13.4 presents a self-assessment tool to help you reflect on the context in which your team is growing.

THE PRIMACY OF PURPOSE

The most effective schools and organizations have a mission and vision that motivates, unifies, and guides all stakeholders in their day-to-day operations. The mission and vision are written in purpose statements and are visible everywhere—on documents, walls, and agendas—and, more important, are alive in the hearts and hands of those doing the work. Short- and long-term goals are created to chart a path to fulfilling the mission and meeting the vision. Staff regularly reflect on the progress they're making toward their goals and identify any modifications that need to be made to the goals or the process for reaching them.

When a school has a living mission and vision, staff members feel as though they are on the same page. They may not always agree on how to do things—there might be heated conflict at times—but they're united around a shared purpose and are headed in the same direction. When hard decisions need to be made, purpose (and not the wants or needs of individuals) offers direction.

A mission and vision are alive only if the people implementing them know what they mean. Purpose statements are notorious for sounding like generic declarations, and many employ the same couple dozen words. Although we don't need to devote hours to revising our statements or conjuring up new phrases, we do need time to make meaning of them together. The process of creating, revisiting, and reflecting on the mission and vision brings them to life.

If your school or organization doesn't have a living mission or vision, your work building a team will be hard. This doesn't mean it can't be done; it just means that you'll need to co-create a strong and compelling purpose within your team, as I described in Chapter 4. You might also consider ways you can advocate for the development of a mission and vision, perhaps seeking out administrators who would be receptive to this work. Unless you're in a top leadership position, you may need to coach up and enroll your supervisors in a conversation about how a mission and vision would bring a group of people together and align efforts. You could suggest the formation of a mission team to lead this work and then offer your support. The strongest and most effective teams are often those nestled within a school with a sharply articulated and widely known mission and vision and also within a district that has the same. While you devote the majority of your energy to what's within your sphere of control, also advocate relentlessly for a compelling, shared purpose.

FOCUS, FOCUS, FOCUS

Effective organizations plan backward. They articulate their mission and vision, identify goals, and create a plan that lays out the actions and activities that will support the goals. Strategic plans include long-term goals (perhaps for 5 years) and annual goals. Good goals are SMARTE—strategic, measurable, attainable, relevant, time bound, and equitable—and limited in number. Based on my experience working in organizational change, I have landed on three as the magic number for school goals.

Goals can provide a focus for our efforts, but to maintain our focus they need to be memorable—not necessarily in the specifics committed to paper (e.g., the percentage of students who will move from X to Y) but at least in the broad strokes. For example, look at Rise Up Middle School's goals (Exhibit 13.1). Although most teachers will not be able to quote the goals word for word, I would expect most to remember the gist: if Rise Up's teachers remember that they're working on improving student reading and making sure that a handful of students have a positive experience in school, they are remembering enough. The goal areas need to be on the forefront of our minds, but we also need easy access to the specifics. Toward this end, goals need to be included regularly on agendas, in weekly or monthly newsletters, and in staff meetings. They need to be read, reviewed, and discussed, and stakeholders need updates on progress toward meeting goals. Goals should drive decision making about initiatives or programs that a school undertakes.

Here's a way to assess whether your school is sufficiently focused. Answer this question yourself, and then ask five staff members: What are we focused on this year? If I asked the staff at Rise Up and 95% of staff said, "We're focused on reading," that's focus. If they said, "We're focused on making people feel happier here," that's focus. If you ask people and they look at you quizzically and wonder what you mean, there probably isn't focus in your school. Look for broad strokes.

Then ask if they know where they can find the school's annual goals. If they can access them fairly quickly, that's good. If they say, "What do you mean? You mean those goals I have to set for my evaluation every year? Or the student goals?" I'd consider this to be an indicator that there's a lack of focus. Unless people remember the focal areas and have the details at their fingertips, the goals may not be present enough in their minds to make an impact on what they do every day.

When you are advocating for focus, it can help to remember that *focus* doesn't mean forgetting about everything else—it just means *focus*. For example, because your school decides to focus on the needs of male students for a year (perhaps because their performance is consistently poorer and they are more frequently sent out of class), you won't plan to ignore girls. We focus so that we can align resources, be strategic, and deepen our learning.

Sometimes schools are unfocused because of competing demands and a lack of shared vision. Sometimes school leaders don't know how to manage these demands and get folks on the same page. If this is the case, you might encourage your leaders to get support and coaching for themselves. By recognizing the level of focus at your site, you can determine where to expend energy. Even if the focus at your school is blurrier than you'd like, you can still set tight goals in your team and get something done.

ALIGNMENT UP AND OUT

Teams can harness individual energies into a collective effort to meet big goals. A team that operates within a school should be aligned to that school's vision, mission, goals, and strategic plans—this could be considered vertical alignment of efforts. Teams also need to align horizontally—what one team does needs to complement another team's work.

Reflect on these questions individually and with your team as you work toward naming a clear purpose for existing:

1. What piece of our school's vision are we working toward?

2. Which components of our mission are we upholding?

3. Which of our long-term or annual goals are we contributing to?

4. What specifically will this team need to do to move our school forward on its vision and goals?

Team members need these connections laid out. When the intersections of purpose and work become clear, team members are more likely to feel energized, motivated, and valued. They can see how their individual and collective efforts will lead to the success of a larger endeavor. They can see how other teams are also contributing and moving the whole school forward. Exhibit 13.1 is an example of how teams in a school are organizationally aligned.

Exhibit 13.1. School Teams' Organizational Alignment: Example of Rise Up Middle School (See Exhibit 4.7)

Our School's Mission:

Rise Up Middle School provides our students with the social, emotional, and academic skills necessary to find joy in life and learning, to build compassionate communities, and to master the skills and knowledge necessary to be successful in high school.

Rise Up's 2014–15 Goals:

1. 100% of our students who attend at least 95% of the school year will make at least a 20% growth in their reading scores as measured by the XYZ reading assessment.
2. On our annual survey of students, families, and community, 95% of respondents will report feeling welcomed, appreciated, and valued at our school.
3. We will reduce suspension rates and office referrals for our 20 focal students by 80%. On our annual survey, these students will each report feeling supported and cared for by at least five peers and three staff members.

TEAM	PURPOSE	RESPONSIBILITIES	MEMBERS * Lead
Leadership team	To uphold our school's mission; to monitor and implement our annual and long-term goals and our strategic plan for achieving these goals. Our team is responsible for all three of our annual goals.	• Analyze student data—for all students and in depth for our focal students • Design and deliver professional development • Lead instructional rounds • Monitor progress toward goals • Evaluate professional development • Serve as communication conduits between teams	Principal* Assistant principal Dean Coaches Grade-level Leads Community partnership liaison

TEAM	PURPOSE	RESPONSIBILITIES	MEMBERS * Lead
Administration team	To ensure the operational and fiscal efficacy of our school so that we can fulfill our mission and achieve our goals. Our focus is on our behavior management systems and on designing interventions for our tier 3 students. Our team is primarily responsible for supporting Goal 3.	• Design and implement behavior management systems • Provide professional development and coaching on behavior management systems • Monitor and disaggregate student referral data • Collect data on our focal students and share with lead team	Principal* Assistant principal Dean
Grade-level teams	Our team is primarily responsible for supporting Goals 1 and 2. (See Exhibit 4.7) We ensure that the conditions for student learning are optimal and that our culture is one of compassion, community, and collaboration among students and teachers.	• Lead culture-building activities with students • Design and implement our advisory program • Align supports for our focal students and analyze their impact	Grade-level lead* Teachers Coaches
Department teams	To ensure curricular alignment between grades; to align literacy practices across the curriculum. Our team is primarily responsible for supporting Goal 1.	• Collect data on our reading initiative and on student achievement and share with lead team • Engage in an inquiry process on our reading initiative	Coaches* Teachers

(continued)

TEAM	PURPOSE	RESPONSIBILITIES	MEMBERS * Lead
Community partnership team	Our team is primarily responsible for supporting Goals 2 and 3. We are the primary links between our staff and our families and external community. We build bridges and connection.	• Facilitate parent leadership groups • Design parent involvement activities • Facilitate parent–teacher–staff communication • Lead home visits for focal students • Access community resources for focal students and others	Community partnership liaison* Grade-level leads Dean

STABILITY

Stability of leadership and staff profoundly influences a school and district's culture. When leadership changes frequently, the organization's mission and vision can become vulnerable. Instability causes anxiety, results in weak follow-through on commitments, and drives individuals into survival mode and sometimes into silos where they become protective about resources. High leader turnover can also mean rapid changes in program and goals. Initiatives begun by one superintendent and carried out for two years might be abandoned when a new superintendent comes onboard. Teacher and leader turnover also means that institutional knowledge is drained from a system.

Those of us who have experienced high leader and staff turnover know well how instability undermines the efforts of team development. It means that we are constantly onboarding new team members, resetting team culture, returning to conversations around norms and goals, and building new relationships with others. This takes time and is mentally and emotionally taxing.

Even though this component of organizational conditions is beyond most team leaders' spheres of influence, it's worth considering for a few reasons. First, simply recognizing that high turnover within a team and within an organization impacts development efforts can help us manage our emotional responses. Second, reflecting on the impact of instability uncovers deep systems issues about why people come and go, which will need to be addressed at some point if we are to truly transform our schools. Third, understanding why people leave a school is useful when we're trying to build teams. Often, staff members leave because they don't feel valued, because their work isn't appreciated, because they don't feel they're making a difference, and because they don't trust each other or feel connected to each other. These are experiences that we can address within a team. If you lead, for example, a math department in a school with high turnover, you can focus on creating a team that is so effective, supportive, and healthy that teachers in your department are inspired to stay at your school. What if you can create a team that helps everyone on it feel safe, supported, and appreciated by others in the group? Can you create a healthy bubble within a dysfunctional system? Can you engage other team leaders in your school and organization to discuss how those conditions can be established elsewhere as well?

LEADERSHIP

Leaders matter. Optimal conditions for teams to thrive require strong, effective leaders at the helm of our schools and districts We need leaders like principals, assistant principals, and associate superintendents who champion team development, who engage stakeholders in building a vision for high-functioning teams, who allocate resources to team development, and who are consistent, outspoken advocates for the importance of functional teams. These leaders also need to appreciate and monitor the work that teams do and push them to refine their work. Finally, these leaders need to be effective at leading teams themselves. Their leadership teams should be exemplars of team effectiveness.

Unfortunately, some leaders in our school systems are underprepared for the scope of their responsibilities Although it can be challenging to enact transformational efforts in the absence of effective leadership, if we focus on what we can control and influence we can still build strong teams. Site and central office leaders often make decisions about time, our most highly valued resource for building teams. Team leaders don't need big budgets to develop a team, but we do need time—and a great deal of it if we want to have the conversations that I've been describing throughout this book. Even if your principal is not a strong team leader, even if he doesn't appreciate or monitor your teamwork, if he will allocate time for team retreats, team meetings, and facilitator preparation then you can do good work in your team.

MEMBERSHIP

One of the more obvious factors that shapes a team is its membership, but it's worth saying anyway: Who is on your team and how each person came to be there affects your ability to lead your team. If you select your team, you'll have a great deal more influence on how the team functions. This might even be a determining factor in your team's efficacy. If you inherit a team or one is assembled for you, you have less control over the qualities and capacities of the members. However, if you get to choose your team, then you also need to choose well and articulate the criteria for membership.

For a team to work well, members need the knowledge and skills to do the tasks that are required. For example, if a leadership team will analyze data, provide professional development, and serve as communication conduits, then members need strong skills in these areas. Of course, skill can be built, but foundational skills needs to exist and might be an important criterion for being on the team. In addition, team members will need baseline skills in collaborating and dealing productively with conflict. Yet sometimes teams are randomly created, and people can be asked to lead a team on which there are wildly ranging skill levels and potentially dangerously low participation interest levels. Who is on a team matters. When membership is intentional, your ability to lead the team will be higher. When people are appointed to serve on teams, or randomly distributed, more challenges will arise.

Furthermore, the number of people on a team matters. Finding the right number is always somewhat subjective, but I've found that eight or nine people on a team is too many. Here's why: Teams need open discussion time. In any open group discussion, if you want to hear from everyone, you need to calculate 3–5 minutes per person. So with a team of 10, you'll need 30–50 minutes to discuss one issue. When this time isn't available, conversations are less productive. In discussions and decision making, there are two main ways that people communicate: through advocacy and inquiry (Argyris and Schon, 1978). Advocacy is all about making your case, which is something we're probably all familiar with. Inquiry happens when people ask questions to seek clarity about another's declarations of advocacy. Argyris and Schon found that when more than eight or nine people are on a team, members advocate a lot more than they inquire. When a team is small, they are more likely to use their time to ask questions and seek clarity. Finally, in groups of more than nine, logistical challenges such as coordinating schedules can be unmanageable.

Your ability to control who is on your team varies according to your role and context. You may or may not be able to exert influence on membership. This doesn't mean you don't work with the people who show up, or, as a colleague used to say, "You dance with the people who come to the dance." Even if they don't want to be there, even if they lack skills, and even when the team is too large you can maintain a growth mind-set while at the same time acknowledging the challenges you face as a leader.

> *Culture is the way we do things around here.*
> BOWER (1966)

A CULTURE OF LEARNING

In Chapter 9, I discussed the importance of cultivating learning organizations in which all participants are seen as learners and see themselves as learners. In organizations that have a strong culture of learning, feedback is regularly given and welcomed. Time for reflection is prioritized. Risks are taken, and mistakes are made. Healthy debate about ideas is common. These elements can exist within a team, and when the team sits within an organization that is truly a learning organization the potential for deep learning is much greater.

Exhibit 9.1 is a tool to provoke reflection. The more indicators of a culture of learning that are present in your school and district, the better. If you are trying to build a reflective team in a culture in which there's little value in taking risks, it is going to be hard to motivate your team members to do so.

As with other organizational conditions, an awareness of where your school or district lies in terms of its stance as a learning organization is useful to manage your mind-set and emotions. If you use the indicators of a learning organization and find that your school scores low in indicators of being a learning organization, you have a couple of options: (1) Focus on what is within your sphere of control and influence—you can strive to create a micro learning organization within your team; and (2) engage site leaders in a discussion about the value in becoming a learning organization. Your ability to shift organizational culture will depend on your role and is an endeavor that can take many years.

> *We can't control the behavior of individuals; however, we can cultivate organizational cultures where behaviors are not tolerated and people are held accountable for protecting what matters most: human beings.*
> BRENÉ BROWN (2012)

Toxic Cultures

The opposite of a culture of learning is a toxic staff culture characterized by individuals working independently all the time, warring camps, divisions across racial or ethnic lines, perpetual negativity, hostile faculty meetings, gossiping, and misdirected values—focusing on enforcing rules, teaching basic skills, and serving a small group of elite students (Deal and Peterson, 2009). Toxic cultures are contagious. New teachers can become acculturated in only weeks because of the strong negative personalities of the informal leaders in a faculty. Positive staff members tend to leave or are driven out.

Toxic staff cultures are hard to shift because people find meaning in negativity—but it can be done by a strong leader with some aligned allies. The question for you, as a team leader, is how much influence you have over shifting the culture and how much energy you can devote to it. Positional leaders can have more influence; a department head has less. Although toxic cultures need to be shifted for the sake of the children who have to attend these schools, you can create boundaries around how much abuse you take and how much effort you invest in this challenge. You don't need to martyr yourself or stay in a situation that makes you physically ill—as I have seen leaders do as they battled against toxic school cultures. The questions in Exhibit 13.2 can help you reflect on how toxic your culture is.

Exhibit 13.2. Am I in a Toxic Culture?

Overall ...

1. Teachers conduct routine, boring classes.
2. Staff obsess about enforcing rules about student behavior.
3. There's a focus on unimportant outcomes.
4. Concern is expressed only about small groups of students (often elite students such as advanced band students, gifted and talented students, or athletes).
5. Teachers are siloed in classrooms, departments, or grade levels.
6. Staff organize into antagonistic camps.
7. Staff perpetuate negative attitudes toward students and work.
8. Staff are disengaged and just go through the motions.
9. Students are disengaged and just go through the motions.

10. Faculty meetings are hostile.
11. Anyone who tries to improve the school culture is attacked.
12. Old grudges between people are right below the surface and explode easily.
13. Negative stories are told about kids, parents, the past, current leader, and the district.
14. Students are seen as a burden.
15. In the staff room, negative stories are told about students.
16. Gossip is rampant.
17. The good old days are talked about.
18. A this too shall pass attitude is expressed about new initiatives, programs, or leaders.
19. The heroes are those who oppose change.
20. Teachers arrive just as school starts and leave right when it ends.

As I approached the end of the two years that I coached the humanities team, I recognized that the toxicity levels in the school were exceptionally high. My responses to the questions in Exhibit 13.3 were all affirmative. No one in a position of leadership had the skills or will to shift this culture, and I'd reached my tolerance levels. As I acknowledged the limitations in this context, I also knew that there were other places where I could have an impact and support adults so that they could meet the needs of children. I have seen too many committed, skilled educators stay in toxic contexts for too long. Please know that you have permission to leave unhealthy organizations, and there's a good chance you will find a place where your efforts will be welcomed and where your work can greatly impact children.

TRUST

For teams to thrive, a baseline quantity of trust needs to exist in an organization. Researchers Anthony Bryk and Barbara Schneider (2002) write that "trust is the connective tissue that holds improving schools together" (pg. 144). When there's little trust across a school or in an organization, it will be much harder to build strong trust within your team.

Exhibit 13.3 will help you assess trust at your site. You can use this tool for self-reflection and also to understand other team members' perspectives. You might find that individuals hold different perceptions of the level of trust that exists in your school.

Exhibit 13.3. Indicators of Trust in Schools

Rate the statement on a scale of 1 to 5, with 1 being lowest (strongly disagree) and 5 being highest (strongly agree).

INDICATOR	SCORE 1–5
Related to Colleagues	
1. My colleagues are willing to go beyond their formal roles and responsibilities for the sake of our school and students.	
2. My colleagues put the best interests of students ahead of their own, especially when difficult decisions are made.	
3. I can be vulnerable with my colleagues.	
4. I feel comfortable telling my colleagues that I don't understand something that we're working on.	
5. I hear colleagues say they don't know or understand something.	
6. I can challenge a colleague on an idea, and we can have a healthy debate.	
7. My colleagues listen to me.	
8. My colleagues care about me personally. I can share personal thoughts, feelings, and experiences with them.	
9. My colleagues care about me professionally. I believe they want to see me be successful.	
10. I know that if I ask a colleague to do something, he or she will do it.	
11. I know that if I ask a colleague to do something, he or she will do it and do it well.	
12. My colleagues appreciate me and share their appreciation regularly.	
13. I hear colleagues apologizing for their actions or behavior.	
14. I can disagree with a colleague about an idea or something that happened, and I know that our personal and collegial relationship won't be damaged.	
15. I feel comfortable apologizing to colleagues and taking responsibility for something I didn't do well.	

INDICATOR	SCORE 1–5
Related to Administrators	
16. I regularly get feedback from my administrators that helps me in my work.	
17. I feel that my administrators know my work—they regularly visit my classroom or observe me engaged in my practice.	
18. I feel that my evaluators are fair when they come to my evaluations, and I respect their feedback.	
19. I feel that my evaluator has my best interests at heart and wants to support my professional growth.	
20. I know that if my immediate supervisor agrees to do something, he or she will do it. This includes promptly responding to emails or requests.	
21. I know that if my immediate supervisor agrees to do something, he or she will do it well.	
22. I feel that my immediate supervisor listens to me.	
23. I hear our leaders apologizing for their actions or behavior.	
24. I hear our leaders expressing that they don't know something.	
25. My leaders regularly ask for feedback in multiple ways. I know they want my honest feedback.	
26. My leaders appreciate me—I feel satisfied with way they appreciate me and how often I'm appreciated.	
27. I can be vulnerable with my leaders.	
28. I feel that the administrators at my school trust each other and are on the same page as each other.	
29. I feel that the administrators at my school work well together.	
30. I feel that the administrators at my school appreciate each other.	
31. I feel that the administrators at my school manage their moods well.	
32. I feel that the administrators at my school are skilled at developing positive relationships with staff, parents, and students.	
33. I feel that administrators at my school set, review, and monitor staff expectations.	
34. I feel that administrators at my school take action to address staff who are not meeting expectations.	

(continued)

INDICATOR	SCORE 1–5
Related to the Whole School	
35. I never hear gossip.	
36. I have meaningful conversations with other staff members about teaching and learning.	
37. I hear staff disagreeing with each other professionally during appropriate times.	
38. I feel that differences of opinion and perspective are valued.	
39. I feel that differences of opinion and perspective don't become barriers to getting things done.	
40. Staff members are courteous with each other.	
41. Staff communicate appropriately through established structures: emails sent to all staff are about business and information.	
42. Personal conflicts between individuals are discussed in private or with a conflict mediator.	
43. I can't remember the last time someone was really disrespectful to another staff member.	
44. I can't remember the last time someone was really disrespectful to a student.	
45. I can't remember the last time someone was really disrespectful to a parent.	
46. When there's a decision to be made, the amount of power different stake-holders have is always clear.	
47. Decision-making processes are always clear, explicit, and transparent.	
48. Decisions are made using an articulated process that's appropriate for the decision, and we use different decision-making processes (e.g., consensus, voting, compromise) in our work together.	
49. We are able to make decisions within a time frame that feels reasonable to me.	
50. If a decision has to be made and I can't attend the meeting in which it's being made, I know that my colleagues will make the best decision.	
51. We honor times when we've agreed to come together. We rarely start or end late.	
52. If people are asked to prepare or bring something to a meeting, they do.	
53. I believe that everyone at my site *wants* to do his or her very best.	
54. I believe that everyone at my site *is able* to do his or her very best.	
55. I believe that everyone at my site is engaged in fulfilling our school's mission.	

Dealing with Gossip

Mike Robbins, author of *Focus on the Good Stuff* (2007), suggests there are two categories of gossip: negative mental judgments about others spoken aloud; and the retelling of negative stories or rumors about someone else. He writes, "Gossip to an organization is like cancer to the body; it slowly eats away at the fabric of the team until the team itself dies" (p. 29).

Robbins also offers an approach to deal with gossip. He suggests creating gossip-free zones in which people commit to not gossiping about others. This means that you remind each other, kindly, if someone slips up and starts to gossip. In a gossip-free zone, you and those around you commit to speaking positively about other people. If you have an issue or complaint about someone, you take it directly to that person, get some coaching or feedback from someone else about how to resolve the issue directly, or simply let it go. When I implemented this approach in a school that I supported, there was a lukewarm response to the suggestion at first, and then there was enthusiasm as staff discovered how easy it was to stop gossiping. The phrase, "This is a gossip-free zone," was used and heard all over campus and reminded staff of their commitment to change their conversations. As teachers recognized the positive impact, they introduced the idea to students, who also appreciated the notion of the hard parameters around a zone. "We just don't do that here," was a sentiment expressed by teachers and students. By just cutting out gossip (or reducing it substantially), the school's culture shifted toward greater health and kindness.

DECISION MAKING

As a team leader in a school, you'll most likely need to communicate decisions from your site administrators or from central office decision makers to your team. You may be asked to act on decisions made in your school or district and to get your team committed to those decisions. Decision making and trust go hand in hand. How decisions are made outside of your team affects your team. If decisions are made in a transparent way, if stakeholders give input, there's likely to be more trust in the decisions. However, if the process for making decisions is not clear in your school or district, if the people on your team don't understand why decisions are made, if they disagree with many of them, and if they feel like new work is heaped on them by outside forces, then your ability to develop a team will be hampered.

You might also find yourself at some point in the uncomfortable middleman position of implementing a decision you don't understand or disagree with. Yet you may be expected to appear in support of it. Depending on the decision and your level of discomfort, you might have hard choices to make. If you voice your disapproval of the decision, you may risk a negative response from those who made it, who expect you to support it. If you speak in approval, you may feel you're compromising your integrity.

TIME

The most important resource for a team is time—both for the facilitator to prepare and for teams to collaborate. Teams must meet consistently and focus their time on what matters—implementing their work plan, learning together, and building strong relationships with each other. Unfortunately, in many schools team meetings are regularly canceled because things come up or team meetings are co-opted for other tasks that have nothing to do with their goals. Urgent matters that require immediate attention will always come up in schools: The challenge is to stay in a proactive mode and recognize that developing teams and doing the work that a team has committed to is equally important. Preserving time for teams to meet and stay focused is a battle worth fighting.

Facilitators also need time to plan and prepare. I use the ratio of 1 to 2 hours of planning and preparation time for every hour of Professional Development I lead or team I facilitate. Sometimes this ratio is much higher. If you've been asked to lead a team, something needs to be taken off your plate so you can have the time to prepare.

When I work with school leaders on team development, I'm often asked, "How can we find the time to do all of this?" They reference the conversations necessary to develop norms, to make decisions, to manage unproductive conflict, and to reflect on how teams are working together. They are right—the activities that I've described in this book take time, large amounts of it. The challenge isn't in finding the time, however; it's in prioritizing how we use time. If we're not getting what we need from the time we spend together (and if we aren't seeing the results in student learning), then we need to reexamine how we're spending it. This kind of reflection will help us make the most of a fixed and precious resource.

It's also important to remember that many teams need more time in the early stages of their formation for engaging in reflection and developing healthy patterns of communication. As teams move through the stages of development (and if membership remains stable) and become high-functioning teams, they require less time to manage. Healthy interpersonal dynamics and effective patterns of working together sustain the team.

Organizational conditions change. With a clear understanding of these when you're trying to build a team, you can have perspective on your own efforts. I hope that by recognizing the many factors that can enable or erode your team-building efforts you'll be kinder to yourself and also better able to see your areas for growth. Acknowledging the lay of the land doesn't exempt us from refining our skills or working to influence what might seem to be outside of our control—it just helps us get clarity so that we can manage our emotional responses, determine the most strategic course of action, and move forward.

Transformational Coaching Team, 2013

At the end of our team meeting, on a Friday just before winter break, I said, "I've made a decision that I need to share. As you know, this year our work has been challenged by some leaders in the district. As a leader, I've been asked to do things that conflict deeply with my core values and beliefs. I can no longer do these things, and I've made a decision that at the end of this school year I will resign from the district."

My voice conveyed my emotions—sadness and frustration. "I know this will affect all of you," I continued. "You'll still have jobs if you want them, although your role might change." I wanted to hold space for coaches to process their reactions, but I was also aware of how much I was feeling and of my limited capacity to take care of others at that moment. Almost 2 decades had passed since I'd started working in the Oakland Unified School District. I'd long assumed that I'd retire from this district to which I had committed so much time and energy.

Two years earlier, when I had designed the transformational coaching initiative that I led in our schools and for which I hired the coaches, organizational conditions to support our team were strong. Our team was nestled in a department called the Office of School Transformation, which had purpose, focus, effective leadership, alignment, stability, and trust. Conditions seemed optimal for us to have a deep impact on the children that our schools served. However, as the new school year began and the coaching team's work was launched, the Office of School Transformation was abruptly dismantled. Our leader was removed from his position, our team was relocated into a different department, and conditions deteriorated.

Within our new location in the organization, our existence was tenuous. For a year and a half, I held outside forces at bay. The leaders who were now above us ranged from being disinterested in our work to wanting to direct every element. Our work did not align with efforts on a horizontal or vertical plane. The decision making outside our team was obtuse, and our input was not welcome. As a leader, I was asked to enact decisions with which I strongly disagreed, decisions that conflicted with what I held to be effective change management. It was a relief, in a sense, when I acknowledged the direction the winds were blowing and that my sphere of influence had shrunk to a domain too small to be meaningful. I knew it was time to go, although I didn't know where I'd go.

Exhibit 13.4. Organizational Conditions for Effective Teams

Rate each element on scale of 1 to 5 (with one being lowest and five being highest) based on how strongly you agree with the indicators.

Element	Indicators	Rating	Evidence and Comments
Purpose	• Everyone in our school or organization knows what our vision and mission is. • Our goals are posted in many places, and we reference them regularly. • I can see how everything that everyone is doing leads to meeting our goals.		
Focus	• Our school or organization has fewer than four annual goals. • These goals build on previous years' work and are easy to remember. • Annual foci are determined based on student (or client) needs and through a clear decision-making process.		

Element	Indicators	Rating	Evidence and Comments
Alignment	• Every team works to meet our school or organization's goals. • I understand the work that every team is doing and am updated regularly on the work done in other teams. • The work of other teams complements ours, and it doesn't feel like there's any redundancy in teamwork.		
Stability	• Our site or organization leadership and staff have remained stable for at least 5 years. • Staff turnover has been less than 10%. • For the most part, implementation of our core programs has been consistent for several years.		
Leadership	• Our site or organization's leaders have many strengths. • They are vocal advocates for team development and set a vision for effective teams. • They allocate resources for team development. • They are effective team leaders. • They monitor the work of teams, appreciate our work, and push us to refine our work.		
Membership	• The majority of team members have the skills necessary to engage in collaboration. • Members want to be a part of the team. • It feels like the right people are in our team.		
Culture of Learning	• On the *Indicators of a Learning Organization*, Exhibit 9.1, there is evidence of two-thirds of the indicators. • There is no evidence of a toxic culture.		
Decision-Making	• There are articulated and transparent decision-making processes in our school or organization. • Outside of our team, we understand why decisions are made and sometimes have input into them.		

(continued)

Element	Indicators	Rating	Evidence and Comments
Trust	• On the *Indicators of Trust*, Exhibit 13.3, there's evidence of 35–40 of the elements.		
Time	• The team's facilitator always has time to prepare for meetings. • Team time is sacred and rarely canceled. • Team time is exclusively focused on work that will lead us to meet our goals. • We have enough time to meet our goals.		

CONCLUSION: COMING TO AN END

All teams come to an end. Sometimes a group's work comes to a conclusion, and disbanding feels voluntary; sometimes a significant change in a team's membership indicates a transition; sometimes teams are dismantled or broken up. Regardless of why the team folds, it is our job, as leaders, to help members feel closure about their experience together.

For one of the most vital ways that we sustain ourselves is by building communities of resistance, places where we know we are not alone.

BELL HOOKS

As we approached the end our time as a team of transformational coaches, I asked the group for their input: "What gives you feelings of closure? What would you like to do on our final day together?" There was a lot of sadness about the fact that our team was ending and, for some, anger that we were being prematurely disbanded. I felt responsible for attending to the feelings that were surfacing. I also wanted our final day to be collaborative, and I knew that members of the team had great ideas.

I knew it was essential that everyone reflect on his or her learning and growth during the two years we had worked together. It is empowering to leave a situation or position and say, "I learned so much." I wanted the coaches to construct their own narrative of their work in Oakland, to create a story that would serve them as they moved into other jobs. In the week preceding our final day, coaches had up to an hour each with our team to share—in any format—what they'd learned about themselves and about teaching, coaching, and leadership. At the end of each presentation, the other team members wrote an email to the presenter describing the impact he or she had on them and what we appreciated about him or her.

The final day was a combination of rituals to let go of the past and acknowledge what we'd gained from the experience of being a team and a celebration. We made a collage, ate a big lunch together, and played a game. A photographer took our photo. Then at the end of the day, we sat around the oval table that had been the setting for so much of our learning together, and I passed around a red strand of embroidery thread. As we took the strand in our hand, we shared in just a few words what the team meant to us and what they'd be taking from it into our future. "This team is my community of resistance," I said, "A place where I never felt alone. You are my beloved community." When everyone had spoken, I asked them to pick up a pair of scissors and cut the string. When that was done, I said, "Our time as a team is over."

That evening we gathered with our families for a barbeque at Anna's house. We were no longer a team, but the bonds that developed would surely endure.

TEN TRUTHS ABOUT BUILDING TEAMS

Team building is hard work because there are few direct, prescriptive routes to take. To build effective teams, we'll need to explore different approaches, modify plans along the way, and be open to unexpected twists and turns. That said, I do believe that 10 truths about building teams can guide our efforts. These have been discussed in this book, and I've offered strategies for implementing these ideas. Let me know declare the following to be truths:

1. *Teams that work in or with schools exist to serve the social, emotional, and academic needs of children.* We might have all kinds of things that we do in our teams and organizations, we may also care for the adults in the mix, but we exist to serve children.

2. *Learning is the primary work of all teams.* Whether you're in a leadership team, a data team, a department, or a curriculum design team, your work is to learn. The only way we'll make a dent in the mountain of challenges we face in schools is if

we—the educators—never stop learning. Our work as team leaders therefore is to create optimal conditions for adults to learn.

3. *Who you are as a leader has the greatest influence on a team*. Your emotional intelligence as a leader is the key knowledge and skill set from which all others emerge. Leaders must learn to recognize and manage their emotions and recognize and manage the emotions of others.

4. *All teams exist within systems and power structures*. A team has transformational potential only with an understanding of those systems. Teams can do satisfactory work without attending to power—but if they aspire to be transformational, team members and their leaders need to hone their understanding of power and how it manifests in organizations and structures (including the team structure) in order to interrupt inequities.

5. *Teams thrive with trust*. With trust, a team can become a true learning organization in which team members can give each other hard feedback and engage in healthy conflict; teams can become resilient communities. This means that team leaders need to pay close and careful attention to levels of trust and need to intentionally build trust.

6. *Building teams takes time*. Teams need time to figure out what they're going to do together, why they're working together, and how they'll work together. Team members need time to develop relationships. We must prioritize time for team development if we want to accomplish our goals of transforming schools.

7. *The health of a meeting reflects the health of the team*. We need to thoughtfully plan and prepare for meetings and ensure that what happens in them is meaningful. We need to reflect on our leadership of meetings and invite team members to reflect on how they work together. *We must hold good meetings*—that's the moment in which teams thrive or die.

8. *A team's collective emotional intelligence is the key factor in its level of performance*. A group's ability to recognize and manage the emotions that surface when the members are together has great impact on the quality of work they do. It is critical that leaders pay attention to the collective emotional intelligence of a team and work to increase it. This is an area of learning for most teams and their leaders.

9. *Communication between team members is the thread that connects everything*. We need to pay close attention to what we say and how we say it. We need to hone our

abilities to communicate effectively and take time to explore our communication with each other.

10. *Conflict can be healthy, but unhealthy conflict needs to be managed.* We need to learn how to have healthy conflict—it's a necessary part of the journey of transforming our schools. We also need to learn how to deal with the kind of unhealthy conflict that erodes trust and communities.

Which of these truths resonates with you based on your experiences? Which feels daunting? Which of these truths would you like to take steps toward implementing?

The unnamed, overarching truth on which this book rests is this: *We need to build teams.* We need to build healthy, effective teams so that together we can figure out the challenges facing our schools. We also need to build teams for our own emotional resilience. The work of transformation is hard. It is emotionally, cognitively, and sometimes physically demanding. We all need communities of resistance, places in which we know we are not alone; we need communities that nurture and hold us, that will sustain us as we create equitable schools that attend to the needs of each and every child.

AMID THE REDWOODS

The transformational coach team needed a day of learning and reflection in an environment more inspiring than our office. I decided that our Friday meeting would take place in the forest—it was only a 10-minute drive from our office to a regional park in the Oakland hills that is blanketed with redwoods like the ones pictured on the cover of this book. I created an agenda and outcomes, and it was a structured meeting with activities including the following:

Walk with a partner and talk about X for 8 minutes each.

Sit on the forest floor and write about Y for 10 minutes.

Read this article and make connections to your work.

Walk in silence through the redwoods and let it all sink in.

Our team meetings always ended with appreciations. We stood in a circle at the end of the trail, our minds oxygenated and enlivened with new reflections. Manny offered me an appreciation: "We talk about teaching the whole child," he said, "I feel like you attend to us as whole adults. We needed this."

The redwoods have always been my place of solace, rejuvenation, and inspiration; since I went to college, I have never lived far from these ancient trees. Many years ago, a friend explained that when a redwood dies of natural or unnatural causes the roots shoot up and grow into new trees forming a ring around the site of the original tree. You can see these if you walk in the redwoods—circular groves creating a cathedral. They are a reminder that below the surface an extensive network of roots is activated when needed, a reminder that death may not be the end we think it is, a reminder that healing and transformation are possible.

Building resilient teams may be the greatest challenge we face in school transformation efforts because it entails attending to our emotions, developing ourselves as transformational leaders, prioritizing time, slowing things down, listening to each other, and speaking skillfully. Where to start? Lao Tzu reminds us, "The journey of a thousand miles begins with a single step."

So onward—with a vision, a plan, some poetry in hand, and the company of other kindred souls. Onward.

APPENDICES

Printable versions of these tools may be found on the author's website, www.elenaaguilar.com

APPENDIX A

Facilitator Core Competencies

There are three components to this tool to help you identify strengths and opportunities for growth as a facilitator: (1) skills and knowledge; (2) emotional intelligence; and (3) will and capacity.

I. Skills and Knowledge		
Domain	**Element**	**1–5** **1 = low** **5 = high**
(A) Team Development and Facilitation	(1) I can engage colleagues in the development of a shared vision for our team.	
	(2) I can facilitate the creation of goals that are aligned to our school's or organization's goals.	
	(3) I use various strategies to ensure that all members are invested in our team's work and that all take responsibility for their part in it.	
	(4) I can design effective meeting agendas with clear and meaningful outcomes.	
	(5) I can facilitate meetings that stay focused and meet outcomes.	

(*continued*)

I. Skills and Knowledge		
Domain	**Element**	**1–5** **1 = low** **5 = high**
	(6) I assess and support the will, skill, knowledge, and capacity of team members so that meetings are inclusive of all.	
	(7) I effectively develop and model norms and community agreements within meetings.	
	(8) I ensure there is a process to reflect on our holding of norms and community agreements.	
	(9) I intentionally work to develop trust within the team as well as between me and team members. I have various ways of intentionally developing and assessing levels of trust.	
	(10) I address the group's affective needs in meetings through structures such as a check-in, dyad, grounding, and intention setting.	
	(11) I use various structures and processes for collaboration.	
	12) I can facilitate healthy decision-making processes using a variety of strategies.	
	(13) I apply knowledge of team development theories to make decisions about meetings and processes.	
	(14) I apply knowledge of adult learning to design and lead learning activities.	
(B) Communication	(1) I use active listening effectively: I summarize and reflect back what's being said accurately.	
	(2) I use a range of questions to promote open discussion and clarify issues.	
	(3) I use structures to ensure equity of participation in meetings: I deal with disruptive or overly talkative group members and draw out quieter members of the group.	
	(4) I am aware of and can address dynamics of race, class, gender, and power in a group.	
	(5) I can confront difficult issues and have hard conversations.	

I. Skills and Knowledge		
Domain	**Element**	**1–5** 1 = low 5 = high
	(6) I can model language that encourages accountability and solutions instead of blame.	
	(7) I can address deficit thinking and actions by moving others to more productive, asset-focused language and action.	
	(8) I can support others in questioning beliefs and examining the intended and unintended consequences of beliefs and actions.	
(C) Conflict and Commitment	(1) I remain open and flexible to multiple options and points of view in order to challenge assumptions and beliefs.	
	(2) When there's unhealthy conflict, I seek to understand different perspectives, I acknowledge views from all sides, and then I have strategies to redirect the energy toward our shared ideals.	
	(3) I mediate, manage, and depersonalize unhealthy conflict between adults effectively.	
	(4) I encourage divergent thinking, multiple perspectives, and productive conflict about ideas.	
	(5) I intentionally develop peer-to-peer accountability.	
	(6) I hold others accountable for their actions.	

II. Emotional Intelligence		
Domain	**Element**	**1–5** 1 = low 5 = high
(D) Self-Awareness	(1) I recognize and am aware of my emotions, especially those that surface when I'm facilitating a team.	
	(2) I am aware that my emotions are contagious.	
	(3) I recognize my strengths and limits. I know when I need to ask for help.	

(continued)

II. Emotional Intelligence		
Domain	**Element**	**1–5** **1 = low** **5 = high**
(E) Self-Management	(1) I can establish a positive, calm climate for a meeting right from the start.	
	(2) I can manage my emotions—especially difficult ones—so that I can effectively facilitate a team.	
	(3) I have a range of strategies to help me manage the emotions that arise from dealing with change, setbacks, and challenges.	
	(4) I can choose appropriate emotional responses to situations and create the space for others to choose appropriate responses.	
	(5) I can be transparent about my emotions in appropriate times for the sake of building a team and to model self-management.	
	(6) I seek feedback on my leadership and facilitation; I adjust and change my actions based on feedback.	
	(7) I can admit to mistakes, faults, and my own areas for growth as a way to build trust and model emotional intelligence leadership skills.	
	(8) I persist in the face of adversity and am frequently described by others as perseverant, resourceful, action oriented, committed, and passionate.	
	(9) I honor obligations by following through, being responsible, and being willing to be held accountable by others.	
	(10) I display optimism, confidence, and a positive, solutions-oriented attitude.	

II. Emotional Intelligence		
Domain	**Element**	**1–5** **1 = low** **5 = high**
(F) Social Awareness	(1) I demonstrate empathy authentically and regularly.	
	(2) I can sense the unspoken emotions of others.	
	(3) I enable others to engage in self-reflection and evaluation, leading toward greater individual and collective responsibility.	
	(4) I recognize power relationships in the interactions of others and pay close attention to how they impact an individual's participation in the group; I have strategies to address power dynamics if they are negatively impacting the group.	
	(5) I have various strategies for cultivating an emotional climate where everyone gets what he or she needs to be a contributing member of the group.	
(G) Social Management	(1) I recognize the emotional undercurrents in a group, and I'm responsive to the feelings and needs of others.	
	(2) I model emotional self-management to manage the group.	
	(3) I use various strategies to enroll everyone in the group; I use these during meeting times as well as at other times to get buy-in.	
	(4) I am genuinely interested in developing every member of this group. I learn about everyone's strengths, goals, and areas for growth to do so.	
	(5) I can advocate for change even in the face of opposition. I've found effective ways to overcome barriers to change.	

III. WILL AND CAPACITY

These questions are intended to help you reflect on your will and capacity to facilitate a team.

1. How did you feel about becoming the facilitator of a team when you were first asked to do so? If you volunteered to facilitate a team, what made you want to do so?
2. What feelings come up for you regarding the team and your leadership in the team?
3. What hopes and concerns do you have for yourself as facilitator of the team?
4. How do you see this team as a vehicle for helping your school realize its vision, mission, and goals? What connections can you see between the work this team can do and the improvement of children's experience and outcomes at your school?
5. What connections are there between your core values and your role as team facilitator?
6. What do you feel that you need from your administration to be an effective facilitator? How much of what you need do you currently have?
7. Given your roles and responsibilities, will you have ample time to plan and prepare for, facilitate, and reflect on team meetings? Has time in your schedule been allocated for this work?
8. On a scale of 1 to 10, with 1 being low and 10 being high, how *willing* do you feel to facilitate this team? Explain your response.
9. If your number was lower than 5, what would it take to increase your willingness? Is there anything within your sphere of influence or control that you could do to increase your willingness?
10. On a scale of 1 to 10, with 1 being low and 10 being high, how much *capacity* do you feel you have to facilitate this team? Explain your response.
11. If your number was lower than 5, what would it take to increase your capacity? Is there anything within your sphere of influence or control that you could do to increase your capacity?
12. Why does this team matter—to you, to your colleagues, and to students?
13. Why might you be the right person right now to facilitate this team? What unique qualities, insights, and skills do you bring as a facilitator?

Team Effectiveness Self-Assessment

TEAM: _____ DATE: _____

TEAM MEMBER: _____

TEAM EFFECTIVENESS SELF-ASSESSMENT		
Rate the following elements on a scale of 1 to 5, with 1 = strongly disagree, 2 = disagree, 3 = neutral, 4 = agree, and 5 = strongly agree. Wherever possible, offer examples that illustrate each element.		
Element	**Rating**	**Examples and Comments**
1. **Purpose** We understand and agree on our team's purpose and goals.		
2. **Results** We accomplish what we set out to achieve.		
3. **Procedures** There are effective procedures to guide team functioning.		
4. **Meeting Process** Meetings are well facilitated and focused and result in clear outcomes.		
5. **Decisions** We have clear agreements about how decisions will be made.		

(continued)

TEAM EFFECTIVENESS SELF-ASSESSMENT		
Rate the following elements on a scale of 1 to 5, with 1 = strongly disagree, 2 = disagree, 3 = neutral, 4 = agree, and 5 = strongly agree. Wherever possible, offer examples that illustrate each element.		
Element	**Rating**	**Examples and Comments**
6. **Commitment** Team members buy into decisions without hidden reservations or hesitation; actions reflect our commitment.		
7. **Member Contributions** Member contributions (ideas or information) are recognized and utilized. Different styles are embraced.		
8. **Creativity** We experiment with different ways of doing things and are creative in our approach.		
9. **Collaboration** Team members share our experience and expertise in ways that enhance team productivity and development.		
10. **Respect** I feel valued as an individual member in this group. People treat all individuals with respect.		
11. **Interpersonal Communication** Communication between members is open and balanced at meetings.		
12. **Productive Conflict** Members engage in unfiltered debate around ideas and issues related to the work.		
13. **Unproductive Conflict** We work constructively on issues until they are resolved.		
14. **Accountability** Team members hold each other accountable.		
15. **Evaluation** We often evaluate our team process and productivity.		

APPENDIX C

Community-Building Activities and Random Grouping Strategies

COMMUNITY-BUILDING ACTIVITIES

The following activities are those I most often use to energize a team and help a team get to know each other.

Compass points: This activity can be found on the National School Reform Faculty's website (http://www.nsrfharmony.org/content/compass-points-activity) and is one of my favorites to do with a group of anywhere between 3 and 300 people. It helps people understand their styles when working in a group and the styles of others and thus cultivates empathy and understanding. It's one of my always-do activities when working with a new team.

Poetry: I love to start or end a learning session or meeting with a poem. I look for poems that have themes related to whatever we're talking about that day and always invite participants to discuss the poem with each other afterward. I prompt them to read aloud passages that resonated with them, to make connections, and to share "what came up for you."

Artifacts: Team members bring an artifact from home that they feel reflects a part of who they are that otherwise would not be seen by colleagues. It could be an object, a photo, an item from their kitchen, or a childhood toy. This kind of show and tell can be really fun and builds understanding and appreciation for each other. Tip: If someone forgets to bring an artifact, I suggest doing a quick sketch of the item.

Pennies: In this activity, a team is given a small pile of pennies (perhaps twice the number of pennies as there are people in the team) and participants are invited to "tell a story from your life—or your family's—about the year on the coin you select." If you're working with a group of young teachers, you'll want to check the years on your pennies to ensure that at least most of them are from the lifetimes of the participants.

Something from your wallet or purse: This is an easy on-the-spot activity because it doesn't require you to provide anything. You simply ask a group of people, "Find something in your purse or wallet that reflects a part of you that we might not know about, and share a story about it." Some examples include photos, key chains, coupons, and membership cards.

M&M game: You need to provide a bag of M&Ms for this game and the following color-coded key: red = something about yesterday; orange: something you do well; yellow = something about your childhood; blue = something you learned last week; brown = something you can't live without; green = something you watch or listen to. Pour an M&M into each person's hand, and take turns responding to the prompt all together or in pairs.

Symbolic thinking: Inviting people to think through metaphors and symbols is a great way to prompt new insights. For easy and quick check-in prompts you can ask questions such as:

- "If our team were a meal, we would be ... "
- "If I could have a super power it would be .... "
- "If I were an animal today, I'd be a ... "
- "In my next life I want to be a ... "
- "Today I feel like [what kind of supernatural or mythic being] ... "

Images: I collect stacks of postcards, calendars and photos that I offer with a range of prompts to stimulate conversation. For example, I share images of forces in nature (e.g., volcanoes, rivers, lightning) and ask people to select the one that most reflects how they feel about change. I also have images of animals, movie posters, and food to prompt conversation. Using images, symbols, and metaphors offers us a way into our thoughts and feelings that sometimes reveals interesting information.

Storytelling: A simple prompt like, "Tell a story about ... " is a great way to give people an opportunity to share with each other. These stories can be brief and a precedent to other activities, or they can be extended. For example, let's say you're going to analyze first-quarter data reports with a team of teachers. You can give participants 3 minutes each to share with a partner about their experience as children taking tests. This allows people to connect and tell their stories about learning, and it invites them to connect with the emotional experience that children have when taking tests. It can generate empathy and multiple perspectives.

Visual life maps: This activity is good for a team that will work closely together and will benefit from really getting to know each other. Each person creates a life map that shows 8–10 pivotal moments from his or her life. Images with captions representing those moments can be included to describe the event.

My life as a book: This activity asks people to reflect and tell their stories through writing—but in this case, they are asked to write only the titles of chapters for their life as a book. They can choose the genre of the book and then name the chapters. This can be shared silently and everyone reads each other's table of contents, or participants can explain what they created.

Tower building: For this activity you need a stack (or several) of index cards. You can do this with one team or break a team into groups—ideally with no more than four people in each group. Tell the group they'll have a limited amount of time (maybe 8–10 minutes) to silently build a tower with the cards. They can't use any other supplies, can communicate only nonverbally, and are in competition with each other to see who can build the tallest tower. It's important to offer reflection prompts. Simple ones work fine: What did you notice about how you worked together? What did you notice about your own participation? What was challenging? You can also do this activity again but remove the competitive aspect, or ask them to build something interesting. This activity allows team members to get different understandings of the roles they play in their team.

Pass the sound: This gets everyone up and being silly. Stand in a circle and pretend to throw an imaginary object to another teammate and make a sound along with it. The person who catches the imaginary object has to imitate the sound you made and then throws it to someone else with a new sound. People can make animal noises or any kind of silly sound.

Boom whackers: Boom whackers are long, plastic tubes that are tuned to different notes. When you whack them on anything (e.g., the floor, your leg, a table), they make a sound. This is an easy way to make music with a group, especially one whose members might not think they are musical people. Playing with boom whackers is easy and always gets people feeling happy and energized. They can also help a group feel more cohesive since instinctually people try to make their sounds work in rhythm with those of others.

Walk and talk: I incorporate this activity into team meetings or Professional Development agendas if we will be meeting for more than 2 hours together. People need to move, or else their brains get stagnant; I haven't found too many group physical energizers that I like. This could be because standing in a group of people and doing goofy movements is usually outside of my personal comfort zone, but I haven't found too many other people who love those energizer activities either. However, most love the invitation to take a quick 10- or 15-minute walk and talk. I am usually intentional about grouping people in pairs or trios—I don't want them to have to find their own partners all the time, which can be hard—and I usually offer a simple and open-ended prompt to talk about. Sometimes I suggest that they set a timer on their phone so that they'll each have equal time to talk and will arrive back on time.

Two secrets: Everyone writes one secret on a card and gives it to the facilitator. The facilitator reads each card, and the group nominates two or three people they think are the authors of the card. If they are nominated, they stand up. After a few nominations, the facilitator asks the real author of the secret to remain standing (or to stand up) and the others to sit down. You can do this throughout a meeting (or across a series of meetings) by picking a few secrets every time you transition after a break or lunch and for an opening or closing for each day.

Step in, step out: The facilitator chooses key phases that describe qualities, roles, wishes, or anything else that individuals in the group can relate to. The facilitator reads one phrase (e.g., I am a parent, I teach elementary, I struggle with ... , _____ brings me joy), and if the members agree with that statement they step into the middle of a circle. If the statement doesn't represent them, they step out. This activity can also help a group see disagreements among the members without having to make people say anything. You can start with easy, fun, and light statements and move to more controversial ones.

Repeated question: Members form pairs, and the facilitator gives the pairs a question prompt that the members can answer with one word or short phrase answers. Each pair has 3–5 minutes for each person to be the question asker and the answerer. This is used when you want members to become more aware about their beliefs or feelings about a particular topic because they keep answering the same question over and over and end up surprising themselves with the answers that come out after their initial answers. Usually they go deeper into themselves.

Restorative justice (RJ) community circle: The RJ community-building circle can be used at the beginning of meetings. Everyone sits in a circle, ideally in chairs (not desks), and the process opens with a poem, meditation, or song, which is followed by a check-in question for the group. After everyone who wants to quickly shares in response to the check-in question, the group is asked a bigger question such as, "How are you feeling about the proposed changes for next year?" A talking stick is passed around the circle, and only the person holding it can speak in response to the question. The speaker can talk for as long as he or she wants and is usually encouraged not to respond to what others have said (to prevent the feeling of a discussion). If you're interested in RJ circles, you can find more information online, perhaps starting here: http://rjoyoakland.org/restorative-justice/.

Check-in whip around: Opening up meetings by simply giving everyone a chance to respond to a prompt is a way to hear from each person and connect. You can generate questions and invite the team to create prompts. Here are some to get you started:

- Share a moment in which you felt good about your work in the week.
- What's important to you?
- What's your ultimate concern?
- What do you hold sacred?
- If we could really know you, what would we know?
- If you could *really, really* know you, what would we know?
- What do you need from someone else to know that you're being listened to?
- What are we not talking about that we should be?

RANDOM GROUPING STRATEGIES

To help group members get to know each other, you'll frequently need to create pairs or small groups—you don't always want to leave who they share or work with up to chance or up to who they are sitting next to. Most of the time I create random small groups or pairs (although occasionally I intentionally group people together). Here are the strategies I most often use.

1. **Birthday line-up:** In silence, within a defined period of time (usually a few seconds longer than the total number of people in the group) ask people to line up according to their birthday month and day. Designate one corner of the room to be the January

starting point and another to be the December ending point. You can't use anything other than nonverbal communication. After the group has formed the line, have them say their birthday month and day aloud to check that it's correct, and then go down the line and group people into twos, threes, or fours. Sometimes I tell people that this is astrological sorting and that they should probably get along with each other. This is fast, fun, and easy to do with groups up to 150 people.

2. **How hot do you like it?** This is a fun activity that I learned from author and professional development expert, Marcia Tate. Ask people to line up according to their preference of spiciness: one end of the room represents those who think that ketchup is spicy and the other end represents those who chew on habanero chilies (the hottest chili there is) with no sweat. People can talk to each other while they do this and can create their own categories. After they've lined up, ask a few people to share their spiciness preference and then group them by threes or fours. This activity is also fast and easy with large groups, and people always love talking about food.

3. **How far were you born from this spot?** Again, invite participants to line up according to the distance in miles of their birthplace from the place they're standing at that moment. People can talk to each other while they do this—and then you can break them up into whatever number group you want. This invites people to share stories about their place of birth and can be extended so that people can make connections.

4. **Barnyard babble:** This activity is from the tribes program. You'll need cards with farm animals on them, which you can make with index cards and stickers. Create sets of animals with the number of people you want in each small group—so four horses if you want a team of four. Randomly pass out cards, tell everyone to look at his or her card, and then when you say go each person makes the noise of the animal and finds the other people making their same noise. This is loud and fun.

5. **Matching cards:** I buy decks of Go Fish cards to create groups of three, four, or six. Simply shuffle the cards and then ask everyone to draw a card and find his or her group.

APPENDIX D

Facilitation Planning Tool and Facilitation Observation Tool

FACILITATION PLANNING TOOL

1. Meeting Design *Most design elements are visible in the participant's agenda.* *Some will be visible only in the facilitator's agenda.*		✓	Evidence Comments Questions
Element	**Indicators**		
Why	The content of the meeting enables progress on the organization's goals, mission, or vision. This may or may not be directly stated.		
	The content of the meeting may reflect external input sources (e.g., feedback from surveys or previous meetings, input from stakeholders outside of the team).		
	The meeting is designed with an awareness of where the group is in its stage of team development. Activities and structures are intentional about developing the team.		
	The purposes for each section of the meeting are clearly articulated. Sections of the meeting are clearly distinguished, for example, learning, decision making, discussion, and information.		
What	Activities are sequenced to reach meeting outcomes.		
	The emotional, cognitive, and energy needs of participants are anticipated. For example, breaks may be scheduled according to anticipated energy needs, energizers may be placed midday, or snacks may be provided.		
	Activities are planned that will best navigate the group's dynamics. This planning may reflect an awareness of how power dynamics may manifest in this group and may seek to interrupt these dynamics.		
	The facilitator's agenda includes procedural notes, precise timing, and scripts for items including the framing of different sections, transitions, and connections between segments. Facilitator's notes may anticipate participants' needs and reactions at different points.		

1. Meeting Design *Most design elements are visible in the participant's agenda.* *Some will be visible only in the facilitator's agenda.*	✓	Evidence Comments Questions
Element | **Indicators**		
How and when feedback on the meeting will be gathered are indicated.		
Various structures are used that reflect best practices for the purpose of the meeting. For example, if the purpose of the meeting is to learn, then best practices in adult learning are applied. If the purpose is to make a decision, then protocols for decision making are used.		
How | Plans include various structures to ensure equitable participation. Everyone will have a chance to speak during the meeting (although not necessarily in the whole group; it may happen in breakout groups or pairs).		
The group's affective needs are addressed through structures such as a check-in, dyad, grounding, or intention setting.		
Team norms are included on the agenda, and a process for using them is indicated. Roles may include a process checker, or participants may be asked to identify a norm to hold for themselves.		
Facilitator agenda may include notes about room set-up. For example, group may sit around one large table or in small configurations.		
Roles such as timekeeper, notetaker, process checker, and facilitator may be identified. (If roles are used then it is assumed that the group has clear understanding of the expectations for the roles.)		
Who | Roles such as timekeeper, notetaker, process checker, and facilitator may be identified. (If roles are used then it is assumed that the group has clear understanding of the expectations for the roles.)		

FACILITATION OBSERVATION TOOL

2. Meeting Execution *Observable during meeting*		✓	Evidence Comments Questions
Element	**Indicators**		
Key Facilitation Skills	Meetings stay focused and outcomes are met within the allocated time on agenda.		
	Participants are given time to make connections between a single meeting and the team and school's goals, vision, and mission.		
	Norms and community agreements are referenced during meetings; different structures are used to reflect on how the team holds norms.		
	Sections of the agenda make clear why the team is engaging in each activity and how it connects to larger goals.		
	Discussions and decisions are anchored in the needs of all students.		
Communication	Facilitator uses active listening and questioning that promotes open discussion.		
	There are structures to invite equity of participation.		
	Participants interact through various structures such as whole group, small group, pairs, and written processes.		
	Facilitator addresses unproductive discourse such as blaming and deficit thinking and moves discussion to problem solving, asset-focused language, and action.		
	Facilitator questions beliefs and prompts the group to examine the intended and unintended consequences of beliefs and actions.		

2. Meeting Execution *Observable during meeting*		✓	Evidence Comments Questions
Element	**Indicators**		
Conflict Mediation	In moments of conflict the facilitator seeks to understand different perspectives, acknowledges views from all sides, and has strategies to redirect the energy toward shared ideals.		
	Facilitator manages disruptive or overly talkative group members.		
	Facilitator draws out quieter members of the group.		
	Facilitator addresses power dynamics in the moment or at other times if they are negatively impacting the group.		
Emotional Intelligence	Facilitator seeks feedback on every meeting and on his or her leadership skills.		
	Facilitator appears to be positive and calm right from the start of a meeting.		
	Facilitator displays optimism, confidence, and a positive, solutions-oriented attitude.		
	Facilitator honors obligations by following through, being responsible, and being willing to be held accountable by others.		
	Facilitator manages his or her own emotions particularly in moments of conflict, challenges, or setback.		
	Facilitator admits to mistakes, faults, and areas for growth.		
	Facilitator demonstrates empathy authentically and regularly.		
	Facilitator engages team in self-reflection and evaluation, leading toward greater individual and collective responsibility.		
	Facilitator appears genuinely interested in developing every member of this group.		

APPENDIX E

Activities for Meetings

E1. The Consultancy Protocol

E2. The Feedback Protocol

E3. Chalk Talk

E4. Dyads

E1. THE CONSULTANCY PROTOCOL[1]

30 min.	45 min.	60 min.	What	How
1	2	1	**Opening**	Facilitator reviews protocol and adjusts time as desired by presenter or as fits the group. The group may decide to spend more time on the preparation section or in the discussion. Timing also depends on how many are in the group.
(5)	(5)	(5)	**Previous Presenter Report Back** (optional)	If desired, the presenter from the previous week's consultancy can report on how she used the ideas generated in her consultancy. Teams often feel invested in hearing what happens as a follow-up to the consultancy and a report back can meet this need.
(2)	(3)	(5)	**Presenter Preparation** (optional)	If the presenter knows ahead of time that he will present, then he can arrive to the consultancy with the dilemma written. If this is not the case, the presenter might want a few minutes to think and write in order to identify what he would like the group's support on.
5	8	9	**Presenter Shares**	1. Presenter shares the dilemma—verbally shared or as a written document. If a written description is shared, presenter can also verbally add anything before or after the group reads the document. It's appropriate for the group members to take notes about what they're hearing. Presenter might also share an artifact such as a transcript of a coaching conversation, an email, or a plan for a conversation. 2. Presenter can ask for feedback or input in one area or key question. Asking for specific feedback or support can help a discussion stay focused and useful.

30 min.	45 min.	60 min.	What	How
3	5	5	**Clarifying Questions**	Group asks presenter clarifying questions. • Clarifying questions are yes–no or require very short answers. • The facilitator needs to interrupt if probing questions are asked and can remind the group that probing questions can be noted and raised during the discussion.
5	5	5–18	**Group Reflection and Preparation** Silent planning and reading time	1. If the group is using a tool such as the Coaching Lenses, the presenter can ask that specific lenses be focused on—or the group can agree to divide up the lenses so that they will all be covered. 2. The facilitator restates the presenter's request for specific feedback or input on one area, if this was requested, and reminds the group to focus on this area. 3. The group silently reflects on the presenter's dilemma and prepares for discussion. It's appropriate for group members to note questions and comments to contribute in the discussion. a. **This time can be extended for an additional 20–30 minutes to do reading or research to inform the discussion.** 4. Group can be prompted to write out a big understanding, question, or insight from their lens.

(continued)

30 min.	45 min.	60 min.	What	How
13	18	20	**Group Fishbowl Discussion**	1. Presenter moves his or her chair outside of the circle and can take notes if desired. 2. The facilitator reminds the group of the presenter's key question. 3. The facilitator can open this section by suggesting that each group member briefly (in about 1 minute) share his or her initial thoughts on the dilemma, and the group can whip around so that all can share a thought before opening into a less structured discussion. 4. In the discussion, group members can raise probing questions, share the insights they gained through using the lenses, and voice any other comments or reflections they came up with. 5. Facilitator needs to ensure that discussion stays focused on the presenter's dilemma and, if requested, on his or her key question. Facilitator may also take actions to ensure equity of participation.
1	1	1	**One Minute of Silence**	Group holds 1 minute of silence so that the presenter can collect his or her thoughts and return to the group.
3	6	6	**Closing**	Presenter shares any reactions, insights, and feelings about protocol or what was said; he or she doesn't need to respond to questions that were raised in the group discussion. If time permits, group can share reflections on process.

[1] This protocol is modified from one created by the National School Reform Faculty.

E2. THE FEEDBACK PROTOCOL

45 min.	What	How
2	**Opening**	Facilitator reviews protocol and adjusts time as desired by presenter or as fits the group. The group may decide to spend more time on the preparation section or in the discussion. Timing also depends on how many are in the group.
5	**Presenter Introduces Artifact**	Presenter frames the artifact—the lesson plan, agenda draft, video, or transcript—and offers contextual information. • The presenter can ask for feedback or input in one area. • The presenter can ask for a tool to use used—such as a rubric for assessing lesson plans, the team facilitation planning tool, or a coaching rubric.
5	**Clarifying Questions**	Group asks presenter clarifying questions. • Clarifying questions are yes–no or require very short answers. • The facilitator needs to interrupt if probing questions are asked and can remind the group that probing questions can be noted and raised during the discussion.
10–20	**Presenter Shares Artifact**	Group reads agenda, lesson plan, or transcript or watches video.
10	**Group Reflection**	The group silently reflects on the presenter's artifact and prepares for discussion. The group can use the assessment tool at this time if it was requested. It's appropriate for group members to note questions and comments to contribute in the discussion.
18	**Group Fishbowl Discussion**	6. Presenter moves his or her chair outside of the circle and can take notes if desired. 7. The facilitator reminds the group of the presenter's specific request for feedback if relevant. 8. The facilitator opens this section by inviting each group member to share his or her observations of the artifact. 9. Following each group member's sharing, the group can engage in an unstructured discussion. 10. Facilitator may take actions to ensure equity of participation.
1	**One Minute of Silence**	Group holds 1 minute of silence so that the presenter can collect his or her thoughts and return to the group.
6	**Closing**	1. Presenter shares any reactions, insights, feelings about protocol or what was said; he or she doesn't need to respond to questions that were raised in the group discussion. 2. Group reflects on process.

E3. CHALK TALK

Objectives

- To hear everyone's voice in a short period of time
- To provide a way for people who don't feel comfortable verbally expressing themselves to do so
- To generate ideas about a new topic to study or discuss
- To respond to other people's opinions and ideas

Activity

1. Consider the questions you want people to respond to. They could be about their opinions, experiences, thoughts, or a response to an activity or reading.

2. Write the questions at the top of chart paper. A good ratio is one piece of paper for every three people. You can repeat questions if you have only three questions and 30 people.

3. Post the papers around the room or on tables.

4. Provide a marker to every person.

5. Go over expectations for the exercise.

Expectations:

- Move around the room and respond to the prompts on the paper.
- No more than three people at a piece of paper at a time.
- The room will be silent.
- Write your response to the question on the paper. You don't have to answer every question if you don't want.
- As you move around also read what other people write.
- You can also respond to what other people write—as long as it is only about their ideas. You cannot correct spelling, grammar, or handwriting or make any comments that are disrespectful. You can use symbols to respond such as ! or ? or ***.
- When you are finished (you've responded to all the questions that you want to respond to and you've read over what other people have written), have a seat and rest quietly.

6. Allow time for people to move around and do the exercise.

7. Facilitator also participates and models responses if participants are stuck.

8. When participants are seated, reflect on the experience and have people share what they learned or something they read that surprised them.

E4. DYADS

Based on the work by Julian Weissglass (1990)

Constructive listening is a form of communication where people can construct understandings and deal with their feelings. A dyad is the exchange of constructivist listening between two people.

I agree to listen to and think about you for a fixed period of time in exchange for your doing the same for me. I keep in my mind that my listening is for your benefit, so I do not ask questions for my information.

Dyad Guidelines

- Each person is given equal time to talk. *Everyone deserves attention.*

- The listeners do not interpret, paraphrase, analyze, give advice, or break in with a personal story. *People are capable of solving their own problems.*

- Confidentiality is maintained. (The listener doesn't talk about what the talker has said to anyone else or bring it up to the talker afterwards.) *To be authentic, a person needs to be assured of confidentiality.*

- The talkers do not criticize or complain about the listeners or about mutual colleagues during their time to talk. *A person cannot listen well when he or she is feeling attacked or defensive. Problems are to be addressed in a different structure, based in dialogue.*

A Few More Things

- The time belongs to the speaker. If the speaker wants to diverge from the suggested prompt, that's okay. If the speaker wants to sit in silence, that's okay!

- Sit facing each other, knee to knee, with nothing in your hands.

- Know that many people feel uncomfortable or awkward doing dyads when they first experience them; often this dissipates.

APPENDIX F

Recommended Resources

ON EMOTIONS AND SELF-KNOWLEDGE

Bradberry, Travis, and Jean Greaves. *Emotional Intelligence 2.0*. San Diego, CA: TalentSmart, 2009.

Brown, Brené. *The Gifts of Imperfection*. Center City, MN: Hazelden, 2010.

Foster, Rick, and Greg Hicks. *How We Choose To Be Happy*. New York, NY: Perigree, 2004.

Olivo, Erin. *Wise Mind Living*. Boulder, CO: Sounds True, 2014.

There are numerous free online questionnaires based on the Myers-Briggs Type Indicator, but not all are considered equally valid. I recommend http://www.16personalities.com but also suggest you try taking a number of them to see if your results are consistent.

Dr. Martin Seligman's website: http://www.authentichappiness.sas.upenn.edu

ON LEADERSHIP

Block, Peter. *The Answer to How Is Yes*. San Francisco, CA: Berrett-Koehler, 2002.

Deal, Terrence, and Kent Peterson. *Shaping School Culture*. San Francisco, CA: Jossey-Bass, 2009.

Fullan, Michael. *The Principal*. San Francisco, CA: Jossey Bass, 2014.

Goleman, Daniel, Richard Boyatzis, and Annie McKee. *Primal Leadership*. Boston, MA: Harvard University Press, 2002.

Heifetz, Ronald, Alexander Grashow, and Marty Linsky. *The Practice of Adaptive Leadership*. Boston, MA: Harvard Business Press, 2009.

Kouzes, James, and Barry Posner. *The Leadership Challenge*. San Francisco, CA: Jossey-Bass, 2007.

McKee, Annie, Richard Boyatzis, and Fran Johnston. *Becoming a Resonant Leader: Develop Your Emotional Intelligence, Renew Your Relationships, Sustain Your Effectiveness*. Boston, MA: Harvard Business Press, 2008.

Teacher Leader Model Standards. http://www.teacherleaderstandards.org/

ON BRAIN SCIENCE

Hanson, Rick. *Buddha's Brain: The Practical Neuroscience of Happiness, Love & Wisdom*. Oakland, CA: New Harbinger Publications, 2009.

Hanson, Rick. *Hardwiring Happiness: The New Brain Science of Contentment, Calm, and Confidence*. New York, NY: Crown Publishing, 2013.

Medina, John. *Brain Rules: Twelve Principles for Surviving and Thriving at Work, Home, and School* (2nd ed.). Seattle, WA: Pear Press, 2014.

ON MANAGING CHANGE

Duhigg, Charles. *The Power of Habit*. New York, NY: Random House, 2012.

Heath, Chip, and Dan Heath. *Switch: How to Change Things When Change Is Hard*. New York, NY: Broadway Books, 2010.

Ryan, M. J. *How to Survive Change You Didn't Ask For*. San Francisco, CA: Red Wheel/Weiser, 2014.

ON SYSTEMS THINKING

Senge, Peter. *The Fifth Discipline: The Art and Practice of the Learning Organization*. New York, NY: Doubleday, 2006.

Senge, Peter, Nelda Cambron-McCabe, Timothy Lucas, Bryan Smith, and Janis Dutton. *Schools That Learn: A Fifth Discipline Fieldbook for Educators, Parents, and Everyone Who Cares about Education*. New York, NY: Crown, 2012.

Waters Foundation. *Habits of a Systems Thinker*. http://watersfoundation.org/systems-thinking/habits-of-a-systems-thinker/

ON COMMUNITY BUILDING

Fleishman, Paul. *Seedfolks*. New York, NY: HarperCollins, 1997.

Pollack, Stanley, and Mary Fusoni. *Moving Beyond Icebreakers*. Boston, MA: Center for Teen Empowerment, 2005.

ON MEETINGS AND FACILITATION

Boudett, Kathryn Parker, and Elizabeth City. *Meeting Wise: Making the Most of Collaborative Time for Educators*, Boston, MA: Harvard Education Press, 2014.

Delehant, Ann. *Making Meetings Work*. Thousand Oaks, CA: Corwin, 2007.

Lemov, Doug, Erica Woolway, and Katie Yezzi. *Practice Perfect*. San Francisco, CA: Jossey-Bass, 2012.

Lipton, Laura, and Bruce Wellman. *Got Data? Now What?: Creating and Leading Cultures of Inquiry*. Bloomington, IN: Solution Tree Press, 2012.

Tate, Marcia. *"Sit and Get" Won't Grow Dendrites: 20 Professional Learning Strategies That Engage the Adult Brain*. Thousand Oaks, CA: Corwin, 2012.

Wellman, Bruce, and Laura Lipton. *Data-Driven Dialogue*. Sherman, VT: MiraVia, 2004.

Weinschenk, Susan. *100 Things Every Presenter Needs to Know about People*. Berkeley, CA: New Riders, 2012.

ON COMMUNICATION

Abrams, Jennifer. *Having Hard Conversations*. Thousand Oaks, CA: Corwin, 2009.

Kegan, Robert, and Lisa Lahey. *How the Way We Talk Can Change the Way We Work: Seven Languages for Transformation*. San Francisco, CA: Jossey-Bass, 2001.

Patterson, K., Joseph Grenny, Ron McMillan, and Al Switzler. *Crucial Conversations*. San Francisco, CA: McGraw Hill, 2002.

Showkeir, Jamie, and Maren Showkeir. *Authentic Conversations*. San Francisco, CA: Berret-Koehler Publishers, 2008.

RACE, RACISM, AND SYSTEMIC OPPRESSION

Alexander, Michelle. *The New Jim Crow: Mass Incarceration in the Age of Colorbindness*. New York, NY: New Press, 2012.

Boykin, A. Wade, and Pedro Noguera. *Creating the Opportunity to Learn: Moving from Research to Practice to Close the Achievement Gap*. Alexandria, VA: ASCD, 2011.

Coates, Ta-Nehesi. "The Case for Reparations." *Atlantic*, June 2014.

Coates, Ta-Nehesi. *Between the World and Me*. New York, NY: Spiegel & Grau, 2015

Delpit, Lisa. *Other People's Children: Cultural Conflict in the Classroom.* New York, NY: New Press, 1995.

Delpit, Lisa. *The Skin That We Speak: Thoughts on Language and Culture in the Classroom.* New York, NY: New Press, 2002.

The National Equity Project offers powerful and engaging workshops: www.nationalequityproject.org

Rios, Victor. *Punished: Policing the Lives of Black and Latino Boys.* New York, NY: New York University Press, 2011.

Steele, Claude. *Whistling Vivaldi and Other Clues to How Stereotypes Affect Us.* New York, NY: Norton, 2010.

Tatum, Beverly D. *"Why Are All the Black Kids Sitting Together in the Cafeteria?" and Other Conversations about Race.* New York, NY: Basic Books.

Wise, Tim. *White Like Me: Reflections on Race from a Privileged Son.* Berkeley, CA: Soft Skull Press, 2008.

FOR INSPIRATION

Loeb, Paul Rogat. *The Impossible Will Take a Little While.* New York, NY: Basic Books, 2004.

Palmer, Parker. *The Courage to Teach.* San Francisco, CA: Jossey-Bass, 1998.

Wheatley, Margaret. *Turning to One Another: Simple Conversations to Restore Hope to the Future.* San Francisco, CA: Berrett-Koehler, 2009.

Wheatley, Margaret. *Perseverance.* San Francisco, CA: Berrett-Koehler, 2010.

Wheatley, Margaret. *So Far from Home.* San Francisco, CA: Berrett-Koehler, 2012.

Wheatley, Margaret, and Deborah Frieze. *Walk Out, Walk On: A Learning Journey into Communities Daring to Live the Future Now.* San Francisco, CA: Berrett-Koehler, 2011.

APPENDIX G

Plan for Team Building

FOR LEADING A NEW TEAM

1. How do you feel about working with the team? How much choice did you have over who is in the team? What is your history (if any) with them?

2. What do you anticipate will be challenging about working with this team? What strengths or assets do you suspect team members have?

3. What is your understanding of the team's purpose? What direction have you been given on why it exists and what it's supposed to do?

4. What do you think this team needs to do? What has informed your opinion?

5. What might you need to learn to help determine the team's purpose? Who might you talk to? What data might you need to gather?

6. What do you feel accountable to in your leadership of this team?

7. How might the work this team engages in have a positive impact on children?

8. How can you ensure that your team will have the time it needs to develop norms and make agreements about the team's purpose?

9. How will you introduce yourself to the team? What will you say, exactly, to communicate what your role with the team is and your vision of how the team will work together? Write this out.

10. What kinds of trust building steps will you take, and when will you take them?

11. How will your approach to trust building be informed by current organizational conditions for effective teams?

12. What kinds of power dynamics do you think will be present in this team that you'll need to be aware of? How might your role and position impact power dynamics?

13. What kinds of decisions do you anticipate this team will need to make?

14. How and when will you discuss healthy communication with your team? How will you introduce that discussion?

15. How can you cultivate the group's emotional intelligence from the very first meeting? Which strategies can you employ right away? Which will you use on a regular basis?

16. When you prepare for meetings, what do you think might be most important for you to keep in mind, given your previous leadership experiences and what this team needs to do?

17. How can you ensure that the work this team does is aligned to work that other teams in the school are engaging in? How can you share your team's work?

18. Who else in your school or organization could be a thinking partner for you as this team develops? Who could troubleshoot with you or provide a listening ear if things get challenging?

19. What are your greatest and wildest dreams for this team? What do you really hope will happen?

20. Who do you want to be for this team? What do you want team members to say about you and your leadership 5 years after you finish working together?

Now, list out the action steps you'll take to develop your team and plot them on a weekly timeline.

WHEN CONTINUING TO LEAD A TEAM AND IDENTIFYING NEXT STEPS

1. How do you feel about working with the team? How much choice did you have over who is in the team? What was your history (if any) with them?

2. What has been challenging about working with this team?

3. What strengths or assets do team members have?

4. What is the team's purpose? What do you think this team needs to do? What has informed your opinion?

5. What data have you used to understand or communicate the team's purpose?

6. How bought into the purpose are team members? How much say (if any) did they have in why the team exists or what it is supposed to do?

7. What are the team's norms or community agreements? How are these upheld? Are they effective at helping the group engage in meaningful work together?

8. What do you feel accountable to in your leadership of this team?

9. How does the work this team engages in have a positive impact on children? What evidence do you have that this team's work has a meaningful impact on children?

10. Does your team have the time it needs? What do you think your team needs more time to do? How could you create the time for that to happen?

11. What stage of development would you say the team is at? What might you do that could push the team into the next stage of development?

12. How much do you trust the members of your team?

13. Which specific trust building steps could you take with the team?

14. How is your approach to trust building informed by current organizational conditions for effective teams?

15. What kinds of power dynamics do you think are present in this team? How does your role and position impact power dynamics?

16. What kinds of decisions has this team made? What processes have you used for decision making? If decision making has been contentious, what needs to happen to improve the process?

17. What are communication patterns like in the group? Do you think it would benefit the team to explore healthy communication?

18. How would you assess group's levels of emotional intelligence? What could you to increase it?

19. What is your process for preparing for meetings? How could you refine your meeting planning processes?

20. How often do you ask your team for feedback? How do they give you feedback? What do you do with the feedback?

21. How is the work this team does is aligned to what other teams in the school are doing? How do you share your team's work?

22. How can you build leadership capacity in other members of the team?

23. Who supports you as a leader? Where can you go when you face leadership and team development challenges? How could you advocate for your own support as a leader?

24. What are your greatest and wildest dreams for this team? What do you really hope will happen?

25. Who do you want to be for this team? What do you want team members to say about you and your leadership 5 years after you finish working together?

Now, list out the action steps you'll take to develop your team and plot them on a weekly timeline.

ACKNOWLEDGMENTS

My participation in many communities has informed my thinking about healthy teams; therefore, the origins of this book are rooted in the vast expanse of my personal and professional life. At times I've found myself contemplating the way the Chilean exiles who played folk music in my childhood living room affected my understanding of resilient communities. Yet acknowledgments that extensive would require an entire book. For now, I want to express my gratitude for those who most recently directly supported the birth of this book.

That Caitlin Schwarzman crossed paths with an early draft of this manuscript can be attributed only to divine intervention. I can't fathom what this book would have been without her honest and thoughtful feedback on that early draft and then on many later versions.

My experience working with Jossey-Bass as my publisher could not be any better. Kate Gagnon, my editor, has also been a thought partner, resource provider, unwavering champion, and friend.

My gratitude to the members of the team of transformational coaches is extensive and profound. Over the two years, this team included Noelle Apostol Colin, David Carter, Rafael Cruz, John Gallagher, Anna Martin, Manny Medina, Angela Parker, Han Phung, and Michele Reinhart. This book would never have been born had it not been for their magnificent hearts and open minds.

In recent years, a number of friends and colleagues have generously offered encouragement, insights, and advice on the content of this book as well as on the direction of my professional life. I am most grateful for conversations with Jennifer Abrams, Lisa Ahn, Laurelin Andrade, Davina Goldwasser, Zaretta Hammond, Lisa Jimenez, Lettecia Kratz, Jennifer Nguyen, Shane Safir, and Jody Talkington.

Over the last couple of years, since the publication of *The Art of Coaching*, I've had the opportunity to meet coaches across the country. I'm grateful to those who have vulnerably asked questions in my workshops, who welcomed me so warmly into their worlds, and who shared the impact that *The Art of Coaching* has had on their practice. My long-distance and virtual community of kindred spirits in the work of transforming schools has grown tremendously, and for that I am so grateful. In particular, I thank those in the Salem-Keizer Public Schools in Oregon and the Aurora Public Schools in Colorado; it has been a gift to work with you. I also thank all of those who traveled to Oakland, California, to attend my coaching institutes. I have learned so much from all of you.

A group of teachers and administrators from The Urban School in San Francisco played a role in my development as a leader of which I doubt they were aware. Their willingness to reflect on their practices and to explore equity in their school was inspiring and energizing at a critical period in my life.

During my two years at "Wilson Middle School," a few colleagues made a huge impact on my ability to think clearly, feel sane, and develop my skills as a coach and leader. Among those were Angela Parker, Leslie Plettner, Mark Salinas, and Ken Yale.

My appreciation for the following leaders is profound: Javier Cabra, Yanira Canizalez, Tina Hernandez, and Paul Koh. I am humbled by your leadership, inspired by your commitment, and grateful for your courage. I am honored to be a witness to your journey.

Steve Sexton, the co-founder and transformational leader of the remarkable Lighthouse Community Charter School, in Oakland, CA., influenced me in ways that have greatly affected my life. While the light that he brought to our world will endure, his passing came far too early. Like a redwood tree, the roots of what he planted have already shot up and are forming a ring around his legacy. I am deeply grateful to have known Steve and miss him terribly.

I must acknowledge a handful of family members for their role in this book. My mother was a community builder extraordinaire. She brought people together from all corners of the world around our dining room table. She was a skilled listener who drew out people's stories—stories that fueled my commitment to social justice. I aspire to emulate the compassion she demonstrated and to embody her ability to foster bonds between people.

My team at home—my husband and my son—make it possible for me to do what I do. Together the three of us have built a nest where we nurture and care for each other. My husband, Stacey Goodman, anchors me in my most authentic self and keeps me feeling hopeful and inspired. There are no words to express my gratitude at being on this journey of life with him. My son, Orion, anchors me to the present moment, energizes me with his wackiness, and fuels my commitment to do whatever I can to create a more just and equitable world where he—and all children—can thrive.

ABOUT THE AUTHOR

Elena Aguilar is a teacher, coach, and consultant with more than 20 years of experience working in schools. She has taught Grades 2–10 and has a particular love for middle school students. She has been an instructional coach, a leadership coach, and a central office administrator.

Elena is the founder of Elena Aguilar Consulting (www.elenaaguilar.com). She and her associates facilitate professional development for coaches, teachers, and administrators in public, charter, and private schools across the United States. Elena also consults with districts that are developing a coaching program and with leaders engaging in transformational change. She continues to coach school leaders in the San Francisco Bay Area.

Elena is the author of *The Art of Coaching: Effective Strategies for School Transformation* (Jossey-Bass, 2013). She has been a frequent writer for *Edutopia* since 2008 and writes a blog on *EdWeek Teacher* for coaches. Elena lives in Oakland, California, with her husband and son.

REFERENCES

Abrams, J. *Having Hard Conversations*. Thousand Oaks, CA: Corwin, 2009.

Aguilar, E. *The Art of Coaching: Effective Strategies for School Transformation*. San Francisco, CA: Jossey-Bass, 2013.

Argyris, C., and D. Schon, *Organizational Learning: A Theory of Action Perspective*. Reading, MA: Addison Wesley, 1978.

Bambrick-Santoyo, P. *Leverage Leadership*. San Francisco, CA: Jossey-Bass, 2012.

Bass, B. M., and Riggio, R. E. *Transformational Leadership*. Mahwah, NJ: Lawrence Erlbaum Associates, Inc., 2005.

Bens, I. *Facilitating with Ease!* San Francisco, CA: Jossey-Bass, 2012.

Block, P. *Flawless Consulting*. San Francisco, CA: Pfieffer, 2000.

Bower, M. *The Will to Manage*. New York, NY: McGraw Hill, 1966.

Bradberry, T., and J. Greaves. *Emotional Intelligence 2.0*. San Diego, CA: Talent Smart, 2009.

Briggs Myers, Isabel. *Gifts Differing: Understanding Personality Type*. Mountain View, CA: Davies-Black Publishing, 1995.

Brookfield, S. D. *Understanding and Facilitating Adult Learning. A Comprehensive Analysis of Principles and Effective Practice*. Milton Keynes: Open University Press, 1986.

Brown, B. *Daring Greatly*. New York, NY: Gotham, 2012.

Brown, S. *Play: How It Shapes the Brain, Opens the Imagination and Invigorates the Soul*. New York, NY: Penguin, 2009.

Bryk, A., and B. Schneider. *Trust in Schools: A Core Resource for Improvement*. New York, NY: Russell Sage Foundation, 2002.

Covey, S. *The Speed of Trust*. New York, NY: Free Press, 2006.

Cozolino, L. *The Neuroscience of Human Relations*. New York, NY: W.W. Norton & Company, Inc., 2014.

Darling-Hammond, L., R. C. Wei, A. Andree, N. Richardson, and S. Orphanos. "State of the Profession: Study Measures Professional Development." *Journal of Staff Development*, 2009, 30(2), 42–50.

Deal, T., and K. Peterson. *Shaping School Culture: Pitfalls, Paradoxes, and Promises* (2nd ed.). San Francisco, CA: Jossey Bass, 2009

Dewey, J. *How We Think*. New York, NY: D.C. Heath, 1933.

Druskat, V. U., and S. B. Wolff. "Building the Emotional Intelligence of Groups." *Harvard Business Review*, March 2001, pp. 81–91.

DuFour, R., and R. Marzano. "High-Leverage Strategies for Principal Leadership." *Educational Leadership*, 66(5), 62–68, 2009.

Fullan, M. *The Principal*. San Francisco, CA: Jossey Bass, 2014.

Fullan, M. *Choosing the Wrong Drivers for Whole System Reform*. Seminar Series 204. Melbourne, Australia: Centre for Strategic Education, 2011.

Garmston, R. "For Principals, the Trick Is Knowing When to Pass on the Facilitator's Hat." *Journal of Staff Development*, Winter 2005, 26(1), 63–64.

Garvin, D. "Building a Learning Organization." *Harvard Business Review*, 1993, 71(4), 78–91.

Garvin, D., A. Edmondson, and F. Gino. "Is Yours a Learning Organization?" *Harvard Business Review*, March 2008, 109–116.

Goleman, D., R. Boyatzis, and A. McKee. *Primal Leadership: Learning to Lead with Emotional Intelligence*. Boston, MA: Harvard University Press, 2002.

Hackman, J. R. *Collaborative Intelligence: Using Teams To Solve Hard Problems*. San Francisco, CA: Berrett-Koehler, 2011.

Hall, E. *Beyond Culture*. New York, NY: Anchor, 2007.

Hall, T., and Campano. G. "Some Thoughts on a 'Beloved Community.'" *Reading and Writing Quarterly*, 2014, 30, 288–292.

Hanson, A. "The Search for Separate Theories of Adult Learning: Does Anyone Really Need Andragogy?" In R. Edwards, A. Hanson, and P. Raggatt (Eds.), *Boundaries of Adult Learning: Adult Learners, Education and Training Vol. 1*. London, UK: Routledge, 1996, 99–109.

Hanson, R. *Buddha's Brain: The Practical Neuroscience of Happiness, Love, and Wisdom*. Oakland, CA: New Harbinger Publications, 2009.

hooks, b. *Yearning: Race, Gender and Cultural Politics*. Cambridge, MA: South End Press, 1990.

Hubbard, R., and B. Power. *The Art of Classroom Inquiry: A Handbook for Teacher Researchers*. Portsmouth, NH: Heinemann, 2003.

Jarvis, P. *The Sociology of Adult and Continuing Education*. London, UK: Croom Helm, 1985.

Jarvis, P. "Malcolm Knowles." In P. Jarvis (Ed.), *Twentieth Century Thinkers in Adult Education*, 144–160. London, UK: Croom Helm, 1987.

Jones, S., and K. Rainville. "Flowing toward Understanding: Suffering, Humility, and Compassion in Literacy Coaching." *Reading & Writing Quarterly*, 2014, 30, 270–287.

Kidd, J. R. *How Adults Learn* (3rd. ed.). Englewood Cliffs, NJ: Prentice Hall Regents, 1978.

King, C. *Testament of Hope: The Essential Writings of Dr. Martin Luther King*. New York, NY: HarperCollins, 1986.

Knowles, M. *The Adult Learner: The Definitive Classic in Adult Education and Human Resource Development*. (8th Edition) New York, NY: Routledge, 2015.

Kotter, J. *A Sense of Urgency*. Boston, MA: Harvard Business Review, 2008.

Lencioni, P. *The Five Dysfunctions of Team*. San Francisco, CA: Jossey-Bass, 2005.

Lencioni, P. *The Advantage: Why Organizational Health Trumps Everything Else in Business*. San Francisco, CA: Jossey-Bass, 2012.

Martin, C. *Do It Anyway: The Next Generation of Activists*. Boston, MA: Beacon, 2010.

Merriam, S., R. Caffarella, and L. Baumgartner. *Learning in Adulthood*. San Francisco, CA: Jossey Bass, 1999.

Parker P. *The Courage to Teach*. San Francisco, CA: Jossey Bass, 1997.

Patterson, K., J. Grenny, R. McMillan, A. Switzler, and S. R. Covey. *Crucial Conversations*. San Francisco, CA: McGraw Hill, 2002.

Robbins, M. *Focus on the Good Stuff: The Power of Appreciation*. San Francisco, CA: Jossey Bass, 2007.

Ryan, M. J. *How to Survive Change You Didn't Ask For*. San Francisco, CA: Red Wheel/Weiser, 2014.

Schein, E. *Organizational Culture and Leadership*. San Francisco, CA: Jossey Bass, 2010.

Senge, P. *The Fifth Discipline: The Art and Practice of the Learning Organization*. New York, NY: Doubleday, 2006.

Showkeir, J., and M. Showkeir. *Authentic Conversations*. San Francisco, CA: Berret-Koehler Publishers, 2008.

Siegel, D. 2007. *The Mindful Brain: Reflection and Attunement in the Cultivation of Well-Being*. New York, NY: W.W. Norton & Company, Inc.

Tennant, M. *Psychology and Adult Learning*. London, UK: Routledge, 1988.

Troen V., and K. Boles. *The Power of Teacher Teams*. Thousand Oaks, CA: Corwin, 2011.

Tuckman, B. "Developmental Sequence in Small Groups." *Psychological Bulletin*, 1965, 63(6), 384–399.

Vygotsky, L. *Thought and Language*. Cambridge, MA: MIT Press, 1962.

Vygotsky, L. *Mind in Society*. Cambridge, MA: Harvard University Press, 1978.

Weissglass, Julian. "Constructivist Listening for Empowerment and Change." *Educational Forum*, 1990, 54(4), 351–371.

Zohar, D., and I. Marshall. *Spiritual Capital: Wealth We Can Live By*. San Francisco, CA: Berrett-Koehler Publishers, 2004.

INDEX

Intellectual stimulation, 29
Intention setting, 114–115
Interdependent teamwork, 9
Interpersonal communication, 7
Introversion, 19, 20

K

King, M.L., Jr., 32, 117
King Center, 117
Knowles, M., 188, 193
Kotter, J. A., 81, 82

L

Laissez-faire leadership, 29
Lao Tzu, 295
Leader: developing vision for self as, 41; implications for, 35–36; and *leader* (term), 2
Leadership: and acknowledging identity/role, 27–28; actions, transparency about, 46–47; and defining good, 25–27; exploring terrain of, 23–28; home and family in, 24–25; and reflection on role, 28
Learned abilities, 17
Learning, as meeting component, 163
Learning Forward, 7
Learning gap, 21
Learning organization: and adult learners, 185–187; definition of, 185–187; indicators of, 186–187 exhibit 9.1; reflection on self-assessment of, 187
Lencioni, P., 250
Limbic system, 15, 18
Listening: and fostering culture of, 53–54; listening to, (how do I listen?), 147–148 exhibit 7.4
Longfellow, H. W., 256

M

Majority voting, 174–175
Marshall, I., 265
Martin, C., 202
Marzano, R., xxiv
McKee, A., 34
McMillan, R., 329
Mead, Margaret, 264
Meaning making, 211–212; protocol for, 212–213 exhibit 10.3
Meeting process, 6
Meetings, meaningful: activities for, 205–219; choosing what to do in, 219–233; and example of team's meeting schedule, 208–209 exhibit 10.1; and humanities team, 2009, 205–206; and making meaning, 211–213; and need for meaning, 207; orchestrating, 205–230; and outcomes for team meetings, 209–210 exhibit 10.2; and pairing and grouping, 220–221; putting on finishing touches to,

241–242; and reason for meeting, 207–211; and stages of team development, 221–226; and transformational coaching team, 2013, 226–227; and working with energy, 220
Mindful Brain (Siegel), 114
Multivoting, 172–173
Myers-Briggs Type Indicator (MBTI), 18–19, 251

N

National Equity Project, 77
National School Reform Faculty, 213, 322
Neuroplasticity, 18, 73–77
Noguera, Pedro, 7
Norm building, 95–96; and clarifying what norms mean, 109–110; and community agreements (norms), 96–97; and counterpart to norms: setting intentions, 114–115; and creating structures for accountability, 111–112; decision-making in, 177; and effective norms, 97–99; example of (Rise Up Academy Math Department PLC), 100–108 exhibit 5.2; and examples of norms, 98 exhibit 5.1; and making norms visible, 111; and procedural and behavioral norms, 98; and reflection questions on norms, 113 exhibit 5.4; and return to norms, 257–258; steps in establishing, 100, 109; and time for process, 99–100; and use of norms for social control, 115–117; and when to revise norms, 113

O

Oakland, California, 22, 23
Oakland Unified School District (California), xxi
Organizational conditions: and alignment up and out, 273–276; assessing, 269–290; and culture of learning, 279–281; and dealing with gossip, 285; and decision making, 285–286; for effective teams, 288–290 exhibit 13.4; and humanities team, 2009, 269–270; and leadership, 277; primacy of purpose in, 271; and school team's organizational alignment (Rise Up Middle School), 274–276 exhibit 3.1; and stability, 276–277; and team membership, 278–279; and time, 286–287; and toxic cultures, 280–281; and transitional coaching team, 2013, 287–288
Overtalkers, 139; questions to prompt reflection on challenge of, 139

P

Palmer, Parker, 28, 116
Patterns of participation, 145 exhibit 7.2; reflections on, 146–147 exhibit 7.3
Patterson, K., 329
PDs. *See* Professional development sessions
Personality, 18–21; traits, 19
Peterson, K., 280